DEMOCRACY'S SLAVES

DEMOCRACY'S SLAVES

A Political History of Ancient Greece

PAULIN ISMARD

Translated by
JANE MARIE TODD

Harvard University Press
Cambridge, Massachusetts & London, England • 2017

Copyright © 2017 by the President and Fellows of Harvard College
All rights reserved
Printed in the United States of America

Originally published as *Démocratie contre les experts: Les esclaves publics en Grèce ancienne,* © Éditions du Seuil, 2015.

First printing

Library of Congress Cataloging-in-Publication Data
Names: Ismard, Paulin, author.
Title: Democracy's slaves : a political history of ancient Greece / Paulin Ismard ; translated by Jane Marie Todd.
Other titles: La démocratie contre les experts. English
Description: Cambridge, Massachusetts : Harvard University Press, 2017. | "Originally published as Démocratie contre les experts: Les esclaves publics en Grèce ancienne, Éditions du Seuil, 2015."—Title page verso | Includes bibliographical references and index.
Identifiers: LCCN 2016021053 | ISBN 9780674660076
Subjects: LCSH: Slavery—Greece—History. | Public administration—Greece—History. | Slavery—Philosophy. | Greece—Social conditions—To 146 B.C.
Classification: LCC HT863 .I8513 2017 | DDC 306.3/620938—dc23
LC record available at https://lccn.loc.gov/2016021053

For Lucie D.

Contents

Preface · ix

INTRODUCTION · 1

1. GENESIS · 14

2. SERVANTS OF THE CITY · 35

3. STRANGE SLAVES · 57

4. THE DEMOCRATIC ORDER OF KNOWLEDGE · 80

5. THE MYSTERIES OF THE GREEK STATE · 103

CONCLUSION · 127

Notes · 137
Bibliography · 175
Acknowledgments · 181
Index · 183

Preface

Could the experience of long-ago Athens help us deal with our political misfortunes here and now?

If you were born in the late 1970s, it is unlikely that politics has been the site of the great accomplishments of your personal life. Your elders taught you that politics was an affair of the imaginary, a matter of desire, and that there were few other activities that could lead to an authentic life. For you, however, the words and beliefs they used to transmit their own experiences seem at best to paint a Shangri-la, at worst to pose a series of indecipherable riddles. And just as the political arena ceased long ago to interest you, you have gradually come to dispute the traditional form of political participation, even to reject the principle of representation per se.

Nevertheless, in the daunting crisis of political language you are witnessing, there is one big word, only vaguely defined, that serves as both a principle of action and a perennial aspiration. That word is "democracy." Granted, it is invoked in the most multifarious aims. But provided you refuse to recognize it—as you are invited to do—as the sole promise for civil peace and liberty for all, provided you understand it instead as a radical word designating the principle of the equal distribution of power and the community's effective control over its own destiny, then you will still be inclined to see it as the only worthy political project still in existence. Is it not that imperative, as yet imprecise, that assembled the demonstrators on Puerta del Sol Square in Madrid, on Syntagma Square in Athens, and in Zuccotti Park in New York City?

It seems to you, however, that one of the daily manifestations of the denial of the democratic idea is the pulsing refrain that exalts the reign of expertise and repeats over and over again that public affairs can be conducted only on the basis of a body of knowledge whose nature requires that it be elaborated at a remove from the people's passions. The deliberate circumvention of the speech of ordinary citizens, condemned for being ignorant (of the laws of globalized economics and the rational management of the state), would therefore be constitutive of the art of governing complex societies. Indeed, although it is true that the people's opinion, constructed through a set of mechanisms, continues to be assessed and dissected, it appears inconceivable that a body of knowledge politically useful for the community as a whole could arise from the egalitarian deliberation of nonspecialists. The "reign of opinion" and the government of experts, far from standing opposed, are the two faces of a self-same political order, one that challenges the capacity ordinary citizens might have to construct political competence collectively. And it is truly that day-to-day retreat from democratic expression that makes you the powerless—and thereby consenting—spectator of your own political death.

In fact, the figure of the government expert is only the contemporary face assumed by one of the most ancient aspects of the very notion of the state, that of producing knowledge about the social body. The state, before being protective or absent, the guarantor of freedom or an oppressor, takes the primary form, through its bureaucratic apparatus, of a set of mechanisms of knowledge designed to constitute society as an object from which the state detaches itself while at the same time informing it. Every state, it could be said, is first and foremost a scholarly organization, a state of knowledge, as it were.

It may not be beside the point to observe that the first democracy in history, of which, rightly or wrongly, we claim to be the heirs, conceptualized the link between power and knowledge in terms that are completely alien to us. The figure of the expert so familiar to us, the one whose knowledge supposedly constitutes a mandate to govern, was in fact unknown to the Athenians of the classical age, for whom no specialized competence by itself legitimized the exercise of power over the civic community. We ought to be intrigued by the fact that Athenian democracy was originally constructed in opposition to the figure of the ruler-expert but also in accordance with a conception of the state contrary to our own. That is precisely what I wish to explore in this book, by retracing the history of those who, in their way, were the first civil servants of the Greek cities and who sometimes played the role of true experts. As it happens, these men were slaves.

DEMOCRACY'S SLAVES

Introduction

> Master of the three ways, I carried in the sun, I carried in the fog I carried Manian ants on the red-hot shards. I carried the parasol, I carried the explosive I carried the yoke.
> From Akkad. From Elam. From Sumer.
> —Aimé Césaire, "Depuis Akkad depuis Elam depuis Sumer," in *Cadastre*

Athens, 1861. Not the capital of the young Mediterranean kingdom of the indolent Othon I, but a small town in the southern United States, engaged body and soul in the revolt of the Confederate States. Athens, then, not *Athēnai*. It was founded in the late eighteenth century by John Milledge to bestow on the new university of the young state of Georgia the prestige of the city of Plato and Aristotle.[1] Athens, Georgia, imagined itself an outpost of Old World culture, implanted in the heart of a conquered territory. Despite its prestigious name, however, the modest town resembled most of the cities of the old slaveholding South. Out of a population of four thousand, Athens had about two thousand slaves.

After the Civil War broke out, the old order of slavery fissured. Many owners, unable to support their slaves, abandoned them, and the city's main street became their gathering place. Slaves roaming the public space "like freemen," far from their masters' properties? The patrimonial plantation system as a whole was shaken, sparking the indignation of John Christy, editor of the town's daily newspaper, the *Southern Watchman*: "Everybody knows . . . that negroes who are nominally slaves, but really free, will not work so long as they can find any thing to steal. . . . The negroes are obliged to have something to eat—their inherent love of idleness prevents them from working, and stealing becomes a necessity."[2] The situation was so scandalous that, to keep a lid on it, municipal authorities decided to impose a tax on slave owners for every abandoned slave, who would otherwise be obliged to leave town.

In what was an incongruous event in the history of slaveholding America, the town then set out to acquire slaves for itself. In the early part of 1862, the city council recruited General Thomas Cobb's "boy Joe" "to work the streets, drive and take care of the town mule."[3] It was Joe's master who had the primarily responsibility for supporting the slave. But less than a year later, when General Cobb died in the Battle of Fredericksburg, the little town decided that, rather than emancipate his slave, it would become Joe's owner. For almost three years, therefore, this "boy Joe" was the public slave of Athens.

This street maintenance worker and slave of Athens, Georgia, would have recognized as one of his forebears a figure from classical Athens. Aristotle, in a digression on the Athenian institutions of his time, mentions the existence of a man in charge of clearing away the dead bodies lying in the street and of maintaining the roads.[4] Like Joe, that "civil servant," whose name has been lost to history, was a slave, his owner the city of Athens. This anecdote, which unites the city of Pericles with its modern American stand-in more than two millennia later, is misleading, however. Joe and the anonymous slave of ancient Athens belonged to two radically different slave structures: what was an anomaly in Athens, Georgia, in 1862, a result of exceptional circumstances, was not so twenty-five centuries earlier, in the shadow of the Acropolis.

In classical Athens, between one thousand and two thousand public slaves worked in the service of a community of thirty thousand to forty thousand citizens. To refer to these men, the Greeks used the term *dēmosioi*, a word that invariably linked a function—working for the city—and a status, that of slave. Any stranger arriving in a Greek city might have observed on his own, during the course of his stay, a multitude of public slaves occupied with very diverse tasks. In a sanctuary, he might have noticed a *dēmosios* taking inventory of the god's possessions and, on certain occasions, even officiating as priest. On the Agora, a group of public slaves charged with keeping the peace might have reprimanded him. If he wanted to conduct business, the stranger would have turned to one of the officers' fellows to certify the authenticity of the currency he was using. On the city's major construction sites, he would have seen public slaves engaged in erecting different monuments. In any event, one thing is sure: the relative silence of the ancient literature on the subject of those who, in their way, were the first civil servants says nothing about the scope of the strange institution of public slavery.

One aspect of the landscape would surely have disoriented our visitor: certain tasks entrusted to these slaves required a real expertise beyond the abilities of most citizens. That simple fact sheds light on the peculiar articulation at the heart of the Athenian democratic ideal, between the order of knowledge and the question of power. At this point, the Athenian experiment comes face to face with the most ticklish issues confronting our present-day democracies. Our political distress—I mean in Europe in 2015—lies in the force of a belief expressed on a daily basis in the following terms: the democratic imperative of majority rule is incompatible with the principle of efficacy demanded by the governance of states, which is necessarily complicated, hence dependent on education. Thus the knowledge useful to public affairs would result from specialization, and the fortunate possessors of that knowledge—experts and advisers of every kind—operate in the shadows, beyond democratic control. For the Athenians of the classical age, however, no knowledge could in itself legitimize the possession of power over the civic community; and if some tasks requiring a form of expertise were entrusted to slaves, it was precisely because slaves were excluded from the political community and thus did not threaten the civic order.

Public slavery highlights another essential dimension of the Greek political experiment, touching on the very status of the state in a democratic system. Was the Greek city a state? The response is less clear than it appears, at least if one confines oneself to observing that the city's administration had nothing in common with that of modern states, because its agents, or "civil servants," were excluded from the civic community by virtue of their slave status. This is because the very existence of the state as an "administration," a separate agency, was problematic; in that sense, the figure of the public slave attests to a rejection of the state, a rejection that lay at the heart of the Athenian democratic experiment.

Slavery among the Ancients, the Moderns, and Primitive Peoples

Historians, whether specialists in Greek slavery or in civil institutions, have shown little interest in these social actors of the classical and Hellenistic periods.[5] In most cities, no doubt, *dēmosioi* represented only a small portion of the slave population as a whole, the overwhelming majority of whom were the private property of free men, whether citizens or metics. But the historians' silence is also the result of an ideological and scholarly tradition that has long contemplated Greco-Roman slavery in the mirror of the colonial plantations, where public slavery in any form was unknown. The first studies on ancient slavery were haunted by images from the New World. For Henri Wallon, a fervent advocate of abolition and the future representative of Guadeloupe at the Legislative Assembly during the Second Republic in France, the denunciation of colonial slavery entailed reminding people that slavery in antiquity was the source of the moral corruption of the cities, prior to the liberation brought about by Christianity.[6] In the preface to his monumental *Histoire de l'esclavage dans l'Antiquité* (History of slavery in antiquity, 1847), Wallon wrote: "Slavery among the ancients! It may seem strange that one should venture so far in search of it, when slavery is still among us. In taking that path, we do not divert people from the colonial question; on the contrary, we would like to lead them back to it and get them to fix on a solution. . . . Proponents of the status quo appeal to antiquity in support of their cause. It is not fruitless to see whether, in all the evidence it provides, it corresponds to their claims."[7]

References to antiquity, in fact, were used by both proponents and opponents of abolition. For some abolitionists, the celebration of the Greeks' and Romans' supposed humaneness toward their slaves served to accentuate, by way of contrast, the cruelty of the Atlantic slave trade. In invoking the memory of the ancients, they could thus indict moderns. But their adversaries also found resources in societies of antiquity to legitimize the perpetuation of the slave system; in such cases, the slaves of the Greco-Roman world bore witness to the price to be paid (unfortunate but inevitable) for the greatness of any civilization.

Paradoxically, in the last thirty years comparative studies of ancient and modern slavery have been revitalized by the paradigm of "slave society." Historians of Greco-Roman slavery, following in the wake of Moses I.

Finley, have tended to distinguish between two types of societies: "societies with slaves" (also called "slaveholding societies"), in which slavery, numerically insignificant, is confined to certain marginal spheres of the system of production; and "slave societies," wherein the phenomenon of slavery, demographically widespread, affects all social relations. In slave societies, a regular resupply of slaves is particularly essential for the reproduction of social structures. If one is to believe Finley, authentic slave societies have been very rare. He counted only five: In addition to classical Greece and certain regions of the Hellenistic world, only Rome at the end of the republican period and the start of the empire, the United States until the Civil War, and the West Indies and Brazil during the colonial era were true "slave societies."[8] Such a list, to which most historians of Greco-Roman antiquity still subscribe, unknowingly gives credence to the exceptionalism of Greek civilization. In a schema that inverts the famous "Greek miracle," the privilege of inaugurating Western modernity would once again fall to the contemporaries of Pericles and Plato.

The decisive weight of slavery in the workings of the classical and Hellenistic city is clearly indisputable. Whether one believes that the slaves of classical Athens constituted 20 percent or 50 percent of the population, that they numbered fifty thousand or two hundred thousand individuals, such a numerical difference, however great it might appear, changes nothing as to the role of the institution of slavery at the root of the civic order.[9] Greek slavery in the classical age, moreover, was characterized by large slave markets that, far more than demographic reproduction alone, ensured that the slave population would be continuously replenished. Another fundamental dimension of chattel slavery in the classical age was that slaves were relegated to a place outside the civic community. The slave, property of another man who alone had the power to give him a name, lost his original identity without acquiring a new one (for example, by becoming part of his master's family). Hence slaves really were the outcasts par excellence, embodying the figure of alterity that haunts every aspect of civic life. For all these reasons, the city of the classical age—including Athens, which, like it or not, constitutes the ideal prototype—truly conforms to the model of a "slave society," and, as Finley noted, "a genuine 'synthesis' of the history of ancient slavery can only be a history of Graeco-Roman society."[10]

As pertinent as the notion of "slave society" may be for describing in brief the forms of Greek slavery, the number of societies to which it applies is debatable. The centrality of slavery in the New World cannot conceal major variations in time and space of a quasi-universal phenomenon. For more than thirty years, historians and anthropologists have continually emphasized the scope and extreme diversity of slave structures.[11] From the Iroquois in the Great Lakes region to the outer reaches of the island of Java, that extreme form of dependency and dispossession is the rule rather than the exception.[12] In this respect, the definition given by the Geneva Convention of 1926, which stipulated that slavery is "the status or condition of a person over whom any or all of the powers attaching to the right of ownership are exercised,"[13] is largely inadequate. Centered on the question of ownership and modeled on the experience of the colonial world, it overlooks many societies that practiced slavery.

The notion of slave society itself cannot be considered the sad privilege of the societies of classical antiquity and the New World (nor, indeed, did the West have a monopoly on abolitionist discourse).[14] When the Portuguese entered the kingdom of Kongo at the turn of the sixteenth century, more than one hundred thousand slaves, composing half the kingdom's population, were being used in every sector of production. Three centuries later, the enormous Sokoto Caliphate, southwest of Lake Chad, had almost as many slaves as the United States of America.[15] In Africa, therefore, the slavery of the great Muslim kingdoms and that of the "peripheral" states was not only domestic or military in nature; it also had a productive function and was often similar to plantation slavery.[16] Likewise, in the kingdom of Aceh, west of Sumatra, slaves constituted the principal labor force on the large spice plantations of the seventeenth century. In that sense, the notion of slave society, far from designating solely Greco-Roman societies and those of the colonial world that resulted from the Atlantic slave trade, can legitimately be extended to a considerable number of societies.[17]

Nothing would be more misguided, however, than to place two heterogeneous worlds in opposition: on the one hand, a plantation slavery proper to the New World colonies; on the other, a "precolonial" slavery confined to so-called primitive societies. That temptation has pervaded the abolitionist literature, which has not omitted to construct excessively optimistic representations of non-Western forms of subjugation, in order to better denounce the atrocities of colonial slavery.[18] Yet the history of slavery in Africa and Asia is itself part of the larger history of the trafficking in human beings, and in that respect its study belongs to a "connected history."[19]

The studies on African or Asian slavery have not only redrawn the map of the phenomenon of slave ownership. More than anything, they have scrambled the coordinates by which it was long apprehended, revealing unexpected objects and constructing new tools of analysis. Debt bondage, for example, has come to light as a major phenomenon at the heart of dependency or subjugation.[20] Many studies, ceasing to define slavery in terms of ownership, have emphasized the forms of interaction and domination that govern the master-slave relationship. Through the notion of "social death," for example, Orlando Patterson placed the process of violence and dishonor, said to be constitutive of all slavery, at the center of his study.[21]

With rare exceptions, historians of antiquity have turned a deaf ear to that enormous effort to redefine the slave phenomenon. Even now, the colonial frame of reference usually constitutes the ultimate horizon of any comparative perspective on their part.[22] Undoubtedly, some of the debates raging among Africanists, historians of the Muslim world, and specialists in Southeast Asia are largely irrelevant to studies of the slave societies of antiquity. And yet, the mirror that New World slavery holds out to the historian of antiquity is reductive. Since the early 1970s, the influence of Finley's writings has extended far beyond the study of ancient societies, providing fertile ground for analyses devoted to slave systems of every sort. Is it not time to defamiliarize Greco-Roman slavery by introducing knowledge about other slave systems well outside the Americas? Standing between the Athens of Pericles and that of the "boy Joe" are (among other places) the Sokoto Caliphate, Cambodia of the Middle Period, the Thai Empire, the great Islamic empires, and the West African kingdoms, all societies that practiced slavery extensively, all unique configurations that invite us to rethink Greek slavery.

The project of a comparative analysis of slave systems within which the Greek world would hold pride of place would be overly ambitious in a single work written by a single historian. In this book, I nonetheless aspire to make an attempt, an *essay*, in that direction, by examining a unique institution of the Greek cities, namely, public slavery. The term "comparativism" is currently invoked to cover a set of disparate and sometimes even contradictory methods.[23] Within the narrow limits of this study, comparativism can operate only at low intensity. My aim is neither to place Greek slavery under the aegis of hypothetical general laws common to all slave societies nor to inscribe it within a generic typology of the different slave systems. My method is more modest: it consists of refining the traditional questionnaire on Greek slavery by studying one of its little-known institutions—public slavery—and by placing it in the light of comparable institutions within other slave systems. It thus belongs to a differential comparativism, attuned to dissonance more than identity, and its primary aim is to identify the unique characteristics of Greek slavery, which in the last instance have to do with the specificities of the Greek city's social and political organization.

What Is Public Slavery?

Public slavery has taken root as a major theme within the new anthropology of the slave phenomenon. Social anthropology, whether it calls them "slaves of the crown," "state slaves," or "court slaves," has brought to light the determining role played by the sovereign's slaves as auxiliaries to power.[24] It is hardly an overstatement to say that, outside the New World, all "state" slave societies have had them. In some societies "royal slavery" even predominated numerically over private slavery.[25] Very often, these slaves were the first "civil servants," contributing toward the state's formation. Some anthropologists have gone so far as to see them as the secret behind its establishment: Even before the king's two bodies, the two bodies of the sovereign and his slave may lie at the origin of the state.[26] In addition to the great disparities in the tasks they performed and the modes of ownership applied to them as compared to private slaves, the privileged position of public slaves seems to have been a constant. Slaves enjoying a privileged condition? The paradox is only on the surface once one concedes that, fundamentally, slavery defines a legal status and not living conditions or a determinate place in the structure of production.

Clearly, public slavery in the Greek cities, taken in all its diversity, cannot be identified with royal slavery without a few precautions. The *dēmosioi* were the collective property of the city and not the private property of the depositary of public authority. This difference is far from trivial; it presupposes that the patrimonial regime governing relations between the master and his slave cannot operate in exactly the same way between the civic community as a whole and its servants. Such a distinction was common in many societies, where slaves who were the sovereign's personal property coexisted with others who, attached to his function and not his person, belonged to the entire community.[27] It also existed in a certain manner within personal regimes known to the Greek world. In second-century Pergamon, the slaves owned by the king, called *basilikoi*, were clearly distinct from the slaves of the city, the *dēmosioi*.[28] That distinction reached its canonical form under the Roman Empire where, alongside the emperor's personal slaves belonging to the *familia Caesaris*, were *servi publici*, whose existence dates back to the Republican period and who were the property of the Roman state.[29]

But public slavery in the Greek cities also cannot be conflated with the forms of collective servitude known in many regions of the Greek world. In a famous passage, the fourth-century historian Theopompus, retracing the origins of slavery in Greece, distinguished between these two types:

> The Chians were the first Greeks after the Thessalians and Spartans to rely on slaves, but did not acquire them in the same way as the latter. . . . For the Spartans and the Thessalians can be seen to have developed their slave-corps out of the Greeks who previously inhabited the territory they now control: the Spartans drew their slaves from the Achaeans, while the Thessalians drew theirs from the Perrhaebi and Magnesians; and the former call the people they enslaved helots, while the latter call them penestai. The Chians, on the other hand, have barbarians as their slaves and purchase them.[30]

On the one hand, barbarian slaves who were paid for; on the other, populations collectively subjugated after a territorial conquest: following Theopompus, historians of the Greek world came to distinguish chattel slavery, of which classical Athens would offer the most advanced model, from the enslavement of an entire community, as in Spartan Helotism.

And yet several authors of the imperial period characterized the Helots as the collective property of the Spartans. Strabo claims that "the Lacedaemonians held the Helots as public slaves [*dēmosious doulous*] in a way,"[31] and Pausanias reports that the Helots "became the first slaves of the Lacedaemonian community [*douloi tou koinou*]."[32] One must not be fooled by that belated comparison; the status of public slaves described as *dēmosioi* can in no way be assimilated to collective enslavement of the

Helotic type. The difference lies, in the first place, in the origin of the slave populations. The *dēmosioi* were overwhelmingly recruited from the slave markets, whereas the Laconian or Messenian Helots, like the Penestae of Thessaly, were populations collectively subjugated following a war of conquest. In fact, public slavery was inseparable from the emergence of chattel slavery at the juncture between the archaic and classical periods. The distinction is also functional. Whereas the vast majority of Spartan Helots worked the land for the benefit of citizens, the *dēmosioi* generally performed administrative and policing functions in the city. Finally, the ownership relation that linked the civic community to these slaves was very different. In the classical period, Helots were considered private property, even though they had been collectively subjugated. Citizens were prohibited from selling their Helots on the slave market, but that restriction was part of a set of regulations on private property characteristic of the Spartan regime and did not make Helots the property of the civic community as a whole.[33]

The City in the Light of Its Slaves

The documentation available, thus circumscribed within its proper dimensions—city-owned slaves within the context of chattel slavery—is at first glance very limited: a few thousand individuals dispersed over more than four centuries, known through a few texts and mentioned in fragmentary inscriptions. The fate of public slaves seems insignificant within the overall history of Greek slavery. Why should one be surprised, therefore, that they have sparked little interest in historians? There is one exception, however. In the late 1920s, the Belgian scholar Oscar Jacob devoted a book to Athenian public slaves of the classical period.[34] This is the only general study of the *dēmosioi*, and by virtue of its scholarship, it remains an irreplaceable reference work. Jacob was particularly interested in compiling a list of all the tasks entrusted to the *dēmosioi* and in identifying the specificities of their legal status.

From the standpoint of a contemporary reader, Jacob's book, despite all its fine qualities, contains two lacunae. The first is incidental. It goes without saying that, since 1928, documentation on the subject has greatly increased, thanks both to the discovery of new inscriptions and the reinterpretation of well-known literary and epigraphic sources. The second lacuna, which concerns the historian's general method, is more serious. His very descriptive approach is marked by a dual isolationism. Jacob focuses exclusively on the Athens of the classical period, even ignoring Hellenistic Delos under Athenian control. Although Athens offers the best-documented case, many aspects of that strange institution are worth interpreting in the light of the experience of other cities. Above all, the *dēmosioi*, conceived by Jacob as a unique case and an exception, almost an anomaly, seem to him to be part of a history marked off from that of the classical or Hellenistic city. Jacob wrote a history of public slaves in and of themselves, without delving into the meaning of that peculiar system, which for the city meant entrusting to slaves a not insignificant share of its administration. And the surprising condition of these few thousand individuals, far from being trivial, offers a privileged observation post from which to analyze the lines of tension, even the contradictions, at the heart of the Greek city's operation. At the crossroads of the history of slave status, civic administration, and the order of knowledge in a democratic system, the study of the *dēmosioi* casts a unique light on the very foundations of that misleadingly familiar object, the Greek city.

In the first place, the origins of the institution are worth analyzing for the entire archaic period, from the eighth to the sixth century BCE. From the specialized artisan of the Homeric world to the scribes of the Cretan cities in the sixth century, that era provides a fairly large contingent of technicians and experts possessing specialized knowledge. Their condition was precarious; their skills, made available to the community, at the same time marginalized their possessors. The laws of the archaic period placed these "experts" in a peculiar position. They were usually excluded from the civic community, even though they were granted significant privileges. The figure of Daedalus, an artisan whose technical ingenuity represented a threat to the rulers on whom he depended, condenses in that respect most of the problems linked to the status of these *dēmiourgoi*, who may at times appear to be the ancestors of the public slaves. The advent of public slaves, however, can be understood only in terms of an intersection between these ancient practices and the two revolutions at the end of the archaic period: the development of chattel slavery and the appearance of democratic systems.

I will focus in Chapter 2 on the tasks entrusted to the *dēmosioi* in the classical and Hellenistic cities. Public slaves were remunerated, and their assignments could be extended year after year; they did not hold a magistracy (*archē*). In that sense, whether they were clerks or police officers, archivists, masons, or even at times priests, their skills were not political, although these slaves occasionally possessed a power of constraint over citizens. Their function can be summed up by the strange expression found in an Athenian inscription from the Hellenistic period, *eleutheria leitourgia*. Ought this to be read as a first definition of "public service" in the Greek city?

The performance of these functions in the service of the city was combined with a unique legal status. For Greece at the end of the archaic period, Finley continually posits a necessary connection between the development of chattel slavery, on the one hand, and the advent of freedom and the status of citizen on the other hand. The specificity of the democratic system is said to lie in the absence of any intermediary status between free and slave. Within the classical city, however, the privileges enjoyed by public slaves undermine such a representation and invite us to rethink in broad terms the variety of personal statuses existing there. It is thus the complexity of status hierarchies in the classical city that comes into focus through an examination of the *dēmosioi*'s status.

But public slavery also illustrates the "social epistemology" of the classical city. Some of the tasks for which the *dēmosioi* were responsible required extraordinary skills. In entrusting them to slaves, the city placed certain areas of expertise outside the political field, preventing the practice of such skills from legitimizing the possession of power. The expertise of the *dēmosioi* thus sheds new light on the thorny and urgent question of the political status of knowledge in the democratic commonwealth.

Public slavery, finally, will lead to an inquiry into the very institution of the Greek city in all its generality. Direct democracy as the Athenians conceived it required that all political powers be in the hands of citizens. Based on the principle that the sphere of the *koinon* (community) must coincide with that of the *archē* (command), no state apparatus was to stand between the community of citizens and the realm of power. Inasmuch as they constituted the "bureaucracy" of the cities, the *dēmosioi* embodied precisely the state dimension of the Greek city, but in the form of pure negativity. Paradoxically, then, the institution of public slavery attested to the resistance of civil society to the emergence of the state as a separate agency. Such an arrangement placed the slaves of the city in a unique position. Standing outside the political community while at the same time possessing a "public" status, they played the role of a third-party guarantor of the civic order; and from their designated place, the ultimate horizon of the norm can be articulated.

CHAPTER ONE

Genesis

> The poet, they say, had only to utter his poem to make the palace disappear, as if abolished and blown to bits by the final syllable. Such legends, of course, amount to no more than literary fiction. The poet was a slave of the Emperor and as such he died. His composition sank into oblivion because it deserved oblivion and his descendants still seek, nor will they find, the word that contains the universe.
>
> —J. L. Borges, "Parable of the Palace," from *Dreamtigers*, translated by Mildred Boyer

When one listens to Aristophanes's gentle mockery of the Scythian archers or reads the last words of Socrates praising the humane treatment of the guard who would reluctantly administer the lethal poison to him, one might think that the public slave was a figure familiar to the Athenians of the classical age. And in fact, public slavery seemed so much a part of the natural order of city life that the ancient authors did not even see fit to recount its origins.

No doubt it was during the classical period that most of the cities for the first time acquired slave bodies charged with performing the majority of tasks that, in a handy anachronism, could be called "administrative." But historians have hardly taken the trouble to search for the antecedents to that institution in the archaic world. This is understandable because the undertaking would seem to encounter a long succession of insurmountable obstacles. In the first place, it appears rash to seek an origin for individuals destined for a dual anonymity: that specific to any slave, whose lack of a proper name is constitutive of the stigma of his servile status, and that required by the impersonal service rendered to the abstract entity of the city. Furthermore, it is tremendously difficult to glimpse these figures in a world as poorly documented as the archaic period. The Homeric epic, fragments of legendary accounts, a few inscriptions in dialect, and histories, often composed after the fact: that is all the material one has to go on to make out the silhouette of this book's protagonist at the end of the archaic period.

Specialists on the classical city, familiar with the inner workings of its institutions and with its social structures, may easily become discouraged in the face of such documentary difficulties and may decide to consign the origins of public slavery to the vast category of problems that are insoluble for lack of sources. The state of the documents at one's disposal requires two complementary methods that, when combined, take the unlikely form of a hybrid game, halfway between dominoes and a jigsaw puzzle. First, one must follow a tenuous thread made up of human faces, from the Homeric *dēmiourgos* to the public slave of the classical age. One after another, a few pieces fall into place—the herald Dolon, the legendary Daedalus, the minstrel Phemius, a mysterious slave answering to the name of Patrias—and a narrow path leading to the *dēmosios* of the classical age opens up. At the same time, these figures have to be placed within the largely fragmentary context of the major shifts that occurred during the archaic period. "Slave of the city": that is how most lexicographers paraphrase the term *dēmosios*.[1] This expression indicates the extent to which the appearance of public slavery was the product of two related developments: first, in forms of dependency, from Odysseus's faithful swineherd Eumaeus to the chattel slaves of the sixth century; and second, in the organizational structures of the Greek communities of the archaic period, from the decline of the Homeric *basileus* (king) in the late eighth century to the advent of democratic systems.

Thus, between the early days of the epic and the beginning of the classical age, the origins of public slavery will be revealed in the course of a long journey from one end of the archaic period to the other. Guided by a vague similarity in sound and reassured by a remote affinity of functions, I shall consider in the first place the figure of the *dēmiourgos* as he appears in the great poem of the early archaic period, the Homeric epic.

The Homeric *Dēmiourgos*

Dēmiourgos: the term has its share of mystery, and for more than a century historians have sought in its etymology the rigorous definition of a function and an individual specific to archaic societies. On a literal level, a *dēmiourgos* performs *dēmia erga*, acts concerning the *dēmos*, the city. His function is defined, therefore, not by his dependency on the political community but by the beneficiary of his activity. This distinction may appear secondary, but it is in fact essential. The *dēmiourgoi* were not workers under the people's orders but specialists placing "their skills or their talent in the service of the public."[2]

At the dawn of the archaic period, the Homeric epic twice conjures the term *dēmiourgos*. In book 17 of *The Odyssey*, Eumaeus, speaking to the suitor Antinous, justifies the intrusion into the palace of a poor beggar, who is none other than Odysseus, by portraying *dēmiourgoi* as follows: "Who, pray, of himself ever seeks out and invites a stranger from abroad, unless it is one of those that are masters of some public craft [*dēmiourgoi*], a prophet, or a healer of ills, or a carpenter, or perhaps a divine minstrel, who gives delight with his song? For these men are invited all over the boundless earth. Yet a beggar would no man invite to be a burden to himself."[3] The description draws together poets, doctors, and artisans. This is not at all surprising. In the minds of the Greeks of the archaic period, intellectual and manual activities did not belong to fundamentally different spheres of activity; on the contrary, they had close affinities to each other. If one is to believe Eumaeus, the *dēmiourgoi* were itinerant technicians possessing unusual skills or expertise, temporarily placed in the service of their host communities. Depositaries of a knowledge transmitted from father to son, these *dēmiourgoi* were often actively sought after by the communities, who were prepared to scour "the boundless earth" (*ep' apeirona gaian*) to find them. That was no doubt the case for Tychius, the master bronzesmith from Boeotia, "far best of workers in hide," who is said to have aided in the manufacture of the shield of Ajax,[4] and to whom, much later, the Romans would attribute the invention of the sandal. Itinerancy, then, would be central to the *dēmiourgoi*'s condition. In that respect, the Homeric epic echoes all the narratives that attribute to the temporary sojourn of more or less supernatural foreign communities most of the major technical innovations of the Greek world. For example, the mysterious Chalybes of the Black Sea are said to have been the first to work in bronze;[5] the Cypriot Telchines, on their way from Boeotia to Rhodes, supposedly contributed to the development of metallurgy;[6] and the Greeks would be beholden to the Cretan Dactyls for the discovery of iron.[7]

And yet, when the Homeric poem agrees to put a face or a name to the *dēmiourgoi*, they are not itinerant but are residing near a sovereign. The goldworker Laerces, for example, is summoned to Nestor in book 3 of *The Odyssey* to gild the horns of the animal sacrificed to mark the arrival of Telemachus.[8] And the Trojan carpenter Phereclus (literally, "bearer of glory"), "whose hands were skilled in fashioning all manner of elaborate work," built Alexander's vessels before being killed by Merion in book 5 of *The Iliad*.[9] Of all the *dēmiourgoi* in the epic, however, it is the minstrels and heralds whose silhouettes assume the most distinct shape. First there is the minstrel Phemius, who practices his art for Odysseus in Ithaca;[10] then Demodocus, a public poet for Alcinous, king of the Phaeacians. And heralds, precisely because of their proximity to the king, whom they serve as "loud-hailers," occupy a privileged place in the epic, from the devoted Eurybates, influential adviser to Odysseus, to the despicable Dolon, whose fate is to be killed by Diomedes's arrows. In fact, when the term *dēmiourgos* is uttered for the second time, by Penelope, it refers to the heralds.[11]

When, for the space of a few lines, the Homeric poem turns its attention away from the world of the *aristoi* (best people), it is generally very reticent about the precise status of its various protagonists. But several elements implicitly define what constitutes, if not a homogeneous legal status, then at least the outlines of a singular condition specific to the *dēmiourgoi*. That condition is at first sight difficult to fathom because the *dēmiourgoi* appear to be placed in such contradictory positions in the hierarchy. Some seem to accrue the marks of prestige. For example, Agamemnon, before leaving for Troy, entrusts to his minstrel the task of keeping an eye on his wife, Clytemnestra.[12] Consider as well the bond that unites Odysseus and Eurybates, whom the poem depicts as his closest adviser,[13] or Priam and his herald, at whose side he falls asleep, both "with deep thoughts in their minds."[14] In other contexts, conversely, the poem emphasizes the *dēmiourgos*'s role as servant (*therapōn*) to the *basileus*.[15] According to a hierarchical conception of social status, which historians usually imagine as a vertical scale composed of a series of parallel and hermetic strata—the infamous "spectrum" of statuses—the *dēmiourgoi* may thus be classified "at the very top" or "at the very bottom" of Homeric society. Historians have therefore adopted the most contradictory positions on the status of these specialists or have simply embraced the notion, both convenient and loose, of "intermediate status."[16] In fact, it is risky to try to identify a homogeneous status that could be located in a determinate position on a spectrum of statuses in Homeric society. It is clear that the Homeric *dēmiourgos*, although not an integral part of the *aristoi*, is distinguished from the *thetes*, dependent day laborers,[17] and from the *dmōes*, servant-slaves. It must also be understood that the same individual can only incidentally be a *dēmiourgos*, in that the term designates him specifically in the performance of functions that can be called "public."

Beyond the diversity of their trades, however, the *dēmiourgoi*'s condition was characterized by two elements resembling two sides of a single coin: an extreme dependency on the person of the king, combined with a relative independence from the royal *oikos* (household). More precisely, royal protection, conferred as an individual privilege, was the only guarantee of the *dēmiourgoi*'s status; it was their close dependency on the very person of the *basileus* that assured them a certain dignity. But such dependency did not make them servants of the royal *oikos*. In Ithaca, the minstrel Phemius and the herald Medon did not belong to the class of the *basileus*'s servants, whether loyal ones like Eumaeus and Philoitius or traitors like Melantheus. It is not insignificant, no doubt, that among the Phaeacians the minstrel Demodocus lived outside the palace and that a herald had to go find him at home to summon him to the royal meal in honor of Odysseus.[18] In that sense, the *dēmiourgos* was situated within the all-powerful orbit of the king's sovereignty but without being directly dependent on the master of the royal household. Hence the *dēmiourgoi* are not located "at the summit" or "at the base" of the hierarchy of Homeric society; in their exclusive dependency on the prince, they are on the margins of a society organized around the *oikos*. One episode in particular sheds light on the ambiguity of the Homeric *dēmiourgos*'s condition: that of Odysseus's revenge upon his return to Ithaca.

The Clemency of Odysseus

The scene takes place in the palace of the king of Ithaca where, before the astounded eyes of the suitors, a strange beggar has just won the archery contest, thus revealing his authority as master of the house. Once he has reestablished his identity, the beggar, who is none other than Odysseus, behaving "like a lion that comes from feeding on an ox of the farmstead," sets out to avenge himself on the suitors, wantonly slaughtering them.[19] In the course of the fighting, the priest Leodes throws himself at Odysseus's feet and begs for his life, arguing that he never prayed for the suitors except under constraint. Odysseus refuses to recognize any extenuating circumstances and, picking up a sword abandoned by a suitor, "struck him full upon the neck."[20] The minstrel Phemius begs Odysseus in his turn, promising he will henceforth sing to him "as to a god." He assures him that he never sang for the suitors except under constraint, which Telemachus confirms. Phemius's supplication provides a magnificent *mise en abyme*, which shows the context of enunciation of Homeric poetry and the minstrel's extreme dependency on the prince: "Ready am I to sing to you as to a god," he implores.[21] Having formerly performed his art under threat from the suitors, he will now sing under Odysseus's sword.[22] Finally, it is the turn of the herald Medon, heretofore hiding under an armchair, to throw himself at the feet of Telemachus, in the hope he will persuade his father to spare the herald's life.[23] Odysseus then consents to spare the minstrel and the herald, asking them to remove themselves from the castle and await him in the courtyard. Medon and Phemius comply, and both take their places on the altar of Zeus the Great (*Dios megalou*), from which they witness the conclusion of the massacre.

With respect to the three "public" individuals who did not hesitate to collaborate with the suitors in his absence, Odysseus therefore adopts very different attitudes, punishing the first and sparing the other two. Eva Cantarella has analyzed the entire episode, insisting on the difference in Odysseus's behavior, depending on whether he is faced with suitors, potentially his equals, or with members of his *oikos*, which is to say, his servants. That distinction is said to govern two different logics at work in the reprisals: a ruthless vengeance is wreaked on the suitors, all of whom are killed, while the administration of domestic justice dictates the sovereign's much more merciful behavior toward the servants. Vis-à-vis the members of his *oikos*, Odysseus could "allow himself considerations that have no place within the logic of revenge: he can assess the degree of guilt and calibrate the punishment; if need be, he can absolve someone who provides proof of his innocence." In that case, he would be "guaranteeing order within the group and asserting his role as a leader."[24]

As appealing as that interpretation might be, it has some difficulty explaining the difference in treatment inflicted on Leodes on the one hand and the two *dēmiourgoi* Phemius and Medon on the other. Their behavior in Odysseus's absence and respective positions in service of the community seem to differ little from each other. During the archery contest, Leodes is even portrayed as the only one to have been "full of indignation at all the suitors,"[25] which makes his execution all the more unjust. Perhaps one should understand that in the case of Phemius and Medon, their very status as *dēmiourgoi* protects them, whereas the absence of such a status condemns Leodes to death. The episode would then attest to a certain neutrality attached to the position of the *dēmiourgos*, which might assure him a form of personal inviolability. In that sense, Odysseus's retaking of his kingdom would entail clemency toward these two figures, minstrel and herald, indispensable aides in the exercise of royal sovereignty. The presence of both men on the altar of *Zeus megalou*, god of sovereignty par excellence, speaks volumes. In book 24 of the *Odyssey*, Phemius and Medon will even be called upon to reestablish the legitimacy of Odysseus by jointly addressing the residents of Ithaca.[26]

Dolon Put to Death

Heavily dependent on the royal person's favor but placed in a marginal position, the figure of the *dēmiourgos* can nevertheless become worrisome. This is suggested by the fate reserved in the *Iliad* for the herald Dolon.[27] This unusual figure does not embody the truth as such of the Homeric *dēmiourgos* but rather condenses several of the threatening potentialities attached to him.

The episode occupies most of book 10. During a nighttime council, the Trojans have decided to send a certain Dolon, son of Eumedes, "the godlike herald, a man rich in gold, rich in bronze,"[28] to spy on the positions of the Achaean army. In return, Dolon asks Hector for a considerable reward (*misthos*): the chariot and horses of Achilles. To accomplish his mission, Dolon disguises himself in the skin of a gray wolf and a helmet made of ferret skin. Diomedes, dressed in the skin of a large fiery lion,[29] and Odysseus manage by ruse to isolate Dolon, cutting off his retreat to the Trojan camp. Then begins a nocturnal chase, at the end of which Diomedes and Odysseus seize the herald despite his speed. Taken prisoner, Dolon immediately reveals the layout of the Trojan camp, not without offering a financial reward in exchange for his freedom. But that base suggestion only makes things worse for him. Once the interrogation is over, Diomedes beheads the herald, whereupon Odysseus offers his mortal remains to Athena, hanging them from the branches of a tamarisk tree.

Ever since Louis Gernet devoted a study to this episode,[30] it has given rise to many interpretations, usually emphasizing its ritual and initiatory dimension. In keeping with a polarity that was continually reformulated over time, Dolon embodies in the epic the antithesis of the values of the Achaean warrior, just as, in the Corinthian and Attic imagery of the archaic period, he will serve as the antimodel for the Hoplite citizen.[31] In fact, the chief traits of the character can be interpreted in terms of a system of inversion. In a variation on the ambivalence associated with cunning, Dolon is the incarnation of deceit (suggested by the term *dolos*) and is here the victim of Odysseus's cunning (*mētis*). Rich in gold, Dolon makes money off Hector's assignment, an act that stands in opposition to the noble devotion and generosity of the leaders of the Achaean expedition. The wolf getup surely plays a central role in that scheme: Dolon is a wolf, victim of the lion Diomedes.[32] In broader terms, the episode is presented as a nocturnal chase at the expense of a solitary being, relegated to the sphere of the wild—an "animal being," like those that will appear in Attic imagery[33]—which suggests an underlying scene of initiation.[34] But as Gernet has shown, that disguise also displays a more limited range of meanings. In various contexts, the wolf can represent the animal demon that is pursued and expelled, and Dolon's disguise may therefore bring to mind the figure of the exile, or in the Germanic world, of the *friedlos*. The ritualized execution of the herald, who dies without even doing battle, would thus implicitly evoke a set of rites that stages the expulsion of an individual deliberately placed on the margins of the community.

Clearly, the figure of Dolon, unusual in more than one respect, in no way embodies the condition of all the *dēmiourgoi* who appear in the world of the epic. This episode, however, highlights the potentiality for a radical exclusion linked to the condition of *dēmiourgos* that, no doubt, is not unrelated to the institution of public slavery that will come into being at the beginning of the classical period.

Daedalus, *Dēmiourgos* and Slave?

To pursue this inquiry, I shall attempt to follow the narrow path that leads from the *dēmiourgos* to the *dēmosios*. Before analyzing several figures of public workers in the cities of the archaic period, I believe it is important to take a detour through legend. The figure of Daedalus, it so happens, concentrates in himself several of the characteristics of the Homeric *dēmiourgos*, while paradoxically anticipating certain traits of the *dēmosios* in the classical period. Although the principal features of the Daedalus legend had crystallized by the seventh and sixth centuries, it is the narrative Diodorus Siculus devoted to it in the first century BCE that offers the historian the Ariadne's thread to guide him through the labyrinth of narratives surrounding that character.[35]

The Daedalus legend unfolds in three locations: Athens, Crete, and Sicily. According to Pherecydus, Daedalus was the grandson of the first Athenian, Erechtheus, through Metion,[36] whereas according to Bacchylides, he was the son of Eupalamus, the tenth king of Athens.[37] In any event, he was an Athenian by birth, and his place within the royal lineage is a trait common to all the narratives that mention him. He left Attica because of a crime. Jealous of the inventiveness of his nephew—the first, it is said, to have had the idea for the potter's wheel and the iron saw—Daedalus, a carpenter and sculptor at the time, murdered his nephew, pushing him off the top of the Acropolis. Banished from the city by the tribunal of the Areopagus, Daedalus then took refuge in Crete and "became a friend of Minos," the king.[38]

But that friendship was short-lived, and Daedalus soon entered into conflict with Minos. On the instructions of the king's wife, Pasiphaë, who had fallen under the charm of a bull sent by Poseidon, Daedalus designed the *mechanēma* (machine) that would allow the queen and the animal to mate.[39] From that unnatural union the Minotaur was born, a monster half-man, half-bull, which Daedalus was assigned to conceal and protect by constructing the famous labyrinth. Every nine years, seven young boys and seven young girls of Athens were delivered to the Minotaur in the labyrinth. At this point, the Daedalus legend intersects the Theseus narrative. Upon Theseus's arrival in Crete, Daedalus offered his cooperation to the king of his former country, who had come to confront the Minotaur. Daedalus made the thread that, with Ariadne's assistance, allowed Theseus to escape the labyrinth.[40] According to Diodorus Siculus, the threats that Minos made against Daedalus convinced him to flee Crete.[41] But the most common version of the myth relates that Daedalus, with his son Icarus, was imprisoned by the king inside the labyrinth and that Daedalus designed wings that allowed both father and son to escape. Pausanias recorded a different version, however, in which Daedalus flees in a small boat whose sails he himself had designed, "an invention as yet unknown to the men of those times."[42]

The ancient authors also disagree about the next landing spot for the ingenious artisan after the episode in Crete. If one is to believe Cleidemus, the Athens of Theseus offered its protection to the fugitive.[43] The most widespread version of the legend, however, takes Daedalus to the Sicily of King Cocalus, in whose service he once again displayed his technical ingenuity. In Sicily, Daedalus oversaw the construction of a number of buildings, including the citadel of Camicus, where Cocalus ultimately decided to install his royal palace and store his treasures. Diodorus Siculus writes that during this time Daedalus also stayed briefly in Sardinia, where he built temples, gymnasiums, and tribunals.[44] It was in Sicily, however, that the confrontation between the Cretan king and the brilliant engineer reached its conclusion. Minos, pursuing the architect with a vengeance, arrived in Camicus and demanded that Cocalus hand over his guest. Apollodorus gives a more detailed account of the episode: Minos is said to have brought a shell with him, promising a rich reward to anyone who could pass a thread through it, a stratagem meant to uncover the location of Daedalus, the only one capable of solving such a riddle. When Cocalus admitted to Minos that he had managed the feat with the assistance of an ant, Minos understood that Daedalus was actually living with the Sicilian king. But the old king failed to seize hold of the fugitive, and it was in that distant land that he met his death, drowning in boiling water that Cocalus's daughters poured over him.

From Crete to Sicily by way of Athens (twice over), the Daedalus legend demonstrates several dimensions glimpsed in the *dēmiourgos* of the Homeric epic. Whether a sculptor and carpenter in Athens or a royal engineer and architect in Crete and Sicily, what characterizes Daedalus is a protean technical competence that is continually being placed in the service of ends he cannot control, risking to turn the architect's ingenuity against him (think of Daedalus's imprisonment in the labyrinth). A wanderer and fugitive, Daedalus owes his salvation each time solely to the protection granted him by sovereigns.

Unlike the Homeric *dēmiourgos*, however, Daedalus is placed in the position of an adjuvant to—and not just a dependent on—sovereign power.

That new position allotted to the *dēmiourgos*, who deceives the king to enhance his own power, can be interpreted as the mark of a legendary structure elaborated over the course of the archaic period and characterized by the effacement of the figure of the *basileus*. Françoise Frontisi-Ducroux has demonstrated the bond of mutual dependency that, throughout the myth, unites Daedalus and the different *basileis* who welcome him. Although Daedalus owes his survival to Minos and Cocalus, he is placed each time in the position of an auxiliary to royal power. Not only does Daedalus, in his capacity as royal architect (builder of the prison, the labyrinth in Crete, and the citadel where Cocalus's treasure is kept), assist Minos and Cocalus in the exercise of their power, it is also through him that Theseus acquires sovereignty over Athens by means of an initiation of sorts.

In broader terms, the Daedalus legend conceptualizes the relationship between technical intelligence and power in terms of both complementarity and opposition.[45] In the first place, Daedalus embodies cunning, which is indispensable to the exercise of any sovereignty,[46] and his legend belongs to a mythical structure already present in Hesiod's *Theogony*. Ever since Zeus, who dethroned his father, Kronos, then married (and ingested!) Metis,[47] cunning (*mētis*) had been an essential component of sovereignty in Greek thought.[48] As Jean-Pierre Vernant has shown, "only supremacy in *mētis* seems able to confer on any supremacy the universality and permanence that truly make it a sovereign power."[49] Zeus, god of sovereignty par excellence, is thus the *mētieta* god, composed entirely of *mētis*. But the Daedalus narrative elaborated in the Greek cities conceptualizes to an equal degree, in terms of opposition and conflict, the relationship between cunning and sovereign authority. Daedalus is one of the many faces of *mētis*, which is not immediately bestowed by the capacity to rule; the narrative finds its resolution in the partial victory of the artisan over the king. As Ovid would sing, "Though Minos rules over all, he does not rule the air."[50] In that sense, the Daedalus narrative marks the fault line represented by technical skill—and more generally, technical knowledge—in the order of power.

It is significant that in classical Athens, according to Xenophon, Daedalus could be assimilated to a slave precisely because of the excellence of his knowledge. No doubt Xenophon's remarks are echoed in all the narratives that dramatize the temporary enslavement of extraordinary individuals, such as the poet Aesop. But the invocation of Daedalus is far from innocent:

"But knowledge now, Socrates—that at any rate is indisputably a good thing; for what is there that a knowledgeable man would not do better than an ignorant one?"

"Really! Have you not heard how Daedalus was seized by Minos because of his knowledge and forced to be his slave [*doulos*], and was robbed of his country and his liberty, and in trying to escape with his son lost the boy and could not save himself but was carried off to the barbarians and again lived as a slave [*douleia*] there?"

"That is the story, of course."

"And haven't you heard the story of Palamedes? Of course, for all the poets sing of him: how he was envied for his knowledge and done in by Odysseus."

"Another well-known tale!"

"And how many others, do you suppose, have been kidnapped on account of their knowledge [*dia sophian*] and haled off to the great King's court and live in slavery [*douloi*] there?"[51]

Historians of philosophy have already pointed out the oddity of the skills implicitly attributed to Socrates, similar to the technical or artisanal competence of Palamedes and Daedalus. But the anecdote says as much about the representations of Daedalus in his native land of Athens than about the socratic conception of the link between knowledge and politics. Indeed, in Socratic circles, the mention of Daedalus's royal slavery allowed philosophers to indict a democratic system that did not make knowledge the condition for participation in public affairs. Daedalus, like Palamedes (to whom Plato attributed the invention of the Greek alphabet),[52] thus became the emblem for the evil the democratic system does to those in possession of knowledge, in its refusal to recognize their political superiority. In Athens, Xenophon seems to say, Daedalus would be a slave. Without making the *dēmiourgos* a public slave, Xenophon thus establishes a close connection between the status of slave and technical skill. And that association can be understood only in the light of the development of public slavery in the city of the classical age.

The Foreign Specialist in Service of the Civic Community

I leave Daedalus to his legend, in order to observe more closely the figure of the *dēmiourgos* in the very real world of the Greek cities during the archaic period. It is there that the gradual emergence of the status of public slave becomes evident. Henri Van Effenterre has completed a survey of a set of inscriptions that appear to be "labor contracts" concluded between civic communities and foreign specialists who settled there for varying lengths of time.[53] The aim of these engraved documents was primarily to ensure the protection of the specialists; on each occasion, the cities conferred a number of rights on them (they are generally designated by their profession and not by their native country), in order to secure their services over the long term. Because of their rare skills, these specialists were particularly sought after, and it is hardly an exaggeration to characterize them as the heirs of the *dēmiourgoi* evoked by Eumaeus, whom the cities went searching for over the "boundless earth." Among them are doctors who would settle in a city for a few years[54] or scribes in charge of composing most public deeds. Two inscriptions in particular, which entrust to one of these "specialists" a lasting position in the city's service, call for special attention.

Spensithius the Scribe

A Cretan inscription from the late sixth century mentions the case of the scribe Spensithius, to whom an unknown city and some mysterious *Dataleis* (no doubt a civil subdivision) jointly grant extraordinary prerogatives. I quote only the most important passages.

> A.
> Gods. The Dataleis resolved, and we the city, five representatives from each tribe, pledged to Spensithius subsistence and immunity from all taxes to him and to his descendants, so that he be for the city its scribe and *mnamōn* [*poinikazen te kai mnamoneuen*] in public affairs [*ta dēmosia*] both sacred and secular.
> No one else is to be scribe and *mnamōn* for the city in public affairs, neither sacred nor secular, except Spensithius himself and his descendants [*genia*], unless Spensithius himself, or else the majority of his sons, as many as be adult, should [thus] induce and instruct the city. [The city] is to give as payment annually to the scribe fifty jugs of must and [——] of 20 drachmai value.
>
> B.
> The scribe is to have equal share, and the scribe too is to be present at and to participate in sacred and secular affairs in all cases wherever

the Kosmos may be;⁵⁵ and the scribe is to make the public sacrifices to whatsoever deity a priest does not conduct its own [sacrifices], and is to have the precincts, and there is to be no seizure, and the scribe is not to take any security, and [——], but otherwise, nothing at all.

As lawful dues to the *andreion* he shall give ten axes of dressed meat, if the others also make offerings, and the yearly offering also, and shall [collect the] portion, but nothing else is to be compulsory, if he does not wish to give it.⁵⁶

By means of that deed, the city and the *Dataleis* acknowledged that Spensithius had an exclusive right to a function in the city, that of writing, or consigning to writing (in Phoenician letters: *poinikazein*), and of preserving the memory (*mnamōn*) of "public affairs both sacred and secular." It is quite possible that this position did not entail any oral transmission of the city's laws but rather the management of its archives.⁵⁷ If that was the case, Spensithius was the archivist of the small Cretan city. Through the decree, the scribe obtained significant rights, which conferred on him an enviable status within the community. Spensithius could participate in the *andreion*, an important public meal (the definition of citizenship in archaic Crete was associated with those who contributed to it). This scribe did not fall within the jurisdiction of the *xēnios kosmos*, the magistrate in charge of all legal disputes involving strangers in the city. Nothing clarifies the specific position of Spensithius within the "spectrum of statuses" of the city, however, and it does not appear that his residence there took the form of full citizenship. Above all else, Spensithius and his family were offered extraordinary protection so that he could perform his duties in the community's service.

The essential thing for us, however, lies in the definition of the duties entrusted to him in the city, which were deliberately placed outside the political realm. As a scribe and *mnamōn*, Spensithius did perform a public function (*dēmosia*), but that function in no way belonged to the sphere of the *archē*, that of sovereign power, which was the responsibility of the different magistracies. Since the early days of the archaic period, the political organization of nearly all the cities, whether they were oligarchic or democratic, depended on colleges of magistrates who were replaced on an annual basis. Spensithius's position was distinguished in every particular from such magistracies; remunerated, solitary, conferred for life, and transmissible by inheritance, it belonged in reality to what I would readily call an "off-field" (*hors-champ*) of the political.⁵⁸ The exclusion of the scribe, to whom important rights in the city were granted, is no doubt explained by the danger represented by the technology of which he was the depositary: writing. Such specialists, "marginal in relation to the political magistracies but masters of a *technē* that eluded the ordinary citizen," in that sense constituted "a threat to the always-fragile balance of civic institutions."⁵⁹ That "off-field," which required a form of expertise, would most often have been occupied in the classical period by public slaves, with most of the cities radically separating the space of the political from that of technical skill.

Patrias, Scribe and Slave?

I now turn to the little city of Elis, located in the northwestern part of the Peloponnese. In the early fifth century, the Eleans engraved the following decree on a bronze tablet, displayed in the sanctuary of Olympia:

> The decree of the Eleans. Patrias will be secure, as will his children and his property. If anyone curses him, he will be prosecuted as if he had attacked an Elean. If the highest magistrate and the kings do not uphold his rights, each of them would pay ten minas dedicated to the Zeus of Olympia. The hellanodikes would enforce this, and the college of *damiourgoi* enforce his other rights. If they do not comply, they will pay double to the college of the *mastroi* [at the public audit]. If someone were to mistreat him when his rights were contested, may he be struck with a fine of ten minas, if he mistreated him knowingly. And let Patrias the scribe suffer the same penalty if he commits a crime or misdemeanors against anyone. The tablet [to be] sacred at Olympia.⁶⁰

Written in the Elean dialect, the inscription raises many problems of interpretation, and it is only with great difficulty that one can attempt to reconstitute the context that led to the decree being erected and a protective status granted to Patrias.⁶¹

Patrias's position was that of a *grapheus*, a scribe, and not that of a magistrate.⁶² By virtue of the decree, Patrias undoubtedly became the city's scribe, but one may also presume that he acted for the city in managing the neighboring sanctuary of Olympia, which would explain why the bronze tablet was discovered where it was. The Eleans were once again attempting to guarantee the security of a "technician of public affairs" who was either a foreigner or a former slave. The penultimate clause of the decree may be interpreted in that way. It prescribes that, henceforth, no one shall be able to mistreat (*himaskoi*, a term derived from *himas*, "strap," by which one ought to understand the whip, or torture) the scribe Patrias. In ancient Greece, flogging and torture were punishments constitutive of the stigma of being a slave. Hence the clause makes sense only if Patrias had originally been in a state of dependency and ran the risk of being reminded of that condition by a citizen. With the decree, the Eleans liberated their *grapheus* from his former status. Henri Van Effenterre therefore believed that Patrias must have originally been a slave, a dependent of the god of Olympia, whose services the Eleans had decided to secure for themselves.[63] It could just as easily be construed that Patrias was originally a private slave who, through the decree, became a *dēmosios* of Elis, the city having ensured him legal protection on that occasion. Note that the very name "Patrias" comports very well with this hypothesis: It could be an antonomasia, a change of name by means of which the city attributed a new identity to the *dēmosios*, now in charge of the "writings of the *patria*."

Compared to the privileges granted to Spensithius, those of Patrias may seem modest. The scribe is the object of legal protection by the city, but his status seems in no way equivalent to that of a citizen. Nevertheless, the position conferred on him entailed a change of status. Between the full citizen and the slave Patrias, was it not the very status of the *dēmosios* that was being confusedly defined? That simple observation, however hypothetical, is suggestive. If Patrias had been truly a *dēmosios*, the implication is that his status could in no case be reduced to that of private slaves. This insight opens new vantage points on the status of public slaves, as the Athenian documentation of the classical period will confirm.

Was Tyranny the Origin of Public Slavery?

To be sure, Patrias's case is unclear and isolated. Yet this singular and mysterious individual—the "anonymous servant of the nation"—puts a human face on the gradual shift from the *dēmiourgos* of the archaic period to the *dēmosios* of the classical period. It sheds little light, however, on the spread of public slavery at the pivotal moment between the archaic and classical periods. Should its growth be attributed to a particular type of political system? There is certainly a great temptation to link the appearance of the first public slaves to the development of tyrannical regimes in seventh- and sixth-century Greece.[64] The hypothesis is particularly appealing in that it is reflected in a process abundantly documented by anthropologists, one that associates the emergence of a strong power, or one possessing a certain capacity for constraint, with the rise of slavery. More precisely, the advent of state societies would often have as its corollary the increase of slavery—at first concentrated in the hands of the possessor of political authority—to unprecedented levels. The sovereign, in disengaging masses of men from the traditional bonds of fidelity and placing them in his exclusive service, would create the embryonic forms of a "state apparatus"[65] and would thereby thwart the aspirations of the traditional elite to hold a monopoly on public affairs.

Yet one must refrain from moving too quickly from that anthropological generality to the situation of the cities of archaic Greece. In the cities of the late archaic period, tyrannical regimes did offer the authorities new ways to exercise constraint, but did they contribute toward the rise of public slavery? The hypothesis rests on three documents, all of which are problematic in various ways.

When evoking tyrants, sources from the classical period commonly mentioned the presence at their side of personal guards to ensure their safety. Tyrants often set about disarming the population: in most situations, keeping order in the city became the exclusive prerogative of their militias.[66] In fact, the monopolization of the armed forces was a central aspect of the scandal of tyrannical regimes according to the authors of the classical period, who viewed military service and the possession of arms in the city as inseparable from the status of citizen. Thus in the second half of the sixth century, Polycrates, tyrant of Samos, is said to have had at his disposal more than a thousand professional archers.[67] It is very difficult to know whether this was a personal guard composed of slaves or, more likely, a troop of mercenaries in the city's service. Somewhat earlier, in the mid-sixth century, the Athenian people—if one is to believe Herodotus—bestowed spear-bearers (*doruphoroi*) and club-bearers (*korunephoroi*) on Peisistratus.[68] Later authors also mention Peisistratus's three hundred bodyguards.[69] Some have been tempted to see these different armed groups in the service of the tyrants as the predecessors of the Scythian archers of classical Athens, public slaves who performed a policing function in the city. Such a genealogy is risky, however. As Brian

Lavelle has shown, Peisistratus's bodyguards were undoubtedly citizens, and he had also recruited many foreign mercenaries. There would thus be no trace of slaves among the tyrant's personal guards.[70] It should be added that if the orator Aeschines is to be believed, the Scythian archers were acquired by the city in the wake of the second Median War, that is, more than forty years after Peisistratus's death.[71]

Several ancient authors also mention the existence of tyrannical laws on slavery. According to Nicolas of Damascus and Heraclides Lembus, for example, Periander forbade the citizens of Corinth from acquiring slaves.[72] In such an account, it is very difficult to distinguish between the realities of the seventh and sixth centuries and the antityrannical propaganda of the classical period. For the authors of the classical period, in fact, the tyrants typically abolished the distinction between freemen and slaves.[73] In that sense, Periander's condemnation of private slavery would reveal the servile fate of any civic community under the leadership of a tyrant, and Nicolas of Damascus's account would in that case be merely a digression on an old axiom of Greek political philosophy. If the authenticity of the measure is conceded, however, it may be supposed that the tyrant of Corinth's aim was to monopolize a slave labor force, of which private citizens were thereby dispossessed. But another interpretation is just as legitimate: Periander may have implemented a measure in Corinth somewhat analogous to Solon's laws in Athens, prohibiting any citizen from acquiring another Corinthian as a slave.

The unusual place granted to certain slaves in the tyrants' entourage constitutes more conclusive evidence. Two individuals in particular rouse the curiosity of historians: Maeandrius, secretary to the tyrant Polycrates in Samos in the second half of the sixth century; and Micythus, who belonged to the inner circle of Anaxilas, tyrant of Sicily, in the early fifth century. Maeandrius occupied a preeminent position, and Polycrates entrusted him with important military commands. The tyrant may even have considered naming him his successor as the city's leader. Yet Herodotus describes him as the tyrant's secretary (*grammatistēs*),[74] and the later sources are unanimous in portraying him as one of Polycrates's slaves.[75] According to Herodotus's account, however, Maeandrius's legal status was more ambiguous. Although a portion of the Corinthians believed he was "not worthy to reign" over them,[76] the historian elsewhere characterizes him as a man of the *astu*, the city or commonwealth.[77] The remark suggests either that Maeandrius, although a citizen, had entered into such a close relation of dependency with the tyrant that he was disqualified from any claim to exercise political authority over the old families of Corinth,[78] or that he was a resident of the city of Corinth in the broad sense. One thing is certain: although the status of Maeandrius is difficult to clarify, it hardly seems akin to that of the public slaves in the classical period.

Micythus, in the service of the Sicilian tyrant Anaxilas in the first half of the fifth century, better embodies the traits of a slave who could be called "public." In describing him, Herodotus indicates that he was of the house of Anaxilas, from whom he obtained a prestigious position; the tyrant made him the governor of Rhegium.[79] According to Diodorus Siculus, the tyrant had also entrusted the care of his children to Micythus.[80] Pausanias, partly repeating Herodotus's account, portrays Micythus as the slave (*doulos*) of Anaxilas and explains that the king entrusted the administration of his treasure to him. It was upon his master's death, or following a popular uprising in Rhegium, that Micythus left to settle in Tegea.[81] If one concedes that Maeandrius was in fact Polycrates's slave, it is easy to grasp what connects the two individuals and what distinguishes them from the public slaves of the classical period. Maeandrius and Micythus may have been the servants of tyrants, who endowed them with extraordinary prerogatives, but neither can be called a slave of the city, either of Corinth or of Rhegium. Theirs is a domestic slavery used for political or public ends, but it is not evidence of the existence of public slavery in the strict sense.

Must one therefore refute once and for all the role played by the "tyrannical moment" in the emergence of public slavery? No, of course not. The tyrannical regimes, in explicitly asserting a power of constraint of which citizens were dispossessed, laid the foundations, if only symbolically, of a state apparatus parallel to the sphere of political power, without which public slavery would certainly never have come into being. For the institution to actually emerge, however, the nature and dimensions of the traditional forms of slavery in the Greek world had to change. The source of public slavery's rise lay in the confluence of three phenomena: first, the specificity of the place allotted to the *dēmiourgoi* since the early archaic period; second, the development, on a previously unknown scale, of chattel slavery; and third, the political reorganization of many civic communities at the dawn of the classical period. Furthermore, one cannot rule out the possibility that contact with the Persian Empire, where court slavery on a large scale developed, may have influenced the world of the Greek cities.[82] This complex historical process, similar to a tight ball of tangled threads, has to be reconstituted in order to analyze the development of the institution at the turn of the fifth century.

Public Slavery, Child of the Democratic System

As Finley has shown, the development of chattel slavery cannot be separated from the growth of a new political model, the one to which the name "democracy" is attached and for which, no matter what one says, the Athenian city constitutes the model. In that sense, the progress of slavery "hand in hand"[83] with democracy constitutes the crucial event of the late archaic period, without which the advent of the classical city would be incomprehensible. Taken together the two phenomena inaugurated a vast redefinition of personal statuses within the civic societies of the Greek world; it was because of them that the status of citizen and slave, and citizen and metic, developed in tandem in the late archaic period. The indigent artisan born in Athens was now endowed with political rights equal to those of the aristocrats, irrespective of the size of his fortune or the level of his activity. As a citizen, he became separated once and for all, both legally and symbolically, from foreigners and slaves. At the same time, the status of metic, attested for the first time in the late sixth century, created a radical break between Athenians and resident aliens. In the course of that vast reshaping of the political community, the relative indetermination of the status of *dēmiourgoi* was fated to disappear.

Even more precisely, the development of public slavery can be explained by the new needs of the democratic system, which now rested on very broad popular participation. Every citizen was able to participate in the Assembly, to be called to the Heliaia and the Boulē,[84] and to be selected by lot to become a magistrate. At the same time, however, the democratic system presupposed a swift turnover among those vested with political authority because the Bouleutai (members of the Council of Five Hundred) and the Heliasts (court judges), like the other magistrates, were replaced on an annual basis. In that context, an "administrative" body ensuring the permanent operation of civic life proved to be much more useful than it had been when a restricted elite, composed of a few families, passed civic offices among themselves. The use of slaves also made it possible to install in the city, on a permanent basis, a portion of the itinerant specialists who in the archaic period had sold their skills on demand, going from city to city.

Furthermore, the democratic systems, in giving to the majority access to political participation, established a new relationship between knowledge and power. The skills passed on through long familiarity with power were now ill suited to legitimize political authority. In some realms, no doubt, expertise remained indispensable, but the values of the democratic system prevented these positions from being entrusted to a restricted category of citizens. The Athenians usually preferred to allot them to slaves, which in sum amounted to relegating that expertise "off-field" from the political.

Finally, the new needs of the democratic system could be satisfied by an ever-increasing supply resulting from the tremendous expansion of the slave markets. The existence of that supply, however, cannot in itself explain the use of slave labor to perform a large share of the "administrative" tasks in the city. The object of the following chapters will be to understand the meaning of that arrangement, but it should be noted from the outset that, in reality, the decision to entrust such duties to slaves had the effect of dissimulating, even making invisible, the administrative sphere within the city.

IN OUR SEARCH for the origins of that peculiar institution known as public slavery, the archaic *dēmiourgos* surged up in our path. His condition, fundamentally defined by a relation of exteriority to the community he served and closely associated with the sovereignty of the *basileus*, anticipates in several respects that of the *dēmosios* of the classical period. The advent of that institution, however, must be attributed to the major upheaval of the late archaic period, characterized by the development of chattel slavery and the gradual imposition of the democratic system. From the Homeric *dēmiourgos* to the first *dēmosios* of the classical period (perhaps the mysterious Patrias), our journey has already drawn several lines of tension that will be central to the workings of the classical city, as well as to the relationship between knowledge and power, and the intimate connection between the figure of the slave and the question of sovereignty. They will form the heart of his book.

But the reader is no doubt clamoring for its protagonist to finally be introduced: These public slaves, who were they? What did they do?

CHAPTER TWO

Servants of the City

> I never used to be interested in politics. The politician, whether a deputy in parliament or a cabinet minister, seemed to me like a servant in my house, whose job is to attend to the indifferent matters of life: that the dust does not get too deep and meals are ready on time. Of course, he carries out his responsibility badly, but as long as it is done passably I do not interfere.
>
> —Robert Musil, "Political Confessions of a Young Man," in *Precision and Soul: Essays and Addresses*

It is now early spring, and we are standing in the shade of a portico on a public square in the city of ancient Athens. Three young men, under the watchful eye of two old gentlemen, Socrates and Theodorus, come up with the idea of defining the essence of the statesman. To achieve their ends, the three apprentice philosophers adopt an unusual method, which proceeds by successive dichotomies: In establishing ever more precisely what political competence is not, they hope to arrive at an understanding, negatively as it were, of what it is.

As they press on, the young men are quickly led to identify a series of activities characteristic of life in the city, each of which would be distinct from the authentic royal function (*archē basilikē*), the practice of the art of politics. First are the so-called auxiliary arts. Whether concerned with the production of goods or with ritual practices, they are certainly indispensable to community life, but mastery of them cannot be equated with the art of politics. Among these "auxiliary" arts, one technique in particular is problematic for our young philosophers, that exercised by all those "who become by long practice skilled as clerks and other clever men who perform various services in connexion with the magistracies." Because of their administrative expertise—their knowledge of the inner workings of the state, as we moderns would put it—those who practice this art could claim to posses royal competence. The Stranger acknowledges that it is among "the class of slaves and servants . . . that we shall find those who set up claims against the king for the very fabric of his art," the fabric from which politics proceeds.

But the young apprentices are on the wrong track. Do these experts in public affairs possess authentic political competence? The question has hardly been raised when its response is given by Socrates the Younger: Because they are "servants . . . not themselves rulers in the city," these false rivals of the statesman cannot participate in the royal function in any way. The Stranger is therefore forced to acknowledge that it would be altogether absurd to seek the possessor of *archē basilikē* "in any servile position."[1]

This brief interlude from Plato's *Statesman* is one of the rare passages that Greek philosophy devoted to the administrative aspect of civic organization. Socrates the Younger and the Stranger themselves reveal the reason for that silence, drawing a sharp dividing line between two ethical orders, that of the political, a noble activity worthy of freemen, and that of service or administration. Authentic politics cannot belong to the realm of administrative expertise, however "universal." This equation between administration and servility was a commonplace of the Greeks from both the classical and Hellenistic periods, now translated into Platonic language. In the Athens of Pericles, and in the little cities of Asia Minor at the end of the Hellenistic period, many duties indispensable to the operation of the cities did not fall within the magistrates' areas of competence and as such were excluded from the political field. Most of the men responsible for these tasks were not citizens but slaves, and to designate them, the Greeks used the term *dēmosios*, which referred indiscriminately to a function—that of working for the city—and a personal status, that of slave.

It is a delicate matter to draw up a list and describe the "jobs" of these slaves, and such a task cannot rely on any mapping of civic activities already done by the ancient sources. Oscar Jacob circumvented the difficulty by dividing public slaves into three categories: "workers," members of the "police," and "clerks."[2] Not only does that tripartition fail to include all the functions entrusted to the *dēmosioi*, it also views their activity through the prism of professional classifications that had little meaning in the classical city. Therefore, rather than try to categorize and rank their tasks, a dubious procedure, one must identify the spheres of action in which their skills were performed, discerning in each case the reasons the cities entrusted these different tasks to them.

The Hired Help of Civic Institutions

At the Assembly, at the Council, before the city's courts, even at the gymnasium, the presence of public slaves was indispensable for the operation of the city's institutions. For example, in the small city of Pednelissos, in Pisidia in the first century CE, public slaves assisted judges in the phases preliminary to the presentation of legal arguments.[3] This aspect was by no means restricted to the tribunals of faraway Pisidia. *Dēmosioi* were omnipresent in the workings of Athenian justice in the fourth century. If one is to believe Aristotle, they organized the selection of judges by lot, played a role in their assignment to the various tribunals, and tallied the votes before a verdict was pronounced.[4] It should be added, to complete the picture, that the *dēmosioi* also stood watch outside the tribunals, oversaw the entrance of judges into the courtroom, and very often ushered members of the public to their seats.[5] Within a city that, according to Aristophanes, had raised the legal trial to a fine art, the number of slaves attached to the city's courts was certainly considerable, and there is little reason to be surprised that lexicographers have often seen the duties they performed there as the principal activity of the *dēmosioi* in the ancient city.[6]

Although public slaves seem to have participated little in organizing the deliberative process or the voting in the Athenian Assembly, it was quite a different matter in some other cities during the Hellenistic and imperial periods. In Acmonia at the beginning of the imperial era, it was public slaves who organized the vote count before entrusting the results to the *dogmatographoi*, who entered the decree into the permanent record.[7] And in the fictional Samos of *The Life of Aesop*, a *dēmosios* helps organize the election of the magistrates, which is held at the theater.[8] Athenian documentation has a great deal to say about the slaves who were in the service of the Council. One must imagine a large staff whose activities, alongside those of the prytaneis, were indispensable to the operation of sessions of the Boulē. These slaves were well regarded in the city, so much so that beginning in the fifth century, the Athenians extended to them the privilege of occupying the *proedria* (select reserved seats) at the Theater of Dionysus.[9] As of the late fourth century, these slaves, along with the prytaneis, were even honored by the city, grateful for the work they performed in its service.[10]

Public Writings

It is very difficult to specify the function of the *dēmosioi* attached to the Council of Five Hundred. Some evidently participated in organizing the sessions of the Boulē. In the late fourth century, for example, a certain Antiphates introduced a legal action, a supplication on behalf of another public slave, Eucrates.[11] The largest contingent, however, worked in the Metrōon, the sanctuary of the Mother of Gods, which was also the city's archive. Public slaves, then, played the role of guardians of public memory, a legacy of the position of *mnamōn*, which Spensithius had held long before in Crete. In classical Athens, these archivist slaves were regularly called upon to cater to magistrates in need of a file. The documents listing the rental of sacred lands were thus overseen by *dēmosioi*, who had to bring them when needed to the *apodectai*.[12] Likewise, in the late fourth century, a *dēmosios* was in charge of tracking down the documents regarding the city's ramparts.[13]

As of the mid-fourth century, all these slaves worked under the authority of the secretary of the prytaneis. It may be conjectured, however, that his authority ended where the work of filing, conserving, and copying documents began, a true specialization on the part of the *dēmosioi*, who must have enjoyed a certain autonomy in the performance of their work.[14] "There is an entry in the record-office at the Temple of Demeter, of which the public caretaker is in charge [*ho dēmosios tetaktai*], and a decree in which he is mentioned by name," Demosthenes stated before the Athenian Assembly, referring to a decree for which his famous enemy Aeschines had already secured passage.[15]

In addition to filing and conservation duties, the *dēmosios* played a role in composing the documents. In the late fourth century, an Athenian public slave was entrusted with the assignment of copying a decision deposited in the archives granting *isoteleia* (a privileged tax status) to a resident alien, which would then be engraved on a marble stela.[16] And in the latter half of the second century in Iasos, a *dēmosios* named Diophantus transcribed private documents before they were placed in the archives.[17] The job was not without its risks. In Lycia in the mid-first century BCE, the edict of the Roman governor Quintus Veranius openly attacked a certain Tryphōn, a public slave responsible for the archives of the city of Tlos, who was whipped after inappropriate additions and deletions were spotted in certain documents.[18] The punishment, as the governor explained, would be a lesson to other public slaves who might demonstrate the same carelessness.[19] In broader terms, *dēmosioi* were very often in charge of conserving or destroying records. On the island of Kos, when the deme of Halasarna set out to reengrave the list of priests of the sanctuary of Apollo in the first century CE, he gave a public slave the task of destroying beforehand all the inscriptions illegally commemorating the priesthoods of the previous years.[20]

The city clerk's office was not limited to management of the archives. Among the "various services in connexion with magistracies," as Socrates the Younger put it, the inventory of public goods was a task of the utmost importance. In conjunction with the city's magistrates, it was usually a public slave who compiled an inventory of the goods stored in the sanctuaries, kept the accounts for the major public construction sites, and accompanied magistrates on military missions, listing and overseeing expenses. In 353/352 BCE, the Athenians gave a certain Eucles the assignment of inventorying all the items assembled in the Chalkotheke on the Acropolis;[21] and in the late fourth century two *dēmosioi*, Leōn and Zōpyrion, made a copy of the inventory of the goods in the sanctuary of Athena for its treasurers.[22] Half a century later, below the temple of Athena, in the sanctuary of the hero Asclepius, Demetrius was responsible for inventorying the offerings in honor of the "hero doctor," "so that, these things having taken place, the affairs of the gods shall be handled well and piously by the Council and the People."[23] Meanwhile, in second-century Athenian Delos in the middle of the Aegean Sea, Peritas, a *dēmosios* of Macedonian origin, compiled the inventory of the property of Artemis and Asclepius for several years in a row.[24]

But the *dēmosioi* did not merely play the role of clerks within the city's major sanctuaries. In the Athenian arsenals of the classical period, it was public slaves—such as Opsigonus between 323 and 321—who kept lists of the public equipment purchased or sold by the city on the orders of the Boulē.[25] For major construction sites, these slaves (for example, Telophilus in the sanctuary of Eleusis in 329/328) were sometimes assigned to keep accounting records of the labor performed.[26] For the military operations conducted by the generals outside the city, it was also public slaves who kept an exact count of the expenses incurred.[27] These slaves were responsible for the bookkeeping records used to settle disputes when the magistrates' yearly accounts were closed. It is therefore clear that on many occasions, *dēmosioi* were more than simply clerks but were actual accountants, both assisting and supervising the magistrates during their assignments. It was undoubtedly by virtue of these accounting skills that *dēmosioi* were sometimes put to use levying taxes in classical Athens.[28]

Public slaves held the same post for several years and in that sense embodied the permanence of a civic knowledge or competence that was beyond the purview of the magistrates, who were usually selected by lot and replaced every year. Gustave Glotz did not hesitate to evoke the "secret power" that these slaves exercised over the magistrates, their "apparent masters."[29] These slaves constituted a powerful monitoring instrument available to the civic community to keep an eye on the activities of its magistrates. A legal argument by Demosthenes suggests that the Athenians did not fail to consult these public slaves if they suspected a magistrate of using his position in the city to advance his own interests.[30] It should be noted that inscriptions usually mention by name the *dēmosios* in service during the accounting process. That mention was undoubtedly the equivalent of a signature, by means of which the inventory or bookkeeping operation acquired its legality. In thus participating in the validation of the magistrates' accounts, the *dēmosioi* played a determining role in the smooth operation of civic life.

Civic Stamps and Seals

In addition to these bookkeeping operations, it was the task of public slaves in classical Athens to guarantee the authenticity of the coins in circulation and to protect the standards for weights and measures used in the city. A law promulgated in 375/374 BCE, whose aim was to combat the circulation of counterfeit money, stipulated that two public slaves, one on the agora of Athens and the other at Piraeus, would monitor and attest to the quality of the coins used in the city's commercial zones.[31] These two public slaves were in the service of magistrates but also of ordinary people—shopkeepers or merchants, if they wished. With that law, the Athenians were simply confirming the existence of a function created back in the fifth century: the 398/397 inventories of the temple of the Hekatompedon, located on the Acropolis, mention "the false staters sealed in a box by Lakon."[32] This Lakon was no doubt the "verifier" (*dokimastēs*) who had discovered false staters, which the Council, having confiscated them, stored in the treasury of Athena.[33] The wording of the inscription seems to indicate that the city's seal, entrusted to the slave, was required for the coins to be withdrawn from circulation.

Nearly three centuries later, the Athenians again placed public slaves in the position of guaranteeing the city's commercial exchanges. In the late second century BCE, the task of conserving the standards (*skhōmata*) fixing weights and measures (*metra kai ta stathma*) in use in the city was entrusted to three *dēmosioi*. In three different places of Attica (Piraeus, Eleusis, and the Skias, located near the Tholos on the Agora), they "shall give copies of the [measures and weights] to the magistrates [and to] all [others] who need them."[34] Hence for any disputed transaction, *agoranomoi* and merchants had to go to the *dēmosios* to have the official weights and measures verified. Whether regarding the use of the city's seal, the control of its currency, or the conservation of the standards of civic weights and measures, the *dēmosioi* were closely linked to the sphere of civic stamps and seals.

One Greek term captures better than any other that strange identity between the figure of the slave and the civic stamp: *sphragis*, which can refer both to the public seal and to the brand tattooed on the slave's flesh.[35] Hence a man whose status was literally inscribed *in* the flesh was assigned the task of guardian of the city's stamps and seals; a man deprived statutorily of an identity was responsible for identifying the community's property. The close link between the slave and civic stamps and seals actually appears in the middle of the most complete account we possess of the slave revolt in ancient Greece. In the third century BCE on the island of Chios, which Theopompus indicates was the first city to have practiced chattel slavery, a slave by the name of Drimacus reportedly escaped with several dozen of his fellows. Having taken refuge in the mountains overlooking the island, they went so far as to constitute a kingdom, with Drimacus as their leader. After living several years by raiding and looting the coastal cities, these fugitive slaves finally concluded a truce with the free population of Chios. At that time, the slave king Drimacus, who ordered the production of units of weights and measures (*metra kai stathma*) and a personal seal (*shragida idian*) to inaugurate his new power, solemnly proclaimed to the Chians, by way of reconciliation: "Whatever I take from any of you, I'll take it using these measures and weights; after I take what I need, I'll seal up the storerooms with this seal and otherwise leave them as they are."[36]

A slave king, master of the standards of the city's weights and measures and possessor of the community's seal? In fact, the chronicle of Nymphodorus of Syracuse, whose historicity is a matter of dispute, looks like the foundation story of a *doulopolis*—a city of slaves—and deserves to be interpreted in terms of the origin narratives of the ancient cities. These narratives, when they relate the great deeds that establish a city, generally emphasize the delimitation of the large civic sanctuary and the creation of the new political community's magistracies and institutions.[37] In a way, the fashioning of a civic seal and the establishment of the standards of weights and measures that together founded the sovereignty of Drimacus's kingdom are the equivalents, within an unlikely city of slaves, of the delimitation of the sanctuary of the poliad deity and the foundation of political institutions within the only communities worthy of the name *polis*, those composed of freemen.

Discipline and Castigate

Although some *dēmosioi* were clerks who inventoried public property or guardians of the city's standards and archives, one must refrain from imagining that all public slaves were genteel scholars, experts in bookkeeping and in handling public documents. Very often, they embodied civic authority in its most repressive form. In Rhodian Peraea, public slaves performed the role of police officers for the *ktoina* (a Rhodian civic subdivision), as indicated by a religious regulation that specified: "If anyone violates this regulation, may the *hierothutai* [the priest in charge of sacrifices], the public slave, and any other citizen of the deme prevent him from doing so."[38] Similarly, public slaves kept watch over activities occurring in certain public buildings. In the late Hellenistic period, the uses of the gymnasium extended far beyond physical exercise; it was a place for the celebration of major civic cults, for public funerals, and for gatherings of the community as a whole. Some historians go so far as to grant it the status of a "second agora."[39] It is therefore no surprise to find public slaves working there, as they did in the tribunals and councils of the classical age, whether to keep order in the gymnasium of Pergamon[40] or to stand watch outside the buildings of Delos.[41] *Dēmosioi* were very often the only staff permanently attached to the gymnasium, whose maintenance they performed even while exercising a policing function.

In that respect, the Athenian documentation is once again unsurpassed. In the first place, a large contingent of Athenian *dēmosioi* was placed in the service of mysterious magistrates, designated in the ancient sources by their number and not their function: the Eleven.[42] Selected by lot, they were tasked with arresting men condemned by the Council, the Assembly, or the Heliaia, and also with imprisoning them until the sentence was carried out. Within the context of their mission, they enjoyed extraordinary prerogatives compared to the other magistrates, such as the right to enter and search the homes of public debtors.[43] The public slaves of the Eleven thus make an appearance during famous arrests in Athenian history, such as those of Theramenes and Phocion in the classical period, or much later, that of the apostle Paul.[44]

It was the responsibility of the Eleven to maintain the small building that served as a prison (*desmōterion*), located southwest of the Agora, where a corps of public slaves guarded the prisoners.[45] The delegation of such a task to *dēmosioi* must have been a feature common to many cities, because in the second century CE, Pliny the Younger, governor of Bithynia-Pontus, asked Emperor Trajan whether the custom ought to be respected.[46] A few centuries earlier, Plato's *Phaedo*, recounting Socrates's last days, had provided a vivid portrait of the Athenian penitentiary administration, depicting three of its members: the first, placed at the entrance, held the keys to the building and monitored visits;[47] the second conversed with Socrates for a few moments at the end of the dialogue, before returning with the third, who brought the poison "in a cup ready for use" to the condemned man.[48]

This last figure must not be confused with the man in charge of most of the capital executions in the city. *Koinos, dēmios, dēmokoinos* (the one who carries out common things): In a strange understatement, that is how the ancient sources most often describe the executioner, without always indicating that, before anything else, he was a *dēmosios*.[49] In refusing to specify his true function, in designating only his relation to public affairs, the ancient authors seem to have wanted to avoid giving a precise name to a task ignoble by its very nature. That is in fact the reason it was entrusted to a slave: The Athenians thereby prevented *miasma*, the impurity associated with crime, and one by a citizen moreover, from descending on the city as a whole. The inferiority attached to the status of slave immunized the community against the risk of impurity incurred by the murder of a freeman; the crime, committed by a slave, lost it toxicity for the community.

In fifth-century Athens, the power of coercion placed in the *dēmosioi*'s hands was primarily embodied in an urban police corps composed exclusively of slaves under the authority of the prytaneis.[50] This is bewildering at first sight. The Athenians never imagined that public security could rest on a body of citizens that would hold a monopoly on violence. The city's security as a whole lay with each of its members, who had the fundamental right to bear arms. As a result, Athens in the classical period never had a police force, except for a slave corps placed at the disposal of its different magistrates. *Toxotai* (archers), *Skuthai* (Scythians), and *Speusinioi* (from "Speusinius," the name of the man who founded the corps) were the terms the ancient authors used for these public slaves, which historiography is accustomed to call "Scythian archers." The ethnic composition of the corps is less clear than it appears, however. It is very probable that, in referring to "Scythians," the Athenians were not so much constructing an ethnic referent as designating in conventional terms an "alterity of the generic type."[51] As François Lissarrague writes, "to assume the role of the Scythian within Athenian society was to play at being other in order to better affirm one's own values and identity."[52] The ethnic homogeneity of the corps is actually far from certain, and one cannot rule out the possibility that Thracians or Getae served in a corps that the Athenians persisted in portraying as Scythian.

The police corps was constituted at the initiative of a certain Speusinius between the end of the Median Wars (479) and the Peace of Callias (449).[53] No doubt originally composed of three hundred slaves, it may have reached a thousand (or twelve hundred) archers by the end of the fifth century.[54] Clearly, these "Scythian archers" must be distinguished from the mercenary archers who fought alongside the civic phalanx. Some historians have suggested that these *dēmosioi* at times joined with the Athenian citizens in battle.[55] But the primary mission of the Scythian archers, armed with a whip, probably a bow, and perhaps a small dagger, was to keep public order in the city. One of Aristophanes's scholiasts portrays them as the city's guards (*phulakai tou asteōs*). According to the comedies of Aristophanes, few places in the city of Athens were free from their activity; at the Assembly as at the Council, at celebrations and at the marketplace, these slaves were truly guardians of public order.[56]

Ancient comedy elevated these archers to the rank of comic archetypes. As depicted by Aristophanes, but also by Eupolis, Cratinus, and the comic poet Plato, the character of the police officer—the oafish flatfoot, cowardly under his blustering exterior, constantly ridiculed by those he is supposed to be pursuing—spawned many successors. In that sense, Aristophanes's Scythian archer introduced a long series of pitiful policemen culminating, by way of Guignol's gendarme, in Hergé's Thomson and Thompson.[57] Spineless, fearful, sometimes obscene, often dead drunk, the Scythian archer is unquestionably an antimodel of the citizen.[58] Lysistrata, after ridiculing the Scythian archers who wanted to seize her and her associates, turns to the magistrates in charge of them and says mockingly, "Did you think you were going up against a bunch of slave girls?"[59] Even in the upside down world of *Lysistrata*, an Athenian woman is still superior to a slave!

But the Scythian archer did not only provide the inverted mirror in which the Athenian citizen liked to contemplate himself onstage at the Theater of Dionysus, as a shopworn structuralist reading would have it. Such a view ignores the bonhomie, the fellow feeling, that these archers elicited, incomparable in that respect to the figures of radical alterity manufactured in fifth-century Athenian art. Above all, it fails to see that these Scythian archers—who, if one is to believe later indications, lived in vast tents set up at the edge of the agora of Athens or near the Areopagus—were well integrated into democratic society.[60] In 411 and 404, they demonstrated their loyalty to democratic institutions, and it appears that democracy, restored after 403, did not fail to increase their number.[61]

The last evidence of the activities of the Scythian archers dates to no later than the first two decades of the fourth century. Many historians have deduced that the Athenians dissolved the corps because it had become too costly to maintain. This hypothesis is rather perplexing. Is it not rather that our principal source on the subject, ancient comedy, disappeared in the first decades of the fourth century?[62]

Artisans in the Service of the City

In contrast to the archivists at the Metrōon, many public slaves performed tasks that did not require any particular expertise. Oscar Jacob has categorized them as "public slave laborers (*ergatai*)." The *dēmosioi* under the authority of the *astynomoi*, who did regular maintenance on the roads, surely belonged to that category.[63] Likewise, the status of "laborer" can be attributed to the public slaves who worked in the city's mints. A fragment from the orator Andocides attacking the "demagogue" Hyperbolus briefly mentions them: "Hyperbolus I blush to mention. His father, a branded slave, still works at the public mint [*argurokopeion*]; while he himself, a foreign interloper, makes lamps for a living."[64] The law of Nicophon of 375/374 BCE also specifies that the *dokimastēs* will be remunerated with the same funds as those used to pay the wages of the workers in the mint,[65] which leaves little doubt that they were public slaves.

Dēmosioi were particularly numerous at the city's construction sites, where they practiced various trades. In the mid-second century, for example, Eumenus II of Pergamon gave slaves (*sōmata*) to the city of Delphi to do reparation work in the theater of the Panhellenic sanctuary.[66] A century later, a decree by the Thasians made public slaves available to a certain Stilbon "in view of the reparations and construction" to be completed within the city's sanctuary, no doubt dedicated to Artemis.[67] It is also very probable that many public slaves worked on the sanctuary of Apollo in independent Delos of the third century.[68]

Nothing, however, provides a more lively portrait of the operation of a construction site in the Greek world than the bookkeeping records for Eleusis, engraved by the Athenians in the mid-fourth century. The *dēmosioi* formed a large contingent of the group of slaves working in the sanctuary. Under the charge of an epistates (foreman), who shared their condition, they performed various tasks. Some transported the stones from Pentelicus to the sanctuary of Eleusis; others worked on erecting the Telesterion, where initiations into the mysteries of the gods took place; still others kept track of the expenses of the project; and finally, some *dēmosioi*, working alongside the architect, verified the accuracy of the weigh-ins of the different tools, thus ensuring, on the city's behalf, that he would not make any mistakes.[69] It is very probable that the use of public slaves can be explained in this case by the difficulty the city had recruiting artisans and private slaves, as it had done less than a century earlier on the construction site of the Erechtheion.[70]

The Athenians did not neglect to initiate some of the public slaves into the mysteries of Demeter: "We have initiated five of the *dēmosioi* who work clearing the temple,"[71] the bookkeeping records for the 330s specify. The reason can be easily discerned: These slaves worked in the Telesterion, the heart of the sanctuary, a zone to which only initiates into the mysteries had access.[72] But the needs of the construction site do not in themselves explain that privilege. One cannot fail to observe that, of all the slaves working on the sanctuary, only public slaves were allowed to perform this task, with the condition sine qua non that accompanied it: initiation. Thanks to the ministrations of the city, which provided them with the animals to be sacrificed, these *dēmosioi* could even participate in the celebration of Chōes, a crucial moment in the feast of Anthestheria.[73] In reality, it is very possible that the initiation of the *dēmosioi* indicates that they enjoyed a privileged status that distinguished them from all the other slaves at the work site. And in fact, in the sanctuary of Lagina in Asia Minor during the imperial period, a similar privilege was granted to the *dēmosioi* who, unlike the priests' slaves, were authorized to enter the heart of the sanctuary.[74]

Priests for the City?

Finally, one cannot neglect the *dēmosioi*'s participation in the religious life of the cities. Whether they inventoried the goods consecrated there or participated in the construction of one building or another, public slaves were commonly present in the sanctuaries. In many cases, their presence implied that certain skills had been delegated by the civic authorities, who entrusted part of their labor force to the sanctuaries' authorities. So it was for the *dēmosioi Eleusinothen*, slaves of the city of Athens who were placed in the service of the sanctuary of Demeter and Persephone.[75] In the late second century, the decree of the city of Delphi in honor of Nicomedes III of Bithynia and Queen Laodice specified that the slaves were offered by the king "to the god and to the city."[76] The slaves thus functioned as civic property allocated by delegation to a sanctuary. In Hellenistic and imperial Asia Minor, it is sometimes difficult to establish a functional distinction between the *dēmosioi* and the sacred slaves of the sanctuaries, called *hierodouloi*. For example, in the sanctuary of Zeus Labraundos in the early imperial period, public slaves and sacred slaves under the control of the small city of Mylasa worked side by side. Both were remunerated from the coffers of the sanctuary and suffered the same punishment if they ever failed in their assignment.[77]

The epigraphy of the sanctuaries also describes many public slaves who assisted priests in the management of the sanctuaries. In Athenian Delos of the second and first centuries, the *dēmosioi* played an important role in organizing the cult of foreign deities around Mount Cynthus.[78] Alongside the priests and their *zakoroi* (assistants), a certain Eutuchides was active for three years in a row in the sanctuary of the Syrian Aphrodite on Mount Cynthus in the late second century.[79] In a small Delian sanctuary that is difficult to identify, a public slave was even the epimelete (superintendent) of the site for two years running,[80] whereas in the sanctuary of Asclepius a *hupēretēs* (servant, no doubt a public slave) was active beside the priest and the neocore, in charge of the maintenance of the treasure.[81]

To serve in a sanctuary is one thing, to perform the function of priest quite another. Although in classical Athens the priesthood was primarily conceived to be a magistracy, the priest who officiated over a civic cult occupied the position of intermediary between the community and the gods, which required an unassailable integrity. It is therefore striking that priesthoods were sometimes entrusted to *dēmosioi*, as attested by two inscriptions. In Delos in the second half of the second century (from 139 to 137), the Athenians entrusted the priesthood of the cult of Sarapis to a *dēmosios* for two years in a row.[82] That extraordinary decision no doubt attests to a temporary takeover of the sanctuary by the civic authorities, for a reason unknown to us.[83] Before the priesthood was ultimately handed over to citizens, the city may have taken control of the cult by allowing public slaves to practice it. In any case, the inscription confirms that there was no prohibition against a *dēmosios* becoming the priest of a cult.

An even more stunning example is provided by Rhodes in the early part of the imperial period. Displayed in the urban sanctuary of Zeus Atabyrius was a dedication from a cult association, that of the community (*koinon*) of the *Diosataburiastai*, composed of "slaves of the city" (*tōn tas polios doulōn*). The dedication explains that the *dēmosios* Eulimenus was the priest of Zeus Atabyrius and that he exercised his priesthood under the authority of the Rhodians (*huper tōn kuriōn Rodiōn*). During his tenure as priest, the association had consecrated a bronze ox in honor of Zeus Atabyrius, one of the major figures of the cult of Zeus in Rhodes, celebrated both on Mount Atabyrion and inside the urban sanctuary.[84] Was this cult public or private in nature? It is impossible to determine; but because the dedication specifies that these public slaves were acting "under the authority of the Rhodians," one may imagine that the city had entrusted to its *dēmosioi*, gathered together in an association, the exercise of a civic priesthood.[85] Finally, it cannot be ruled out that public slaves were called upon to represent all the public slaves in Rhodes in the exercise of the cult of Zeus Atabyrius.

The diversity of tasks assigned to the *dēmosioi* is a reminder of an obvious fact: Far from defining a specific place in production, the term *douleia* designated a legal status in the first place. Dozens of public slaves may have worked on the same construction site or in the service of a single institution, while practicing very different trades. In reality, beyond their common status as slaves, little united the conveyor of stone at the Eleusinion and the person in charge of keeping the accounts at the construction site. The degree of specialization or expertise involved in their task—and as a result, the slave's purchase price—was disparate to say the least. Slaves in the city's mints did not possess the rare, sought-after skill of the *dokimastēs* in charge of verifying the authenticity of the coins in circulation in the city. Likewise, while certain public slaves were sufficiently well known by the Athenians to be entrusted with one task or another by a vote in the Assembly, the slaves who swept the streets or hauled stones on the construction sites were simply anonymous faces. A shared slave identity thus masked very different living conditions.

Acquiring Slaves

Is it possible to estimate the number of *dēmosioi* in the city? This is a risky undertaking, since we have only two pieces of statistical data, equally uncertain, about a single city, Athens in the classical period. First, Scythian archers are known to have composed a corps of several hundred slaves, probably between three hundred and twelve hundred. Second, in the mid-fourth century Xenophon proposed that the city acquire large numbers of slaves in order to rent them out to private citizens.[86] According to Xenophon, that plan to turn a profit on public property required that the city become the owner of three times as many *dēmosioi* as there were citizens, which would have entailed a contingent of ninety thousand to a hundred thousand public slaves at the time. The plan, which was never realized, undoubtedly replicated a proposal by an Athenian general by the name of Diophantes in the first half of the fourth century, who wanted all public works projects to be entrusted to *dēmosioi*.[87] Based on partial information concerning only a fraction of the *dēmosioi* and a crude estimate based on a political project that was never realized, the historian can propose only an extraordinarily rough count: in Athens of the classical age, between one thousand and two thousand public slaves worked in the service of the city.

Was Athens representative of the other cities of the Greek world in that regard? One will never know. But two remarks by Aristotle suggest that, in certain cities, the proportion of *dēmosioi* was much higher than it was in Athens. In Epidamnus, Chalcidice, all the men employed on public works projects may have been public slaves; and in Chalcedon, the lawmaker Phaleas is said to have ruled that all artisans had the status of slaves of the city.[88] These two indicators are not corroborated by any other source, however, and they arouse suspicion. It also cannot be ruled out that, in the case of Epidamnus, Aristotle was referring to slavery of the Helotic type, very different from the Athenian slavery model, which was based on chattel slavery.

The inscriptions and literary sources are more explicit on the matter of acquiring *dēmosioi*. It was through the purchase of slaves at the markets, on the one hand, and thanks to gifts from major benefactors on the other, that cities acquired most of their slaves. It is also probable that new supplies of slaves were obtained by incorporating some of the children of *dēmosioi*.[89] Finally, a speech by Demosthenes suggests that some of the slaves confiscated from public debtors became city property. That mode of acquisition was unusual, however, given that cities usually preferred to sell off such slaves.[90] As Oscar Jacob noted about Athens, that was certainly a well-thought-out policy, based on the fear that these slaves, who had had a master and had no doubt established relations of all sorts in the city, would not properly serve its interests.[91] One fact, in any case, can only be surprising, especially in view of the situation of the *servi publici* in the Roman Republic: no written evidence exists of a citizen who became a *dēmosios* in the wake of a criminal conviction.[92] Likewise, prisoners of war who had fought against the city were not integrated into the public slave corps.[93]

The great majority of inscriptions, when they mention the acquisition of public slaves, specify that the city would purchase its future servants at the markets. The 375/374 law of Nicophon on the circulation of currency, for example, says: "So that there shall also be in Piraeus a verifier for the shippers [*nauklēroi*] and the merchants [*emporoi*] and all the others, let the Council appoint one of the public slaves, if one is available, or buy one."[94] In the mid-third century, the Delians purchased a slave to serve at the palaestra in the city's gymnasium.[95] The literary sources confirm the predominance of purchase. Aeschines explicitly notes that the Scythian archers in the early fifth century had been bought by the city;[96] and Xenophon does not envision any other means to constitute a civic slave labor force.[97] One must therefore imagine relatively specialized slave markets capable of supplying the cities with slaves who met the precise requirements for one task or another. In the *Politics*, Aristotle does not omit to establish a connection between the wealth of the cities and the growth in the number of public slaves; other functions, he says "are subordinate, and are the sort of services to which people when well off [*an euporōsi*] appoint slaves [*doulous*]."[98] The development of public slavery in fifth-century Athens is in that respect inseparable from the city's prosperity and imperialist expansion.

But the acquisition of slaves was also very often a result of the generosity of a powerful foreign benefactor. The gift could assume two different forms. The benefactor could offer slaves to the city, as Nicomedes of Bithynia and Eumenus of Pergamon did for the city of Delphi in the second century. But it was also common practice to allot the revenues of an inheritance to a city so that it could procure slaves for itself. Archippe, in establishing a foundation for the city of Cyme in the mid-second century, intended its revenues to provide a regular supply of public slaves to the small Asian city:

> When the talent, by loan of which at interest are to be bought slaves [*katagorasmon tōn sōmatōn*] and the *Bouleuterion* is to be repaired, is given by Archippe's inheritor, let the people passing a decree through the *strategoi* and *synedroi* of that time decide about gathering the sums and their interest and about the yearly overseer [*epistatēs*] in charge of the restoration of the *Bouleuterion* and about purchasing the slaves and their food, clothing and wages, and if any of the purchased slaves should suffer something, let the overseer in charge at that moment, purchase another slave so that they never be fewer than four.[99]

But these transfers of slaves from a private inheritance to the city did not always meet the strict requirements of a disinterested gift. In the little city of Tlos in the first century CE, the *dēmosios* in charge of civic records was "offered" to the city by a certain Apollonius of Patara, who received the sum of 300 drachmae from the city's treasury.[100]

Once *dēmosioi* had been acquired by the city, they were no doubt registered by the civic authorities, their names placed on lists subsequently made available to the magistrates. Thanks to these registries, citizens could choose the slaves suitable for the different assignments to be entrusted to them. Several Athenian inscriptions from the classical and Hellenistic periods specify that the *dēmosioi* performing one function or another were selected by a show of hands in the Assembly or the *Boulē*. This is by no means a trivial matter. It attests that, at times, the qualifications of some *dēmosioi* were known precisely by the entire civic community and were appreciated by them.[101]

"Public Service" in the Classical City?

There is no dearth of reasons to explain the interest the Greek cities had in placing slaves in their service: to ensure that the civic community had an expert keeping an eye on a magistrate; to have someone to perform an ignoble task in the place of a citizen; or to provide a labor force indispensable for the city's large construction sites. Some of these jobs conferred a certain de facto power over the members of the civic community. Nevertheless, as Socrates the Younger affirmed, their function did not lie within the realm of the *archē*. The *dēmosioi* were not magistrates, and their activities were considered divorced from the field of the political.

True, public slaves were remunerated, and at levels rather similar to those of the magistrates during the classical period.[102] What distinguished a *dēmosios* from a magistrate lay elsewhere. In the Greek city, the notion of political time entailed the annual replacement of the magistrates and, for all the magistracies selected by lot, rested on the principle of noniteration; that is, no citizen could hold a magistracy two years in a row. By contrast, *dēmosioi*, because of their specific qualifications, often remained at the same job for several consecutive years. In fourth-century Athens, Opsigonus worked under the orders of two different magistrates in the city's arsenals; and Eutuchides served for three years running in the

Delian sanctuaries during the late second century. In Acmonia during the imperial period, a certain Hermogenes even kept track of the voting in the Assembly for seventeen years in a row! In that respect, the *dēmosioi* had nothing in common with the *paredroi* of classical Athens, who assisted the *archontēs*, were replaced every year, and were subject to a final audit. The *paredroi* were truly considered magistrates.[103]

The *dēmosioi*'s jobs were not performed collectively. The great majority of the inscriptions portray their work as a solitary activity. Even when several public slaves worked together on a common task, there is nothing to suggest they were organized into a collective whose members were jointly responsible for the result. Finally, everything indicates that the procedures for monitoring the magistrates, central to the institutional operation of the cities, did not apply to the *dēmosioi*.

If the function of public slaves did not lie within the field of the political, how did the Greeks conceive of it? Did the cities of the classical and Hellenistic periods formulate the beginnings of a "public servant" status? Plato understands the function of the *dēmosioi* only within the paradigm of "service" (*hupēresia* or *hupēreteia*), a function distinguished from the power of command, the *archē*, possessed by the magistrate.[104] Aristotle, in book 4 of the *Politics*, lists all the functions necessary to civic life, arriving at the most accurate definition of what a magistracy (*archē*) is. The Stagirite then explicitly distinguishes political functions from economic and subordinate functions (*hupēretikai*), ordinarily the lot of slaves. In his conclusion, he dismisses without equivocation that last category from the sphere of the *archai*:

> But the title of magistracy, to put it simply, is chiefly to be applied to all those offices to which have been assigned the duties of deliberating about certain matters and of acting as judges and of issuing orders, and especially the last, for to give orders is most characteristic of authority. One must call above all magistracies all these functions to which is attributed, in a determined field, the power to deliberate, to decide, and to order, and quite especially the latter power, since to give orders, is more particularly the mark of a leader.[105]

It is therefore only negatively, in contrast to the sphere of command and deliberation proper to the *archē*, and not in terms of a positive definition, that the public slaves' sphere of activities is understood.

But the language of Plato or Aristotle is not that of Athenian democratic ideology. Forget for a moment the political philosophy of the classical period and pay heed instead to civic rhetoric, as indicated by the decrees passed in the Assembly. One expression in particular is illuminating. An Athenian decree from the late second century prescribes that the *dēmosioi* in charge of weights and measures should place in the city's archives a copy of the list of items received by their predecessor and which they themselves will transmit to their successor. If they fail to do so, they "shall not be allowed to receive wages for any el [*eutheria leitourgia*]."[106] The expression *eleutheria leitourgia*, in the literal sense of "free service," is hardly comprehensible. In any case, it stands in contrast to an expression much more common in the civic decrees, *politikē leitourgia*, "service to the city," used to refer to the actions of a public doctor or a great magistrate in the service of his fellow citizens. *Eleutheria leitourgia* designates a somewhat different reality than that traditional formulation, and some have not failed to translate the expression as "public service."[107] The translator's quandary is meaningful here: If *eleutheria leitourgia* designates nothing other than "public service" in the city, it is by virtue of a substitution, or an equivalency established between the realm of the public and that of freedom.

That expression, far from being inconsequential, thus gives a glimpse of the peculiar archaeology connecting the status of citizen—the freeman par excellence—and the realm of the public in the city. Yan Thomas has done a superb job of shedding light on that connection at the foundation of the ancient Greek and Roman city. Among the ancients, freedom was not conceived as a fact of nature that the law would be designed to protect. Nothing was more alien to the world of the ancient cities than our naturalistic conception of freedom, which makes it an individual right rooted in the natural order of the world prior to the formation of any political community. "Man is born free, and everywhere he is in chains": The famous opening line of Rousseau's *Social Contract* would have been incomprehensible to a contemporary of Socrates or Cicero. On the contrary, the citizen's freedom was understood as the product of the city's very existence, the result of a set of institutions and practices constitutive of civic life. In legal terms, the citizen's freedom was identified with the public goods that no one in the city could seize; just as public or sacred property was inappropriable, a citizen could not sell himself to benefit a third party and thereby alienate his freedom. At the foundation of every city, wrote Cicero, are "things serving for common use, which we call public."[108] These things were all the public places and goods whose use defined the boundaries of the circle of citizens. In other words, the status of citizen was primarily attached to the use in common of public things and not to an individual quality based in nature that the city's law would have had the obligation to protect. In that sense, writes Yan Thomas, providing a contemporary horizon for that axiom as unexpected as it is fertile, "citizenship is not separable from certain collective services, now called public service, but which, it is clear, originally defined what was irreducible and permanent in the city."[109] If "public" and "free" are equivalents, it is because the circle of citizens ultimately consists of those entitled to what is held in common.

But that slip of the pen, in assimilating the public slave's labor to a "free service," also sheds light on the singularity of his condition. It condenses the paradox at the heart of the "Greek miracle," that of an experience of political freedom whose defining characteristic was to depend on slavery. In order for these public things without which citizenship would be inconceivable to come into being, there also had to be slaves. That simple fact places the *dēmosioi* in a paradoxical situation, that of the excluded third term, guarantor of the civic order. Having been placed in the service of the city, these slaves, whether they verified the coins in circulation, kept order in the city, oversaw the expenses of the magistrates in the field, or attended to the civic archives in the Metrōon, were the depositaries of collective freedom.

To evaluate the specificities of public slavery in the classical city, it is helpful to examine all the assignments entrusted to them, in the light of those placed in the hands of public or royal slaves within other slave systems. The tasks of controlling the civic archives, inventorying public goods, and recording the expenses incurred by magistrates belong to an area of competence regularly associated with public or royal slaves, that of public writings.[110] The policing functions performed by the Scythian archers also had many equivalents in other slave societies, which made slaves the guardians of royal order.[111] From that standpoint, the participation of the *dēmosioi* in the administration of economic life in the city, whether they collected taxes, guaranteed the quality of coins in circulation, or maintained the standards of weights and measures, appears to have been widespread.[112] So too were slaves' contribution to city construction sites and the maintenance of public buildings.[113]

By contrast, all the aulic functions, some of them remarkably sophisticated,[114] reserved for royal slaves rarely appear among the set of tasks entrusted to the slaves attached to the city's major institutions, whose daily operation they nevertheless assured. The absence of *dēmosioi* working the land was also an original feature, which can be explained by the fact that the city itself did not directly exploit public or sacred lands. Above all, the military dimension of public slavery, so widespread in the Islamic world,[115] was wholly absent from the world of the classical city, which made defense of the *polis* a privilege and an obligation constitutive of citizenship.

But the enumeration of the spheres of competence entrusted to the *dēmosioi* in the city says nothing about their real power there, which depended in the first place on their becoming part of the general organization of powers in a society. It was obviously a very different thing to be the servant of a civic community and to be that of a personal sovereign. The *dēmosios* of the Greek cities, in the service of the community of citizens as a whole and placed under the authority of the magistrates, possessed a narrower margin of autonomy than that often granted to royal slaves, who were the direct embodiment of the sovereign's will. Public slaves could not avail themselves of the support offered by a despotic power, which had the capacity to elevate them to a position of authority over the society of freeman generally. Above all, the position conferred actual power only if it took concrete form in a set of statutory privileges, which defined public slaves not only as agents of the sovereign will but as a community that could advance its own interests in society. What was the situation of the *dēmosioi* in that regard in the city of the classical and Hellenistic periods?

CHAPTER THREE

Strange Slaves

> Every owner will procure three free printed forms, on which he will record his *family name* and *given name*, the place and date of his birth, his profession . . . ; the *names* of his slaves, their sex, their age, and the particular signs that can certify their identity: . . . blacks bearing the same *name* will have to be distinguished by number or a *nickname*.
> —Ordinance establishing the registry for the identification of Guadeloupian slaves, June 11, 1839

When, in the wake of Afonso de Albuquerque's expedition, the Portuguese conquistadores took possession of Malacca at the dawn of the sixteenth century, they were dumbfounded to discover the inordinate privileges enjoyed by the Malay suzerain's slaves, the *hamba raja* (king's slaves): "They all remain free at home, bring up their children, and earn a profit on their property; they reported for service only when called," the explorer João de Barros relates. The Portuguese sources attest to these privileges. Any personal assault against royal slaves was punished much more severely than one against a private slave, and their value was fixed by statute at seven times that of any other slave. The stigma of being a slave hardly seems to have applied to these strange servants, and the colonial administration quickly came up with the wholly invented term *aliberdados*, the "almost free," to designate them. Indeed, in the aftermath of the conquest, the Portuguese crown did not hesitate to co-opt them, guaranteeing by decree that they would be "treated justly, with the freedoms and living conditions they had previously possessed, and would not be obligated to perform any services apart from those they rendered in the time of the king of Malacca."[1] The conquistadores' bewilderment is an indication of the disconcerting condition of "slaves of the crown" for European observers in the modern age. With the Atlantic slave trade deporting more men and women to the New World every day, how could they grasp that slaves placed under a prince's absolute dependency owned property or had legitimate offspring?

Explorers and missionaries were not the only ones at a loss to describe the condition of royal slaves. Within the kingdom of Yatenga, one of the Mossi kingdoms of present-day Burkina Faso, "royal captives" represented about 10 percent of the population in the eighteenth and nineteenth centuries. Several of the functions indispensable to the life of the kingdom were in the hands of these "people of Bingo" (*bingdemba*),[2] as they were called. In addition to the duties associated with the court's operation and the protection of the royal relics, they assisted in collecting taxes on commodities and performed a policing function in the service of royal power. In his study devoted to them, Michel Izard expresses his reluctance to call these "royal captives" slaves. The "people of Bingo" could in fact dispose freely of themselves, could "marry and cultivate a plot of land."[3] None could be sold, and nothing about their status would suggest "the absence of a legal personality and the procedure of emancipation."[4] But are these various elements sufficient to exempt the royal captives from the status of slaves? There is reason for doubt. Izard himself remarks that the fate of these captives, "without history and without land," fell within the realm of a social death. After their capture, their existence here below continued "beyond death," solely by royal will; their definitive change in personality, status, and name was symbolized by the shaving of their heads.[5] Through a study of the practice of "companionship deaths," Alain Testart has proposed including the case of the "people of Bingo" within the category of slaves of the crown.[6]

Anthropologists, then, seem no less flustered than the conquistadores when they have to assign a precise status to the servants of the crown on one side of the line separating the freeman from the slave. This is because in our representation of slavery, we automatically conjure up images from the colonial societies of the New World, and we have difficulty acknowledging that certain servants could hold positions of power and enjoy a privileged condition while remaining slaves. Many studies conducted by Africanists and specialists in Southeast Asia have shown, however, that slaves placed in the service of sovereigns often enjoyed a special status.[7] Indeed, the privileged position of "slaves of the crown" or "state slaves" when compared to domestic slaves seems to have been a constant.

The Slave Body

Was the same true for public slaves in the Greek cities? A quick perusal of the civic decrees determining the punishments to be inflicted on *dēmosioi* who committed crimes in the performance of their assignments would seem to indicate the opposite. In the Greek cities, the slave was defined in legal terms primarily as a body, a *sōma*. Nothing is more telling in this respect than the acts of manumission by which a master liberated one of his slaves in consecrating him to a deity. In the sanctuary of Apollo in Delphi in the second century BCE, following a standard form often attested, "Kallicratēs, son of Kallinous, and Praxō, daughter of Klēomēnēs, both from Erineus, consecrated to Pythian Apollo a body of the male sex, which has the name Antiochus [*sōma andrein ōi onoma Antiochos*], for his freedom, after recovering from him the ransom collected by the enemy."[8] Through the disjunction of body, sex, and name, the formula definitively marks the negation that defines the slave's condition: a name, purely an artifact or simulacrum referring to no legal existence, is affixed to the impersonality of a body-commodity.

The slave, merely a body devoid of legal identity, cannot occupy a place in the tribunal, the consecrated site of the civic *logos*, except as a witness and then only under torture. A famous Athenian legal adage provides the justification: "Indeed, if you wanted to contrast the slave and the freeman, you would find the most important distinction in the fact that slaves are responsible in their bodies for all offences, while freemen, even in the most unfortunate circumstances, can protect their persons."[9] The maxim is a reminder of what separates the slave's body ontologically from that of the citizen: the slave's body-as-chattel stands in opposition to the citizen's body, which is inviolable and above all inalienable, given that Athenian law since Solon had prohibited a citizen from voluntarily selling himself as a slave.

The law of most cities did not hesitate to establish an equivalency for the same crime: a fine for citizens, a lashing for slaves. In Andania in the Peloponnese of the first century BCE, if a slave cut timber inside the sacred wood, he would be whipped by the *hieroi*; a freeman would have to pay a fine for the same offense.[10] As chance and the repetitiveness of history would have it, in 1836, the namesake town of Athens, Georgia, established different penalties for black slaves and young white men who went swimming in the Oconee River: whites would pay a ten-dollar fine, while slaves would receive twenty lashes.[11]

In this fundamental distinction of status between the body of the freeman and that of the slave, public slaves do not seem to have enjoyed any privileges. Like any *doulos* in the city, the *dēmosios* was responsible in his own flesh for the offenses he committed in the performance of his duties. The civic decrees were definitive: the penalty imposed in cases where *dēmosioi* did not respect the decree's prescriptions was the lash. The Athenian law of 375/374, which specifies the duties of the public slave who authenticated currency, stipulates, for example: "If the verifier does not sit, or does not verify in accordance with the law, let the conveners of the People [*syllogeis tou dēmou*] flog him with fifty lashes of the whip."[12] In the late second century, the *dēmosioi* charged with overseeing the city's weights and measures would be subject to a lashing by prytaneis or generals, depending on the gravity of the offense committed.[13] In the same way, a speech by Demosthenes unambiguously attests that public slaves testified under torture before Athenian tribunals.[14] Within the penal system, which drew a clear line between free and slave, *dēmosioi* were slaves like any other.

Privileged Slaves

Public slaves did have certain remarkable privileges, however, at least when compared to the typical chattel slave in the classical period.[15] Three elements characterized their condition. First, as a legal minor, the slave was prohibited from playing a role in a trial, except under exceptional circumstances; he could not initiate proceedings, nor could he be charged in his own name. Second, because the slave was the property of a master, most of the consecrated rights related to any property in Athenian law applied to him; the master could use and abuse the slave, sell him or give him away. That there was a law protecting the slave from his master's violence is only a hypothesis. And third, the slave was excluded from the bonds of filiation and kinship that structured Athenian social life; he could neither bequeath nor inherit, and any form of familial cohabitation was dependent on the master's goodwill and was not recognized by the law.

Regarding each of these three aspects, the status of the *dēmosioi* exhibited several particularities, largely as a result of their condition as public property. These distinctive characteristics have been pointed out several times, and historians, puzzled by them, have adopted two different approaches. Some have simply argued that the *dēmosioi*, although slaves, were treated "like metics," that is, like resident aliens.[16] But such a comparison, which projects onto the condition of the *dēmosioi* the forms of a better-known legal status, is unwieldy, even with respect to the metic's status in its essence. Public slaves never enjoyed the protection of a citizen patron (*prostatēs*) who could represent them and defend their interests during a trial. Several historians have therefore preferred to believe that public slaves occupied an intermediate position between free and unfree.[17] Such a representation, irrefutable at first sight, is also problematic because of the assumptions it makes about the topography of Athenian society. The expression "intermediate status" refers to a median position on a continuous scale of hierarchical statuses, from the very top to the very bottom. But the principle of an orderly spectrum of statuses cannot really account for the way society functioned in the classical period. Granted, it is often possible to observe elements of hierarchization—although these are always incomplete—between different groups of citizens. Before the imperial period, however, the structure of Greek societies usually consisted of many overlapping layers, and the great diversity of statuses observed there cannot usually be reduced to a hierarchically ordered totality. Historians of the classical and Hellenistic city, once they examine status longitudinally, will have a great deal of difficulty identifying a homogeneous structure that breaks down every status into a hierarchical order.

Consider by way of contrast ancien régime societies, which have provided so much food for thought for historians undertaking to describe social hierarchies in terms of order or class.[18] Social structures in the modern age are inclusive, in the sense that they make a place for every personal status within the context of a hierarchical understanding of society, conceived as a body. That was the very principle behind the capitation taxes in the kingdom of France, which some thought constituted the "true social hierarchy" of ancien régime society.[19] Conversely, personal status in the classical city came into being within a logic of exclusion and inclusion. In the city, slaves, metics, and citizens do not keep company, that is, they do not form a single society. In the *Nicomachean Ethics*, Aristotle argues that a master and his slave cannot share the bond of friendship (*philia*) necessary for the existence of any community (*koinōnia*).[20] In a broader sense, the space of the political takes shape only from the moment that the boundaries of the body of citizens are drawn; it is there that the question of power, shared among all or reserved for a few, first arises. Yet the composition of the civic community itself is not called into question, except under extraordinary circumstances. For example, when Plato elaborates the plans for an ideal society, assigning to the city's different components complementary functions in the service of a social body conceived organically, he does not include slaves in it. In that sense, slave status does not consist of a position hierarchically inferior to the lowest Athenian censitary category, that of the *thētes*. Rather, it is the result of a radical exclusion, an unequivocal domination.

The status of *dēmosioi*, far from being simply an anomaly, therefore invites us to call into question the conventional representation of society as different groups of homogeneous statuses arranged hierarchically, and it reveals an original social topography of the classical and Hellenistic city.

Slaves, Owners of Property—and of Slaves

It was an axiom of the slave societies resulting from the Atlantic slave trade that the same person cannot be both property and owner. For example, article 28 of the Black Code of 1685 declares that "slaves cannot have anything that is not their master's," before specifying that "everything that comes to them by industry or liberality, from other people or otherwise, in any capacity whatsoever, is acquired in full as a possession of their master; nor can the slave's children, father and mother, relatives, or any other freeman or slave have a claim to anything by inheritance, an arrangement between living persons, or death." This article sheds light on precisely what should be understood by the provisions in the following article of the code, which concern the slave's earnings, always conceived, in the tradition of Roman law, as usufruct temporarily granted and unilaterally revocable solely by the master's will.[21]

And yet, public slaves in the classical and Hellenistic city owned property. In a legal argument by Aeschines, a *dēmosios* by the name of Pittalacus seems to have been in possession of a house.[22] The litigant's terminology, however, is too vague to be interpreted with certainty as a right of ownership that is more than mere possession. Conversely, the mention of a *dēmosios* slave owner can only elicit surprise. It appears in a lengthy, very fragmentary inscription from the years 330–317/316, which gives a list of freedmen who prevailed in the procedure known as *dikē apostasiou*. These freedmen, to confirm their free status against citizens who claimed the right to seize their person, consecrated to Athena a silver phiale worth one hundred drachmas. There have been many discussions about the exact status of this procedure. Several historians believed it was only a legal fiction, and it is probable that the inscription simply regularized a set of acts of emancipation carried out in the 340–330s that had not yet received the blessing of the civic tribunals.[23] In the case in point, it makes little difference whether this was a real or fictive procedure. The inscription unambiguously lists the manumission of "Krateia, residing in Kydathenaion, manumitted from [——]es the *dēmosios* [who] consecrated a phiale worth 100 drachmas."[24] A *dēmosios*, therefore, whose name has unfortunately been lost, owned a female slave by the name of Krateia in Athens in the second half of the fourth century.

From an economic standpoint, this is hardly surprising. *Dēmosioi* possessed modest powers of initiative because they were paid a wage by the city. It is more striking that on this long list of manumitted slaves, nothing seems to distinguish property in the hands of a *dēmosios* from that reserved for citizens or metics, who are also mentioned on the inscription. In that regard, the *dēmosioi*'s prerogatives were no doubt much greater than those of the "privileged" slaves, whom their master could entrust with the management of a shop, as in the case of the perfumer Athenogenes in fourth-century Athens.[25] Their relative freedom, however, never resulted in legal recognition of a right of ownership because the debts contracted by them were in the last instance ascribed to their master who, insofar as he accrued a profit from his slave, could be held responsible to his creditors.[26]

In the first century CE, Ephesus provided further evidence of public slaves as slave owners. In 44 CE, the edict of the Roman governor Paullus Fabius Persicus declared that the public slaves, "who are said to purchase children at a low price and consecrate them to Artemis, such that their own slaves [*douloi*] are supported thanks to revenues from the goddess, shall themselves provide the necessities of life for their own slaves."[27] It was therefore common practice for public slaves, having acquired young slaves of their own, to consecrate them for a time to the goddess, thereby relieving themselves of the burden of supporting them, until these slaves returned to their master's service at a later date.[28]

Finally, an epitaph from Rhodes during the Hellenistic period introduces a certain Epigonus, a former public slave who became a metic. He had assumed responsibility for two choregai in the city, which implies he was in possession of a large legacy. It is probable that part of that wealth was acquired when Epigonus was still a slave in the city's service.[29] It was also in Rhodes, in the early first century, that five public slaves participated in a public subscription alongside metics, which attests to a relative financial autonomy, if not full right of ownership.[30] Likewise, in Metropolis, Ionia, at the turn of the imperial age, a *dēmosios* by the name of Philippus contributed equipment for the gymnasium, donating a *triclinium* (table bed).[31]

How is one to understand the fact that public slaves could themselves own slaves? One may dismiss from the outset the apparent incongruity of this phenomenon, which was not nearly as unusual as the laws of the modern period would suggest. Ethnography attests that it was common for a "self-established slave," one residing away from the master's house and as a result possessing a certain autonomy, to be a slave owner.[32] But these were primarily public or royal slaves. Whether the Malay *hamba raja* in the sixteenth century, servants of the emir of Kano in the nineteenth century, or slaves of the Ottoman sultan within the context of the *devshirme* system, examples abound of slaves of the crown who were slave owners.[33]

Roman casuistry long pondered the legal nature of that property placed in the hands of a property. Did the slave whom another slave purchased with his earnings belong in the last instance to the master? The Roman jurists adopted contradictory positions on the question, as attested by an excerpt from the Digest: "Nerva the son says that they can both possess and usucapt through a slave what he has acquired through his *peculium*; there are, though, those who think differently, since the citizens do not own the slaves themselves."[34] Even so, the question cannot be raised in the same terms for private slaves, placed under the control of a master, as for public slaves, and it is striking that there is no dearth of laws that grant the public slave a specific right to bequeath property. In the Rome of the imperial period, for example, Ulpian says that *servi publici* can bequeath half their earnings in their wills.[35]

In the cities of the classical and Hellenistic periods, no private slave seems to have been a full owner of goods or slaves. Hence this was truly a privilege reserved for the *dēmosioi*, to whom the rigors of private inheritance law did not apply. In the absence of a precisely defined site of legal imputation that could embody the city and play the role of the public slave's own master (*despotēs*), the ownership rights of the *dēmosioi* could be formulated only in specific terms, irreducible to those referring to private slaves.

A "Kinship Privilege"?

Families of slaves living in the house of a single master, although difficult to identify with precision, existed de facto in the cities, although they were not legally recognized by the tribunals.[36] The union of a male and female slave, and the bond of filiation between a slave father and his son, had no legal standing. In that respect, three traits seem to have differentiated the situation of the *dēmosioi* from that of the great majority of chattel slaves, allowing one to imagine the existence of a "kinship privilege" reserved for them.[37]

The civic identity of every citizen in classical Athens rested on a combination of three factors: a name chosen by his father, a patronymic, and a demotic corresponding to the administrative district of the city where his name was listed on the citizenship registries. "Pericles son of Xanthippus of Cholargos" is the complete name of the great fifth-century general Pericles, son of Xanthippus, inscribed in the citizenship registries of the deme of Cholarges. In most inscriptions, only one of the last two elements (the patronymic or the demotic) is mentioned, and epigraphists have traditionally concurred that the mention of a patronymic, although it may not always have indicated citizenship, implied a free condition.

As it happens, the names of a few *dēmosioi* that appear in the inscriptions of the Hellenistic period are followed by a name in the genitive case. On the list for Athenian Delos in the second century is the aptly named Daidalos (Daedalus), son of Demetrius, who acted as an epimelete for a small sanctuary on the island.[38] In first-century Athens, a certain Apollonius son of Apollonius is mentioned at the bottom of a list of the city's magistrates. Unlike all the names that precede it, the *dēmosios*'s name is not followed by the traditional mark of Athenian citizenship, the demotic.[39] For a slave, the genitive can ordinarily designate only the relation of ownership that binds him to his master.[40] The genitive next to the name of a public slave might in this case refer to the magistrate under whose authority the *dēmosios* was placed. The patronymic might then attest to the temporary extension of a private-type relation to a public context, with the magistrate assuming legal responsibility for the slave, like a master for his personal slave. That hypothesis is unlikely, however, because the demotic or patronymic of the magistrate holding such a responsibility is not mentioned. In actuality, the genitive here can be nothing other than a patronymic.

A slave's name followed by a patronymic appeared so strange that several historians believed that beginning in the Hellenistic period, some *dēmosioi* were free, even citizens.[41] The term *dēmosios* itself would then refer to a function—service to the city—and not to a servile status. In the imperial period, it seems that citizens could be called *dēmosioi* when they performed public duties.[42] The mention of the patronymic, however, does not seem sufficient to postulate the *dēmosioi's* citizenship, a status that would contradict all the literature of antiquity, which invariably links the condition of a *dēmosios* to that of slave. The two cases already mentioned are telling. The Delian epimelete's name (Daidalos, which is to say, Daedalus) and the absence of a demotic for the Athenian *dēmosios* indicate that these two individuals really were slaves. It must therefore be assumed that the use of the patronymic is an acknowledgment of the bonds of filiation granted to public slaves.[43]

The hypothesis would be without value were it not possible, first, to identify bonds of filiation between two *dēmosioi*, allowing one to conceive of the existence of slave dynasties in the service of the city. In fact, the *dēmosios* Demetrius, in charge of an inventory in the sanctuary of Asclepius in 221/220,[44] was certainly the father of Demetrius the Younger (*ho neoteros*), who was performing the same duties in that sanctuary five years later (216/215).[45] Furthermore, in the classical period, there were citizens portrayed in polemical contexts as sons of public slaves.[46] If one is to believe a legal argument by Lysias, the famous Nicomachus, in charge of revising the laws of the city from 410 to 404 and again from 403 to 399, was the son of a *dēmosios*. While affirming that "on the father's side he has no connexion with the city,"[47] the orator claims that Nicomachus was introduced into his phratry at a rather late date.[48] Although the *antigrapheus's* slave ancestry was apparent, Nicomachus's integration into a phratry assured him the legal status of citizen. The argument does not allow one to determine whether Nicomachus's father was emancipated by the city before bringing his son into his community or whether citizenship was granted only to his son, while his father was a *dēmosios*. Whichever scenario is envisioned, the extraordinary nature of the transition from slave status to citizenship, bypassing the intermediate stage of freedman, is worthy of note.[49]

Whereas the slave condition of the father of Nicomachus is hardly open to doubt, the case of Hyperbolus, the famous Athenian "demagogue" from the late fifth century, is more uncertain. A scholion to Aristophanes quotes a passage from a speech by the Athenian orator Andocides, who claims that the father of Hyperbolus worked as a slave in the city's mint: "Hyperbolus I blush to mention. His father, a branded slave, still works at the public mint [*argurokopeion*]; while he himself, a foreign interloper, makes lamps for a living."[50] The charge echoes an entire comic tradition that mocked Hyperbolus as a Phrygian or a Syrian.[51] Yet the citizenship of Hyperbolus, from the deme of Perithoidai, cannot be placed in doubt. Andocides's remarks are more pointed than the comic tradition, however; their aim is less to assign an imaginary ethnicity, as most of the poets sought to do, than to disqualify Hyperbolus by evoking a slave ancestry, which the orator claims can still be verified.

Finally, a fragment by Dinarchus attacks Agasicles, a second-rate orator and politician in the 320s: "He was the son of a Scythian verifier of weights and measures. He was born among public slaves and has himself been a verifier up till now in the market."[52] Agasicles is known for having been the defendant in an *eisangelia* (trial for "treason"), because he was registered, perhaps fraudulently, in the deme of Halimus.[53] Despite that accusation, there can be no doubt that Agasicles became a member of the civic community. Is it imaginable that he became a citizen after performing the duties of a verifier as a *dēmosios*? As in the case of Hypereides, the orator seems to be designating a precise function characteristic of the tasks entrusted to the *dēmosioi*.

These three references, although controversial, provide precious evidence about a possible status of public slaves, and several ethnographic parallels can shed light on them. In many societies, it seems, the sons of public slaves constituted a specific category of the population that enjoyed free status. Although the emancipation of public slaves was unusual, if not prohibited in many cases, freedom offered to their sons became a privileged means to grant promotion or honors. In Ottoman Syria during the fourteenth to sixteenth centuries, sons of Mamluks, of free status, bore the specific title *awlad al-n s* (sons of the people).[54] Integrated into Muslim society and, unlike their fathers, given Arabic names, they constituted a privileged group that possessed the right to land ownership. Often close to the ruling elite, they were in a position to defend their own interests within the state. In the Delhi Sultanate of the thirteenth and fourteenth centuries, the children of royal slaves also enjoyed free status and came to hold the most prestigious posts. Called *maulazagdan*, they made up a closed community intent on defending their own privileges.[55] Closer to the Greek cities, the sons of *servi publici* in the last days of the Roman Republic became citizens automatically, according to Léon Halkin.[56] It would be rash to assume that such a rule existed in the classical city, and I have already put forward the hypothesis that there were dynasties of *dēmosioi* in the city's service. One may nevertheless wonder if granting citizenship to the children of *dēmosioi* was not an honor regularly accorded to certain slaves of the city.

The use of the patronymic, the existence of slave dynasties, and the integration of the *dēmosioi*'s children into the citizenry without recourse to the intermediate status of freedman: all three of these elements are indications of a privilege specific to the *dēmosioi* in the order of filiation. This "kinship privilege" distinguished them from the vast majority of Athenian slaves.

"Like Freemen"

Access to the civic tribunals was central to the status hierarchies in the classical city. Fundamentally, it was the possibility of imposing respect for one's rights by initiating a legal action or speaking out in the tribunals that distinguished the status of citizen from that of metic or freedman. Metics and freedmen could only be "represented" by a citizen patron (*prostatēs*), who alone could promote their interests in the arena of Athenian law. In that respect as well, the *dēmosioi* seem to have enjoyed a privileged status, as indicated by the famous legal argument of Aeschines *Against Timarchus*, delivered before the Athenian courts in 345.[57] The orator's target was someone close to Demosthenes, and Aeschines sought to deny his right to express himself in public. The undertaking was in fact crowned with success: Timarchus was condemned to *atimia* at the conclusion of the trial. In the course of his argument, Aeschines happened to mention a certain Pittalacus, described as a public slave (*dēmosios*). This Pittalacus is said to have been one of the many victims of the arrogance of Timarchus who, with his comrade Hegesander, sexually abused him. Pittalacus's legal status has been the object of controversy among historians; some doubt whether he was really a slave and prefer to see him as a freedman or a citizen of very modest condition.[58]

Nonetheless, three noteworthy details in the colorful account given by Aeschines attest that Pittalacus truly was a public slave. In the first place, he is unambiguously described by the litigant, and also by later sources, as a *dēmosios*,[59] although his function in service of the city is never specified. Second, the litigant recalls in elaborate detail one of the humiliations inflicted on Pittalacus: One night, Hegesander and Timarchus entered his house and, after breaking some items, tied him to a column and whipped him.[60] That flogging is not at all insignificant because its aim was to humiliate Pittalacus by reminding him of his slave condition by the use of the lash. Third, the end of Aeschines's account brings the *dēmosios* into the Athenian judicial arena and therefore merits particular attention. Some time after being humiliated in his own home, Pittalacus took legal action against his two assailants.[61] During the trial, Timarchus's accomplice, Hegesander, staged a coup de théâtre, claiming that Pittalacus was his personal slave. To counter that claim, a citizen by the name of Glaucon began proceedings for a "vindication of freedom" (*aphairesis eis eleutherian*) on Pittalacus's behalf. Hegesander and Timarchus, hardly eager to see their shameful actions exposed to the eyes of the citizenry, finally suspended their legal action against Pittalacus.

The use of the "vindication of freedom" procedure has caused perplexity among historians and has led some scholars to doubt whether Pittalacus was a public slave: Nick Fisher and Oscar Jacob believe that, because *aphairesis* applied by definition only to freemen (*eleutheroi*), Pittalacus was free, whether a metic, a citizen of lowly status, or a freedman.[62] Such an interpretation sidesteps the fact that Pittalacus is several times called a *dēmosios*, and the flogging episode spectacularly recalls the stigma of servility.[63] I believe the event lends itself to a completely different interpretation: A procedure normally reserved for citizens whose freedom is in dispute was applied to the slave Pittalacus. The *aphairesis* would have been set in motion by Glaucon so that a slave, claimed by his adversary to be his personal property, would be recognized as public. Pittalacus would thus have been a public slave assimilated at the procedural level to an *eleutheros*, a freeman, which would explain why he himself could consider taking legal action against Timarchus and Hegesander. This assimilation should not cause undue astonishment. It was undoubtedly a way of resolving legally the impossibility of applying to public slaves the traditional provisions specific to private patrimonies. In other words, it was the extrapatrimoniality of the *dēmosioi*—the impossibility of their being the property of anything but the city, an abstract entity legally speaking—that led to their being considered "like freemen" at a procedural level.

This may explain why historiography has sometimes failed to find matter for reflection in the Pittalacus "case" on the question of slave status in the classical city. The postulate of a sharp distinction between citizens and slaves, two legally homogeneous statuses, has meant that commentators have not recognized the specificity of a status proper to the *dēmosioi*, one irreducible to that of all other Athenian slaves. Only that status can explain the astonishing portrait presented by Aeschines. To be sure, Pittalacus was a slave but, by virtue of being public property, he had a number of extraordinary privileges and could be considered the equal of a freeman within the context of certain Athenian procedures.

The Honors of the City

Two decrees from the beginning of the Hellenistic period, one passed by the city of Athens, the other by a garrison based in Eleusis, reveal that the Athenians also did not hesitate to grant honors to public slaves. At the very end of the fourth century, the Athenians honored by decree a *dēmosios* by the name of Epicrates.[64] On that occasion, the decree mentions another slave named Antiphates, placed in the service of the Boulē. He is said to have introduced before the Athenian Assembly a supplication by Epicrates, who had served in the Athenian army twenty years earlier during the Lamian War (in 322), under the orders of the general Leosthenes. Epicrates was undoubtedly one of the *dēmosioi* who accompanied the generals during foreign operations and whose mission it was to oversee their expenses. The fragmentary state of the decree makes it impossible to identify the nature of the honors granted to him by the vote of the assembly. It should be noted, however, that during the same period, in the annual decrees that honored the prytaneis, the *dēmosioi* placed in the service of the Boulē were mentioned alongside citizens.[65]

Some three decades later, at the beginning of the Chremonidean War in 267/266, an Athenian garrison based in Eleusis passed a decree in honor of an individual named Dion.[66] During the first years of the conflict between Athens and the kingdom of Macedonia, the provision of wheat to the various parts of Attica was obviously a matter of the utmost importance for the city.[67] The decree specifies that Dion had for several years running been in the service of the civic treasurers in charge of supplying and distributing wheat. The soldiers praised the efforts he had made to ensure the distribution of wheat and decided to "crown him with a foliage crown, because of his goodwill [*eunoia*] and love of honour [*philotimia*]" for the soldiers. The decree specifies, finally, that Dion would be permitted, if he showed the same zeal, to obtain any benefit "of which he would appear worthy."[68] Dion's duties seem to have been similar to those traditionally entrusted to the *dēmosioi* of the classical and Hellenistic periods. The absence of any reference to his patronymic and demotic makes it difficult to believe he was an Athenian citizen, and the promise of the future privileges he might someday obtain is uncommon in honors given to citizens. It is therefore very likely that Dion was a public slave, and the future honor that the citizens promised to reserve for him might well have been emancipation.[69]

The honorific rhetoric at the heart of Athenian civic ideology could therefore be expressed without difficulty toward public slaves. This is all the more remarkable in that such decrees have no equivalent for private slaves. No doubt these were only "routine honors," like those the city or its subdivisions were accustomed to confer on many magistrates who had suitably performed their job. No public slave was awarded a gold crown, and no statue was erected in a *dēmosios*'s honor, as was done for the city's major benefactors. Nevertheless, these two decrees constitute an exception in the documentation as a whole, and their existence sheds new light on the specificity of the status of *dēmosios*. Some anthropologists and historians, in fact, have advanced honor as the ultimate criterion for distinguishing free status. According to Orlando Patterson, slave status is defined before any other consideration as an absolute, quasi-ontological dishonor.[70] Martin Klein, a specialist in slavery in West Africa, believes that honor drew the dividing line between free and slave; fundamentally, honor would define the "identity of the non-slave."[71] The status of the *dēmosioi* in the Athens of the classical period belies the rigor of such a distinction.[72]

The mark of the specific honor reserved for the *dēmosioi* can also be assessed through a reading of the treatise *Ways and Means* (*Poroi*), composed by Xenophon in the mid-fourth century. The treatise suggests a series of measures for restoring Athenian might. The author envisions public slaves serving in the Athenian armies, not only as oarsmen in the fleet, to which the Athenians had agreed several times in the fifth century, but also as foot soldiers in the city's armies. As Yvon Garlan has noted, Xenophon is "the only Greek author to envision coolly a systematic use of slaves in wartime."[73] Philippe Gauthier calls the proposal unheard-of because it appears to subvert the traditional distinction within the city that reserves conduct of the ground war for citizens, although in theory much more than in practice.[74] But Xenophon's measure, which was never implemented, concerns only the city's public slaves and excludes all private slaves. It is therefore tempting, once again, to recognize here the mark of an honor or privilege accorded to public slaves.

The *dēmosioi* of the classical and Hellenistic periods, then, had remarkable privileges that distinguished them from the common lot of private slaves: They were defined in certain procedures as being "like freemen"; they owned property; and they no doubt possessed, though in a form difficult to determine, a "kinship privilege" that could sometimes extend to the integration of their descendants into the civic community. The honors the civic authorities granted them attest to a recognition of a specific rank. It remains to be determined in what measure the set of privileges identified defines a clearly formalized legal status.

Consider for a moment the case of two cities in Asia Minor at the end of the Hellenistic period. In Ephesus, *dēmosioi* seem to have constituted a category of the population with clearly delimited boundaries, midway between private slaves and resident aliens, in what looks at first sight like a true spectrum of statuses. During the First Mithridatic War (88–86), the Ephesians promised freedom and the status of *paroikoi* (resident aliens) to public slaves who took up arms for the city.[75] By contrast, the law stipulates that if *isoteleis* (metics enjoying tax privileges), *paroikoi*, *hieroi* (people consecrated to a god), *xenoi* (free foreigners), or freedmen enlisted to offer the city their assistance, they would be declared full citizens (*pantas politas*).[76] The *dēmosioi*, then, seem to have held an intermediate status in the city, between that of free individuals who were not citizens, such as metics and freedmen, and that of private slaves.

Fifty years earlier, within the context of the war of Aristonicus (133–131), the city of Pergamon had ruled that the *dēmosioi*, like the children of freedmen and like royal slaves (*basilikoi*), would obtain the status of resident aliens (*paroikoi*).[77] A Rhodian epitaph seems to attest to an identical hierarchization of statuses. A certain Epigonus, a former public slave emancipated by the city, thus became a *xenos* (foreigner), then obtained the status of metic (resident alien) before his death.[78] Once again, the status of *dēmosios* seems lower in the hierarchy than the status of most resident aliens (*katoikoi, paroikoi*, but also mercenaries, *epikouroi*), to whom full citizenship was granted.[79] But the decision is somewhat obscure, in that it offers the same rights to *dēmosioi* as to the children of freedmen, who theoretically ought to have been considered citizens. It cannot be ruled out that these two inscriptions attest at least as much to reluctance on the part of the cities to dispossess themselves of their own servants by a unilateral action as to the inferiority of status of the *dēmosioi* vis-à-vis resident aliens or freedmen.

Such a hierarchical conception of status seems to have been unknown in the Athens of the classical period. Depending on the circumstances, a *dēmosios* could be assimilated to a freeman (at least in the language of the law) or explicitly to a slave, as the punishment of flogging indicates. *Dēmosioi* thus occupied an uncertain position within the traditional status distinctions, which we tend automatically to think of as a scale leading by successive gradations from slave to citizen. How, then, are we to explain the singularities of the status of public slave? Was that status purely and simply an anomaly, an exception devoid of real significance in terms of the status hierarchies in the classical city? Or does it invite us to revise our conception of such hierarchies?

The Slave as Public Property

In the first place, the specificity of the public slaves' status and the privileges reserved for them had to do with their condition as public goods. The notion of something being public was not as self-evident in the classical city as it is to our modern eyes. In the Greek world of the classical age, the city did not have the status of a legal person. Public goods did not constitute public property in the sense we are accustomed to give that term, with the implication that, just like a private individual, a legal subject, the state, can own goods and ensure that its rights are respected.[80] That simple fact has far-reaching consequences for the ownership relation the city maintained with its slaves. On the subject of the *dēmosioi*, a major book on Greek slavery confines itself to noting: "Like any piece of furniture or any building, they were the property of the people, who collectively exercised over them the same rights as a private owner."[81] This remark is unsatisfactory in that it understands public ownership as being similar to private ownership. The patrimonial regime that defined the bonds between a master and his slave cannot be applied without precautions to the ties that bound the civic body as a whole to its *dēmosioi*.[82] In the absence of an embodiment of the state in the form of a person in possession of rights and obligations, the rules of Athenian private law could not be applied to the city's slaves. It is difficult, for example, to identify an agency capable of embodying the entire civic body in its relations with the *dēmosioi*.

The complexity of the status of *dēmosios* therefore plunges us into the thorny question of the city as legal subject.[83] The historian Yan Thomas has insisted several times on the difficulty that the legal institution of the city represented for Roman law in the republican and imperial periods. He brilliantly elaborates the theoretical substrata of public ownership in Roman law, which did not require that the city be defined as a legal person: "What the city possessed, then, was not analyzed in terms of a relation of immediate ownership, which would have implied the real existence of a subject, but rather indirectly, through the idea of inappropriability, which in a certain sense opened onto a void. The determination of that relationship took a negative path and left the very question of its subject in suspense."[84] Hence to characterize property belonging to the city, the law used the concept of *res nullius in bonis*, "things that are not within the patrimony of anyone," a category to which public slaves belonged.[85]

This remark indirectly clarifies the status of public property in the Athens of the classical age, with the notable difference that inappropriability does not seem to have defined the nature of public ownership in the classical city.[86] If within the context of certain procedures Pittalacus could be considered to be like a freeman, it was precisely because the city could not play the role of a patrimonial figure in the same way as a private individual. The public slave was not the coproperty of the plurality of citizens identified as a subject or a person but rather the property of an entity that was, in legal terms, phantasmal: the city.

The power granted to *dēmosioi* to own property is more difficult to grasp. Its origin too undoubtedly lies in the mysterious arcana of the Greek conception of public property. It should be noted in the first place that the distinction between public property and sacred property was particularly fragile in the classical city.[87] That conflation is by no means a trivial matter. Public property and sacred property, *hiera* and *dēmosia*, must no doubt be conceived in a fundamentally similar way, with the emphasis less on their submission to the decisions of the civic community than on their irreducibility to private property generally and on the identical legal arrangement presiding over their operation. In *Ways and Means*, Xenophon places the *dēmosioi*, sacred lands, and public lands in the same category: all are similarly in the hands of the civic community, which can make a profit from them as it wishes.[88]

In terms of the management of sacred property, the *dēmosioi* often seem to have belonged indiscriminately to the gods and the city. For example, public slaves are described as having been offered by King Nicomedes of Bithynia "to the god and the city"[89] in the large Panhellenic sanctuary of Delphi in the late second century, and the Delphians decided to assign the slaves to watch the sacred herds of Apollo. These public slaves thus appear to have been managed by the city on behalf of the sanctuary, but they were not the exclusive property of either because neither functioned as a legal person holding a patrimony. Denis Rousset has called the arrangement a "joint and undivided" ownership by the god and the city.[90] In Labraunda in Asia Minor during the imperial period, the god's funds were used to remunerate the *dēmosioi*,[91] whose duties seem to have been identical to those of the *hieroi*.[92] An inscription even mentions the existence of *dēmosioi* of the god.[93] In Ephesus during the first century CE, support for the *dēmosioi* came indiscriminately from the city's coffers and the treasury of Artemis.[94] The distinction between sacred property and public property is once again very difficult to determine. But just as the sanctuaries owned goods that could be sold,[95] the *dēmosioi* no doubt constituted a form of property that, as if by delegation, could own goods or slaves.

The Status of *Dēmosios*

In broader terms, the specificities of the status of the *dēmosioi* can be understood as a "normal exception,"[96] to use a famous expression, a unique configuration but one that reveals the norms that govern how status generally functioned in classical Athens. An analysis of the specific privileges reserved for the *dēmosioi* should not lead us to minimize the importance of status distinctions in the workings of civic life, as some historiography of classical Athens suggests. Such an interpretation, which is quick to propose an excessively fluid conception of the functioning of society in the classical age, too often makes the city of Pericles the preliminary draft—inextricably democratic and liberal—of the American dream.[97] In projecting a contemporary ideal onto the city of Athens, it constitutes a version, revised to be sure but no less erroneous, of the old Greek miracle.

It is absolutely clear that differential status in the Greek city took a more complex form than a simple, traditional division between metics, freedmen, slaves, and citizens would indicate. But the plurality of legal status in a society says nothing about the social mobility of the individuals who compose it. It remains true that Athenian society as a whole was marked through and through by multiple statuses constituting barriers and allocating to each individual his position within the different spaces of the city. Nevertheless, one needs to define what is meant by the term "status." Status is not class, that is obvious. The term "status" does not define a specific position in relation to the means of production; rather, it delimits the boundaries of a legal power. Nor is status "order," in the sense the Old Regime conferred on that word, assuming an organic conception of society that the Greek cities never formulated. What, then, is a personal status?

In reality, historians of the Greek world have tremendous difficulty giving a rigorous definition of what they mean by that term, even though it is a commonplace of their vocabulary. The writings of the great Anglo-American historian Moses I. Finley have continually vacillated between different definitions of personal status. In *The Ancient Economy*, embracing the use of an "admirably vague word with a considerable psychological element," comprising both a "value system" and a "behaviour pattern,"[98] Finley sought above all to emancipate the representation of ancient societies from a reflection on class. That definition of status, inasmuch as it entailed a mode of life and an expression of prestige, tended to put the emphasis on "rank," or even on the prestige attached to each individual, more than on a specific legal position in the ancient city. And yet that use of the term "status," embraced as loose or imprecise, conceals a different approach that Finley defended from his earliest writings when he undertook to decompose status in the city into a "bundle of privileges, powers, and so on," exercised along a spectrum of the most varied rights. Finley, half jurist, half historian, then called for "breaking up the traditional notion of rights into a number of concepts, including claims, privileges, immunities, powers, and their opposites."[99]

Such a definition raises certain difficulties for anyone undertaking to describe the society of the classical age because, potentially, it conceives of the existence of as many statuses as there are individuals. In any case, it authorizes a fine-grained reading of Athenian society that would no longer focus on vast generic statuses as such—slave, citizen, metic, freedman—each composing an order impermeable to all the others. As a result, the term *timē* (honor, right, or power) appears the most adequate to account for the set of rights attached to each category within the population of Athens. Granted, the full citizen was an *epitimos*, possessing all the *timai* required for full participation in *politeia* (civic life). Apart from the sphere of full citizenship, however, the different statuses appear to be an agglomerate of *timai*, that is, of various rights and capacities, and not a homogeneous totality.

Nothing is more illuminating in that regard than what appears at first sight to be the exact opposite of full citizenship: *atimia*. This was the punishment for a disparate set of crimes or offenses by which a citizen disengaged himself from his civic duties (broadly conceived). Grounds for such a forfeiture of rights included deserting the civic army on the battlefield, stealing public property, bearing false witness, failing to repudiate an adulterous woman, engaging in prostitution, and not providing for the needs of one's parents in old age. But *atimia* did not consist purely and simply of a loss of citizenship or demotion to a hierarchically inferior status, that of metic or slave.

An *atimos* was deprived of his right to political participation. He could no longer take part in the deliberations of the assembly or be named a judge or magistrate.[100] Even some rights that metics possessed, such as testifying as a witness at a trial[101] or being allowed access to the Agora, were taken away from the *atimos*. But he did not lose his citizenship. For example, he enjoyed the protection the law granted every citizen against murder, and most *atimoi* continued to possess land in the city, which was in principle prohibited to metics. The *atimos* retained privileges proper to full citizenship, yet some prerogatives reserved for metics were taken from him. *Atimia* thus defies a representation of personal statuses ordered hierarchically in the city.

Furthermore, *atimia*, far from defining a homogeneous legal status, appears to have been a generic concept, a "grab-bag" term, as the historian Robert Wallace has noted, one that encompassed various cases as a function of the type of honor or capacity (*timē*) of which the *atimos* was dispossessed.[102] Andocides explains, in a digression during a legal argument, that *atimia* could be either complete or partial.[103] If it was partial, specific rights were taken from the citizen, either those having to do with his political participation (the right to be a member of the Council or to speak at the Assembly) or rights that could be called private. For example, *atimia* could consist solely of a prohibition on going to the agora of Athens or, even more precisely, on traveling to Hellespont or Ionia.

Atimia was never anything but the loss of certain *timai*, simply because, as Finley's early writings showed, every personal status took the form of an agglomerate of various powers and rights relating to access to political institutions and the conduct of private affairs. The procedures characteristic of *atimia* therefore give us a glimpse of a composite conception of legal status, for which the *dēmosioi* provide an example because their status aggregated different powers belonging a priori to different categories of the Athenian population. Before the city's tribunals, a *dēmosios* could be treated like a freeman, whereas in a penal context he could be flogged like any other slave. Conversely, the "kinship privilege" granted him and the awarding of honors placed him in a position difficult to determine. Without entailing full citizenship, this position was without common measure to that of private slaves.

In that sense, Athenian society cannot be broken down into homogeneous blocs of status, arranged hierarchically like orders. It was also not an open society in which anyone could emancipate himself from the determinations of his status and move from one to another, thanks to his merit or lucky star. It took the form of a multidimensional social space, traversed through and through by a kaleidoscope of statuses. *Dēmosios* is the name for one of them.

A COMPARATIVE PERSPECTIVE once again provides us with a productive defamiliarization of the classical city, projecting an unexpected light on what had seemed self-evident. The history of royal slavery in the Islamic world (at its Mediterranean center as well as on its fringes) and in the large kingdoms of West Africa offers in abundance accounts of palace revolutions orchestrated by the prince's servants, who took advantage of a decline in dynastic power to seize power on behalf of their own community. In the eyes of a specialist on the African kingdoms or a historian of the Ottoman Empire, the status of the *dēmosioi* in Greek cities appears very strange in that regard: How to explain why, despite the privileges they enjoyed, they never constituted a united community able to advance its own interests in the city? I shall pose that question, certainly naïve, in as general terms as possible: Why was the "Mamluk paradigm" inconceivable in the Greek city?

Although there is no dearth of reasons to explain it, the recourse to slave markets is necessarily foremost among them. For the most part, cities acquired their *dēmosioi* at the markets, and everything indicates that new members were added to the slave corps not by integrating the children of *dēmosioi* but by purchasing new slaves. Such regular turnover made it difficult to form a collective consciousness uniting the *dēmosioi*. Their condition in Athenian society was too disparate for a sense of solidarity to take root in a lasting way.

But that explanation is to a large degree incomplete. There is no lack of examples of slave corps whose growth depended on the slave trade but who were able to form a community of interests or to promote an "esprit de corps."[104] Although there were undoubtedly families of public slaves in which members succeeded one another in the same post, the status of *dēmosios* never gave rise to a "dynastization," that is, a monopolization of certain prerogatives in the form of titles transmissible by inheritance within the group. That is because the very conception of status hierarchies in the Greek city prevented the emergence of a community of public slaves able to assert its own interests. Outside the circle of citizens, society prohibited privileges of status from giving rise to a closed order legally recognized as a community. There was no more a "community" of *dēmosioi* than there was a "community" of metics or freedmen who could advance their interests in the ancient city. It was only negatively, in their relation of exclusion to the sphere of citizenship, that noncitizens were defined, never in terms of an organic conception of the city that would have allocated them a specific place, hierarchically defined within the whole of a society conceived as a body. The unique power that these slaves were able to obtain, therefore, entailed not the recognition of an autonomous community founded on a specific status identity but rather integration into the only "community" that possessed a political authority, that of citizens.

CHAPTER FOUR

The Democratic Order of Knowledge

> What are we to believe in? Nothing! That is the beginning of wisdom. It might be time to get rid of "Principles" and go into Science, Examination. The only reasonable thing (I always return to this point) is a government of mandarins, provided the mandarins know something, even many things. The people are forever legal minors and (in the hierarchy of social components) will always come last, for they are the multitude, the masses, the limitless throng.
> —Gustave Flaubert, letter to George Sand of April 30, 1871, in *Correspondance Flaubert-Sand*

"We have, as far as possible, closed every avenue by which light might enter the slaves' minds. If we could extinguish the capacity to see the light, our work would be completed; they would then be on a level with the beasts of the field and we should be safe." With these words in January 1832, Henry Berry, member of the House of Delegates for the state of Virginia, condemned the antiliteracy laws, one of the most sinister innovations in the slave codes of the southern United States. Most of the states of the Old South, following the model of South Carolina and Georgia, had since the mid-eighteenth century gradually come to penalize any master who taught his slaves to read and write. In the late 1820s, the antiliteracy laws were even extended to all people of color, free and unfree: access to writing and reading became completely bound up with the color of one's skin.

The Greek cities never tried out such laws on their own slaves. At first sight, a passing remark by a scholiast of Demosthenes even provides a spectacular contrast: "The Athenian people were in the habit of buying slaves who knew their letters [*grammata epistamenous*]."[1] Should the two slave societies, that of the ancients and that of the moderns, therefore be contrasted term for term, as some nineteenth-century abolitionists liked to do, celebrating the humaneness of Athenian masters so as to better denounce the cruelty of their contemporaries? No, obviously not. The scholiast's remark concerned in the first place only a tiny fringe of slaves in the classical city, those who were the property of the Athenian *dēmos*. It is even doubtful whether all *dēmosioi* had the level of education attributed to them by the anonymous scholiast. As a matter of fact, Athenian masters did not display much more concern for their slaves' education than did plantation owners in the American South.[2] Finally, despite the antiliteracy laws, some slaves, such as the young Frederick Douglass, did manage to teach themselves to read, sometimes with the aid of missionaries. Some historians have argued that 10 percent of American slaves could read and write, whereas no specialist in ancient Greece would venture such a high estimate.[3]

Nevertheless, the remark of the scholiast of Demosthenes, reduced to its proper dimensions, points to a very real difference between some of the forms taken by slavery in the classical city and those on the colonial plantations. That difference lies not in the greater or lesser proportion of literate slaves but in the uses made of a specific knowledge in the service of the civic community, a knowledge held by slaves and not by most citizens. An Alabama grower or a Martinican *béké* would have been dumbfounded to see expert slaves in classical Athens performing on a daily basis public tasks that a portion of citizens were incapable of doing. And yet, that slave expertise, far from being an anomaly, was a product of the democratic ideology of classical Athens. In entrusting expert tasks essential to the city's administration to individuals who were excluded from the city, the Athenians were only carrying out a part of the democratic program, which refused to allow an individual's expertise to legitimize his claim on power. Public slavery was therefore central to the mechanisms that linked the question of knowledge to the political in the democratic city of the classical period.

In this respect, the Athenian experiment is germane to one of the most burning issues of our present-day democracies. The political status of expertise is at the heart of the contemporary "disenchantment" with representative democracy. The terms "democracy" and "knowledge" usually appear in ordinary language as two contradictory imperatives. The democratic ideal of majority participation in public affairs would seem to be incompatible with the principle of efficacy required in the governance of states, which is necessarily complicated and therefore requires learning. Who can fail to recognize therein the refrain of our own time, which makes the "epistocracy" of governments the insuperable horizon of all politics?[4]

I shall refrain from repeating clichés about the difficult relationship between the people, sole source of legitimacy, and an elite, whose "competence" would be cursed simply because it never finds the mandate to acknowledge it. The controversy has a sharper edge, and the disagreement runs deep. No one, neither the proponents of the forms of popular legitimation nor the advocates of the government of experts, disputes, on the one hand, that expertise informs any good political decision, and on the other hand, that good expertise is characterized by an independence from the political and social arena. The fact that some social actors, in the form of militant collectives, constitute themselves as experts in certain fields of specialization alongside the specialists recognized by the public authorities (think of Act Up or Greenpeace) changes nothing in that respect.[5] The circle of experts may expand to include a few groups of militants or segments of the population, more or less informed, but the knowledge for which they serve as guarantors requires a fundamental autonomy vis-à-vis the social arena. It would seem peculiar, even irresponsible, to claim that politically useful knowledge could result, if only in part, from a deliberative process open to all comers.

It was a different matter for the Athenians. Nothing was more alien to the democratic ideology of the classical age than the figure of the government expert so familiar to us. Clearly, if the Athenians entrusted to slaves tasks that at times required real expertise, it was not because they looked down on such functions, whose importance for the city's administration they well understood; it was in the first place because they wished to keep certain specialized knowledge outside the political field. Above all, it was because unlike moderns, they believed that political deliberation between "nonspecialist" or "amateur" citizens could give rise to a collective knowledge useful for the city.

Every epistemology is a social epistemology, that much is clear: every knowledge is inscribed within unique social configurations, produced by them and at the same time participating in their formation.[6] As a result, as Michel Foucault has magnificently demonstrated, there is "no relation of power without the correlative constitution of a field of knowledge, and no knowledge that does not presuppose and at the same time constitute relations of power."[7] Public slavery, located at the intersection between a specific system of domination (the slaveholding structure of Athenian society) and an original mechanism for organizing knowledge, provides a privileged observation post from which to consider the forms of articulation between knowledge and power in democratic Athens. The public expertise entrusted to slaves prompts us to reflect on the hierarchies fashioned by democratic ideology, between the different types of knowledge and their political use—in other words, to shed light on the "social epistemology" of the classical city.

Slaves and Experts

It is no easy matter to identify figures of expert slaves in the classical city. Civic discourse, both in Athenian inscriptions and in most legal arguments, is generally inclined to celebrate the agents of the *archē*, magistrates, the better to leave in the shadows the anonymous factotums, even though without them the city's administration would have been impossible. The historian is often reduced to imagining the nature of the *dēmosioi*'s work, unable to establish on the basis of documents of what it consisted. Likewise, it is very difficult to determine by what means such slaves came to acquire this knowledge or these sometimes extraordinary skills, which most citizens lacked. It is clear, for example, that the task of archivist required exceptional qualifications: the *dēmosioi* of the Metrōon, in charge of supplying magistrates with different documents on demand, knew precisely the content of public deeds, which they themselves had filed and had often even composed. Few citizens could have done their job. Unfortunately, none of these experts in public documentation is known to us in any detail.

But the situation is less hopeless than it appears at first sight. Thanks to a handful of inscriptions from the classical and Hellenistic periods, a few figures of expert slaves can be brought back to life.

The "Verifier" of Currency

To protect the city's commercial activity, Athenians in the classical age attempted several times to check the influx of counterfeit money. This was such an important issue that they did not hesitate to attribute to Solon, the great lawmaker of the archaic period, incontrovertible words to incite judges to deal with counterfeiters with the greatest severity: "If a man debased that currency [of the city], and introduced counterfeit, the jury had graver reason to abhor and punish that man than one who debased the currency of private citizens."[8] And a law of 375/374 BC indicates that two public slaves, posted on the agora of Athens and at the harbor of Piraeus, were responsible for overseeing the quality and authenticity of the coins in circulation.[9] Several indications even suggest that this crucial function had already been entrusted to a public slave by the second half of the fifth century.[10]

The two *dēmosioi* performed their job as "verifier" (*dokimastēs*) differently. When the city's *dokimastēs* was not required at the Council of Five Hundred, he spent his time among the moneychangers and bankers, whose tables were set up on the Agora. Conversely, his counterpart at Piraeus stayed near the "stela of Poseidon" (location unknown), waiting for merchants and private individuals to come to him to have their coins authenticated. He had to make sure that no counterfeit money would get into the city. In any event, the two slaves were the only ones who could determine in cases of dispute whether the currency used during a transaction was valid.

From the outset, the law stipulated two contentious scenarios: "If anybody present [foreign silver coin] having the same stamp as the Attic . . . let him give it back to the man who presented it. But if it has a bronze or a lead core or is counterfeit, let him cut it through immediately and let it be sacred property of the Mother of the Gods and be deposited in the Council."[11] The Athenians thus distinguished between counterfeits and foreign-made imitations of Athenian coins that were of the same metal, the same weight, and the same alloy as the Athenian coins. If the "verifier" happened upon one of these imitations, he was obliged to return it to its owner, who was authorized to use it.[12] By contrast, if the coin looked to him to be counterfeit, either because a thin layer of silver concealed bronze or lead, or because the proportion of silver was lower than the Athenian standard, the *dēmosios* had to cut the coin in two and consecrate it to the Metrōon on the Agora.

Obviously, Athenians did not entrust that important assignment to slaves out of indifference, or worse, contempt toward it. On the contrary. In the first place, a *dēmosios*, in that he was outside the Athenian social arena, appeared less likely to succumb to corruption than the average citizen. His status placed him in the position of neutrality ideally suited to his assignment of guaranteeing exchanges of currency.[13] But there was another factor, disarming in its simplicity, that explains the use of a slave: Citizens capable of performing the task were no doubt rare. Had the Athenians given the job to a citizen, they would have made individual expertise a qualification for governing and thereby violated the principle of the egalitarian distribution of the *archē* within the political community.

Indeed, the task of *dokimastēs* required exceptional skill. In Petronius's *Satyricon*, Trimalcio portrays the occupation of moneychanger, alongside that of doctor, as the most difficult in the world: "'And now,' said he, 'what do we think is the hardest profession after writing? I think a doctor's or a money-changer's. The doctor's, because he knows what poor men have in their insides, and when a fever will come—though I detest them specially, because they so often order a prescription for a dose of dill for me. The money-changer's, because he sees the copper under the silver.'"[14]

Every numismatist knows how tricky the assignment of seeing "copper under the silver" is. If the coin was simply "stuffed," the lead or bronze merely covered with a layer of silver, the task was easier than if the "proportion of silver" in the coin itself had to be verified, that is, if the silver was combined with bronze or lead when the coin was minted.[15] It is hard to imagine how the *dēmosios* managed to distinguish an imitation from an original, when both of them, as the treasuries of coins have shown, had the same weight and the same alloy; it is often a very difficult task for numismatists who work on ancient coins.[16] Was the *dokimastēs* particularly attentive to the sound the coin made on a hard surface? Would he weigh every coin? Did he taste them?[17] In any event, one thing is certain: his assignment required true expertise. The law itself confirms that the recruitment of such a slave was no easy matter: "So that there shall also be in Piraeus a verifier for the *nauklēroi* [shippers] and the merchants [*emporoi*] and all the others, let the Council appoint one of the public slaves, if one is available, or buy one."[18] The city, anticipating that, among the hundreds of public slaves in Athens, none would be suitable, envisioned turning to the slave markets.

The *dokimastēs*'s activities on the agora of Athens were supervised by the people's inspectors, who had the power to punish him if he did not respect the law: "If he does not approve in accordance with the law, let the conveners of the People (*sylloge is tou dēmou*) flog him with fifty lashes of the whip."[19] Nevertheless, the *dokimastēs* held a considerable de facto power over the operations of the Athenian agora. The law stipulated that "if anybody does not accept the silver which the verifier approves, let him be deprived of what he is selling on that day."[20] Only the public slave, therefore, had the power to guarantee the validity of the coins in circulation. Trusting entirely in his own personal conviction, he alone was able to withdraw from circulation and destroy a counterfeit coin, cutting it in two. Private individuals, who were not supposed to be experts in the evaluation of Attic coinage, were particularly cautious when they acquired coins and had to submit to the authority of a public slave, whose decision was irrevocable: every coin he declared valid had to be accepted by the merchants.

Eucles, Clerk and Accountant

The *dokimastai* of the classical period, however powerful they may have been, have remained anonymous. It is a very different matter for Eucles, a *dēmosios* I will not hesitate to call a public figure of fourth-century Athens.[21] Thanks to three different inscriptions over a period of more than twenty years, he can be seen acting as clerk or accountant in the two most important of the city's sanctuaries, in the service of Athena on the Acropolis and of Demeter and Persephone in Eleusis.

In 353/352, the Athenians named Eucles to draw up an inventory (*exetasmos*) of the objects deposited in the Chalkotheke, at the entrance to the Acropolis. In the presence of many city magistrates (strategi, hipparchs, phylarchs, taxiarchs, treasurers of the goddess of the current year and of the nine previous years) and under the supervision of the prytaneis's secretary, Eucles had to count up and classify all the offerings that had been delivered to the building.[22] The decree mentions that the inventory would be compared to the annual inventories published in stone, which gives a glimpse of the situation that served as a prelude to the designation of the *dēmosios*. The treasurers, having observed discrepancies between what they found in the Chalkotheke and what had previously been engraved on the stone, decided to entrust a new inventory to a specialist considered neutral.[23] It seems, in fact, that Eucles kept his job for several years in a row, given that he was active on the Acropolis in about 350.[24] A discerning connoisseur of all the property in the sanctuary, the *dēmosios* was indispensable to the magistrates in their daily management of the site.

Some twenty years later, Eucles reappears in the context of the construction done in the large civic sanctuary of Demeter and Persephone, in Eleusis. The city's account books for the sanctuary in the 330s specify that the *dēmosios* was to keep track of the magistrates' expenses. The city paid Eucles upwards of three obols a day to perform that task of *anagrapheus*.[25] Above all, the account books specify that he was designated by "a show of hands [*cheirotonia*]" at the Assembly, which suggests his skills were known to all Athenians.

Eucles would no doubt have recognized Peritas, a Macedonian *dēmosios* who officiated in the sanctuary of Delos in the mid-second century, as a distant cousin.[26] Whether he was providing information on the silver phiales deposited in the temple of Artemis[27] or counting up the broken silver offerings in the Asclepieion,[28] Peritas played a not insignificant role in the administration of the sanctuary for three consecutive years. His assignment went beyond the management of the god's property. Peritas seems to have performed a function rather similar to that of treasurer, given that the sacred revenues were paid simultaneously to him and to the administrator of the sanctuary.[29] Eucles's duties in fourth-century Athens, and those of Peritas two centuries later, entailed a singular expertise; and it was because of that expertise—publicly recognized in Eucles's case— that citizens gave them these assignments for several years. The inventories they completed were indispensable, especially for the procedure of *paradosis*, which marked the transfer of responsibility for management of the sanctuary from one magistrate to another. Public slaves, keeping meticulous accounts of the property deposited there, thus indirectly played the role of accountants for the sacred properties.

These two individuals working in classical Athens—the anonymous currency verifier of 375 and Eucles—represent only a small sample of the *dēmosioi* placed in positions of expertise in the city's service. Neither, of course, is representative of public slaves generally. Apart from a shared legal status, such experts had little in common with the *dēmosioi* who worked in the city's mints or hauled stones to the construction site of Eleusis. As part of their duties, these expert slaves often collaborated with citizens in possession of minor magistracies. For example, in fourth-century Athens, *parerdroi* assisted the *archontēs*.[30] Specific tasks were nonetheless set aside for slaves because of the expertise required, and this simple fact exemplifies an essential component of democratic ideology in the classical period: the deliberate exclusion of expert knowledge from the political arena.

Granted, fourth-century Athenians sometimes used the term *politeuomenoi* to describe individuals whose aptitude for public speaking and whose political ambition distinguished them from the *idiotai* generally. But the notion of "political class" was alien to the classical city in every respect, and these *politeuomenoi* never acquired the status of political "professionals." Above all, democratic ideology refused to legitimize their accession to elective magistracies based on any kind of expertise.[31] On occasion, Athenians no doubt had to appeal to a specialist in one field or another and use his skills in the city's service. In the fourth century, some politicians were occasionally entrusted with specialized tasks because of their expertise: In about 350, for example, Eubulus was appointed to manage the funds of the *theorikon* for three consecutive years.[32] In addition, the treasurer Lycurgus was responsible for the city's financial administration (*ho epi tē dioikēsei*) from 336 to 324, no doubt because of his knowledge of finance. But civic ideology pretended to be unaware of the role played by this specialized knowledge in the workings of civic life. When one reads the orators of the classical period and listens to the regular droning of the decrees passed by the city, it might seem as if the democratic city never needed specialists to run its administration. And when, at the initiative of a certain Stratocles, the Athenians passed an honorific decree for the great Lycurgus in the late fourth century, they praised his devotion, his courage in battle, his virtue, his sense of justice, and the kindness he had demonstrated toward the city, not the special *technē* he had placed in its service.[33]

Nicomachus the Jurist

Although specialized knowledge was put to use by the city, therefore, civic discourse did not allow it to become a qualification to govern and, apprehending it as a threat to the democratic order, preferred to remain silent about its importance. Nothing is more telling in that respect than the controversy sparked by Nicomachus, a major figure in late fifth-century Athens. For more than ten years, the Athenians entrusted the delicate assignment of compiling the set of laws of the city to that son of a *dēmosios* of uncertain legal status. He is known primarily through the speech composed by Lysias on the occasion of the charges of treason (*eisangelia*) brought against him in 399.[34] But Nicomachus was famous (and controversial) enough in the late fifth century to be the object of a violent attack from Aristophanes in the last scene of *Frogs*, during which Hades urges Aeschylus to give him a rope with which to hang himself.[35]

From 410 to 404, the Athenians had assigned to a special commission the task of revising and republishing all the city's laws.[36] Among the commission's members, Nicomachus had acquired a special position, so much so that a rumor circulated in the city that he had introduced unknown provisions into the venerable corpus of Solonian laws. If one is to believe Lysias's legal argument, the *anagrapheus* "assumed supreme authority over the whole code," to the point of himself becoming a lawmaker.[37] Nicomachus should have simply compiled and recopied all the laws in force in the city, but he was alleged to have placed the civic community under his influence and perverted the ordinary functioning of Athenian justice: "We were brought to such a pass that we had our laws dispensed to us from his hands, and parties to suits produced opposite laws in the courts, both sides asserting that they had obtained them from Nicomachus."[38] In 403, democracy having been restored, the Athenians reelected Nicomachus regardless, this time giving him the assignment of revising the city's traditional calendar, without setting any time limits.[39] The *anagrapheus*, according to Lysias, then added new cults to the city's ritual calendar.[40]

The power acquired by Nicomachus was certainly unusual in view of how Athenian justice ordinarily functioned. The Athenians never conceived of lawmaking as a science but rather as a practice consubstantial with the civic ideal and, like other political practices, belonging to the sphere of the *dēmos*'s sovereignty and within the purview of all citizens. Athenian justice was thus placed in the hands of nonprofessionals; although it was possible to appeal to a logographer to compose one's speech before the Heliaia, the citizen-judges, numbering six thousand and selected by lot every year from among all citizens, had no specific training in law other than that procured by regular participation in civic institutions. In that context, Nicomachus seems with good reason to have been the only expert that Athenian law in the classical period ever had.

As Stephen Todd has noted, that position as expert placed Nicomachus in a paradoxical situation. His position, while granting him considerable authority, did not constitute a magistracy in the usual sense of the term. Renewed from one year to the next, it did not fall under the rule of noniteration, as Lysias does not omit to note: "Though it is not permissible for the same man to act twice as under-clerk to the same magistracy, you authorize the same persons to have control over the most important affairs for a long period."[41] Nicomachus may have even been exempted from the traditional audit that concluded the exercise of a magistracy.[42] The logographer's virulence can be explained precisely by the ambiguity of the position acquired by the *anagrapheus*: in holding real power without being in possession of a magistracy, he undermined the separation between the order of the administration or service (*hupēresia*) and that of the *archē*.

The selection of Nicomachus to conduct such an undertaking owed nothing to chance. "You have chosen Nicomachus for the transcription of our ancestral rites, when on the father's side he has no connexion with the city," the orator affirms; the slave ancestry of the *anagrapheus*, son of a *dēmosios*, certainly explains why such an assignment was entrusted to him. A *dēmosios* through his father, Nicomachus remained tainted by the indelible stigma of the slave: "You . . . carry insolence to such a pitch that you regard the city's property as yours, who are yourself its slave!"[43] the litigant proclaims, adding that Nicomachus's natural place was at the slave markets. Nicomachus was actually a citizen, but the litigant's insistence on his supposedly servile background is highly significant. It is as if the task that had been entrusted to him could only be that of a slave. The conclusion of the legal argument was incontrovertible: "And yet from a slave he has become a citizen, and has exchanged beggary for wealth and the position of under-clerk for that of lawgiver!"[44] That formulation, linking slave status term by term to administrative service for the city, in order to better contrast both to the legislative activity reserved for citizens, resolves any ambiguity about the position of the *anagrapheus*, whose ancestry ought to have prohibited him from playing a political role in the city. Above all, it casts a harsh light on a polarity constitutive of Athenian democratic ideology, which relegates the administration of the city to the rank of servile tasks and places expertise on the fringes of the political arena. The figure of the expert slave, unusual as it might be, was thus emblematic of a unique system that governed the political use of knowledge in democratic Athens.

Democratic Epistemology: Protagoras, or the City of Auletes

We now arrive at the residence of the rich Athenian Callias. Let us open the door and slip in among the many guests gathered on this day in 431. Amid the vast assembly composed of illustrious Sophists and young admirers who have come to listen to Protagoras, master of Abdera, another intruder has already taken his place: Socrates. Introducing himself as guide to the young Hippocrates, he wishes to listen to the lessons of the "wisest of our generation, most learned of our contemporaries."[45] He ingenuously asks the great Protagoras about the substance of his teachings. Without batting an eyelid, Protagoras replies that he teaches a man "good judgement in his own affairs, showing how best to order his own home; and in the affairs of his city, showing how he may have most influence on public affairs both in speech and in action"—the art of politics, in short.[46]

This definition does not satisfy Socrates, who doubts that the art of politics can be taught. And in Athens, in fact, knowledge in no way determines participation in political life; in the democratic assemblies, anyone at all, whatever his knowledge, can speak out.[47] To Socrates's dismay, the Athenians, although they refer to the most learned technicians when they have to build a ship or temple, do not grant any preeminence when community affairs are at stake to those who might possess a specific knowledge about the city's administration. Protagoras, to respond to that first objection and thereby justify his own conception of political skill, tells his interlocutors a myth, that of the creation of the mortal race by Prometheus and Epimetheus. The Sophist's narrative, which diverges appreciably from the versions of the myth given by Hesiod or Aeschylus before him, provides an original reinterpretation of the Promethean legend, which may with good reason stand as a founding myth of the democratic city.

For Hesiod as for Aeschylus, the Promethean legend is an opportunity to reflect on the hubris of human beings. The punishment of Prometheus, whose liver would be devoured by an eagle night and day, exacted a price for the sin par excellence of humankind when it aspired to equal the gods. Protagoras provides a completely different denouement to the epic of Prometheus, whose punishment is not mentioned and who appears in the guise of benefactor of humankind. Men, possessing technical knowledge thanks to Prometheus's theft of fire, prove powerless to ensure the reproduction of the human race over the long term. Although in possession of *dēmiourgikai technai*, they are incapable of founding a stable political order. Zeus, the quintessential figure of sovereignty, is called upon to intervene to preserve humankind. He then offers men *politikē technē*, the mastery of which rests on two qualities in particular, *aidōs* (modesty, respect, or shame)[48] and *dikē* (justice). It remains to be determined, however, how these two qualities are to be distributed among human beings. Must one imagine, on the model of medical science, that a single person can possess political ability and cultivate it for the good of everyone else, or rather that Zeus distributed that ability equally among men? It is the second possibility that Protagoras chooses in his narrative.

The myth of Protagoras has three striking aspects related to the context of its elaboration within the Athenian democratic system. First, political ability proceeds from a radical break with the order of *dēmiourgikai technai*, specialized knowledge placed in the service of the community. The political, within the twofold dimension of *aidōs* and *dikē*, is now conceived as an ability offered to humankind by the gods. In that sense, it constitutes not a specialized knowledge but an ability that requires regular practice: "They do not regard [this virtue] as natural or spontaneous, but as something taught and acquired after careful preparation by those who acquire it."[49] Finally, it is distributed among all men; therein lies its specificity. Protagoras's narrative thus provides a legendary foundation for a cardinal value of Athenian democratic ideology, *isonomia* (the equal sharing of political duties).

Protagoras, having now abandoned the realm of myth, is invited by Socrates to present his own conception of virtue and how it can be taught. The Sophist makes a comparison with learning to play the flute (*aulos*): "Suppose that . . . we were all flute-players, in such sort as each was able."[50] Can learning virtue be understood on the model of mastering the flute? To be more precise, the Sophist proposes a model of teaching by which citizens, like a group of flutists, would collectively and individually come to acquire the quality of virtue, without which no city could exist: "Suppose that everyone were giving his neighbour both private and public lessons in the art [of flute playing], and rebuked him too, if he failed to do it well, without grudging him the trouble—even as no one now thinks of grudging or reserving his skill in what is just and lawful as he does in other expert knowledge; for our neighbours' justice and virtue, I take it, is to our advantage, and consequently we all tell and teach one another what is just and lawful."[51]

According to Protagoras, then, the teaching of virtue meets conditions different in every way from those presiding over *technai* in the world of artisanship. Whereas *technai* require the knowledge of a master, who inculcates in his disciples the basic tools of mastery, the teaching of virtue comes about "diffusely and repeatedly at every possible level in a man's life."[52] *Dēmiourgikai technai* are acquired through a vertical transmission of knowledge established once and for all, whereas virtue is learned by means of a horizontal circulation among equals throughout one's lifetime. Protagoras uses language acquisition as a model by which to understand that strange skill, which can dispense with a master: "Why, you might as well ask who is a teacher of Greek; you would find none anywhere,"[53] he exclaims to Socrates. Just as one does not need to be taught by the best linguists to learn one's mother tongue, virtue is acquired through a socialized learning process involving all members of the community, who possess that skill to varying degrees.

In that sense, the imperfection of each citizen's virtue is not a drawback, except insofar as his own abilities cease to improve through continuous contact with his peers. Above all, no definition of the essence of virtue could serve as a prerequisite for the intense circulation and exchange by means of which that quality is actualized in the civic community. Protagoras's reflections thus promote a social epistemology that valorizes the circulation of knowledge, even incomplete knowledge, among equals. The half-educated teach those more ignorant than they, for the city's greater good: such is the core of that democratic epistemology, which defends an associationist theory of political competence.

The Alchemy of the Political

That curious pedagogy was reflected in the institutional organization of the city of Athens. One of the notable traits of Athenian democratic life was the multiplicity of the deliberative structures that organized any decision-making process. From the assemblies at the deme or phratry level, sometimes comprising ten or so citizens, to all the private associations and the many colleges of magistrates, all the way up to the Assembly, in which all citizens could participate, civic life was marked through and through by an intense deliberative practice. According to Josiah Ober, it was precisely that capacity to organize collectively the heterogeneity of knowledge that was the key to the success of the Athenian democratic system in the classical age.⁵⁴ For lack of a state apparatus that could produce a common body of knowledge, it was the responsibility of all these deliberative agencies to aggregate and synthesize the knowledge distributed among the population of Attica and to convert it into a politically efficient knowledge to the city's benefit. The extraordinary density of the communities of Athenian society, composed of multiple groups, both private (*thiasoi, orgeōnes, gēnē*) and public (demes, phratries, tribes), weaving countless networks among the different components of the civic body, may have played a determining role in the implementation of all available knowledge to serve the common interest.⁵⁵ In organizing the maximum number of social interactions on very diverse scales, Athenian democracy, in this view, favored the generation of politically useful public knowledge.

If one is to believe Ober, one institution in particular played a central role in the aggregation and synthesis of all the knowledge dispersed throughout Athenian society: the Council of Five Hundred. In the classical period, that Council played a determining role because no decision could be passed by the Assembly without being discussed there beforehand. Composed of five hundred citizens selected by lot irrespective of fortune and proportioned equally from each of the different parts of Attica, the institution lay at the heart of a vast and constant circulation of the knowledge dispersed throughout Athenian society as a whole. Within the Council, the most diverse kinds of knowledge could be put to use by the city to aid in collective decision making.

But Athens' success did not lie solely in the aggregation of the most diverse skills within the framework of civic institutions and on an extraordinary scale. It did not provide a living demonstration of Condorcet's famous jury theorem, which holds that the probability that the majority of a jury will pronounce in favor of the most just proposal increases with the number of jurors. That is because for Condorcet, the elaboration of the pertinent decision depends in the last instance on the level of expertise of each of the participants in the deliberative process: "Let us consider voters who render their verdict by a simple majority. If it is more probable that each voter will judge in conformance with the truth, then the greater the number of voters, the greater the probability of the truth of the decision; conversely, if it is probable that each voter will err, the probability of the decision will diminish, eventually falling to zero."⁵⁶ In other words, it is only to the extent that each of the jury members demonstrates competence and independence that the majority can produce the most just decision. The theorem therefore neglects the production of knowledge that occurs in the deliberative process itself, independent of the level of knowledge of each participant. That process was at the heart of the Athenian political model.

Indeed, in the epistemic model put forward by Protagoras, the essential thing was not so much the aggregation of individual expertise on a broad scale as the Athenian system's capacity to create, by multiplying the number of deliberative spaces that involved all citizens on very different levels, the alchemy that brings a collective knowledge into existence. In book 3 of the *Politics*, Aristotle takes his place in the Sophist's school when he compares the city to a community picnic, with the plurality of participants creating on their own a new collective entity capable of producing superior judgments:

> For it is possible that the many, though not men of political worth, yet when they come together may be better, not individually but collectively, than those who are so, just as public dinners to which many contribute are better than those supplied at one man's cost; for where there are many, each individual, it may be argued, has some portion of virtue and wisdom, and when they have come together, just as the multitude becomes a single man with many feet and many hands and many senses, so also it becomes one personality as regards the moral and intellectual faculties. This is why the general public is a better judge of the works of music and those of the poets, because different men can judge a different part of the performance, and all of them all of it.[57]

Hence a chorus of men "without political worth" is always better than the monody of an elite, even a learned one. Granted, collective knowledge is the beneficiary of each citizen's individual expertise, but the alchemy composing the political rests primarily on a general deliberation that transforms the aggregation of individual bodies of knowledge, which are always incomplete, into a knowledge useful for the community. Not only can individual expertise not constitute a qualification for governing, but its civic utility is revealed only at the end of a distillation process that occurs within the framework of deliberative practice.[58]

The *Dēmiourgos* Philosopher

The limits of the Socratic interpretation of the democratic phenomenon thus come into better focus. In condemning the Athenian regime as a "regime of ignoramuses," Socratic philosophy indisputably identified the core democratic principle, which separates the question of the legitimacy to govern from the possession of knowledge. But the "dictatorship of ignoramuses" is simply the name Platonic philosophy gave to a specific epistemological regime, of which Protagoras's "city of auletes" provides a glimpse. That regime, promoting a form of "peer learning" in the city's multiple deliberative institutions, was certainly based on a radical break from *dēmiourgikai technai*, which were excluded from the sphere of the political. It nonetheless defended an ambitious and specifically democratic conception of what public knowledge is.

An excerpt from Xenophon's *Memorabilia* illustrates spectacularly the dissensus between Socratic philosophy and the democratic system, making the philosopher's enslavement the logical consequence of his possession of a body of knowledge. Here Socrates is compared to the *dēmiourgos* par excellence, embodied in the figure of Daedalus. His fate, to be "seized by Minos because of his knowledge and forced to be his slave," then taken to the Great King where he was again enslaved, thus prefigures the fate of the philosopher, sacrificed by the democratic mob because of his knowledge.[59] In the Hellenistic period, Duris of Samos would embroider on that disturbing identity, claiming that Socrates had been a slave and stonecutter in his youth.[60] The philosopher as *dēmiourgos* and slave: that highly polemical association marks the impossibility of integrating someone who possesses authentic knowledge into the democratic order. At the same time, it announces the Socratic program, whose early phases will be realized by Platonic philosophy: the restoration of specialized fields of knowledge as a model for all politics. Whereas Protagoras conceived of the political apart from the *dēmiourgikai technai*, Plato believed it was continuous with these specialized fields, arguing that the authentic statesman should first prove his skill in delimited areas of specialization before laying claim to a leadership role in the city.[61]

The Meaning of the Slave's Knowledge

Ultimately, the same conception of the political is at work in Protagoras's relegation of the *dēmiourgikai technai* outside the field of the political and in the dedication of expert *dēmosioi* to service to the city. In its way, Platonic philosophy perfectly understood the issues at stake, even placing the slave's knowledge at the center of its polemic about the democratic city's epistemological regime. And now, rising up in our path is a monument of the philosophical tradition toward which the historian, intimidated, can advance only with caution. That monument is the first formulation of the theory of reminiscence, located in Plato's *Meno*. This totemic scene, already dissected a thousand times, merits rereading in light of the controversy surrounding the city's regimes of knowledge.

Allow me briefly to set the scene. While passing through Athens, the young Thessalian Meno, an admirer of the Sophist Gorgias, has a conversation with Socrates about virtue: "Can you tell me, Socrates, whether virtue can be taught, or is acquired by practice, not teaching?"[62] When Socrates sends the question back to Meno, the young Thessalian proposes the idea that it is impossible to learn anything other than what one already knows. To resolve that paradox, Socrates is led to formulate the theory of reminiscence, according to which learning occurs through the recollection of a previously acquired knowledge. Socrates questions one of Meno's young slaves, a (literal and figurative) embodiment of that theory, leading him to discover on his own a geometrical proposition that consists of constructing, from a given square, a second square with twice the area.

Many historians of philosophy have viewed this scene as the birthplace of a Platonic philosophy finally emancipated from Socratic control. The theory of reminiscence, repeated and developed further in *Phaedo* and especially *Phaedrus*, would in this view bear the mark of the young Plato concealed behind a Socrates mask. But I shall not attempt initially to consider this first formulation of the theory of reminiscence from the standpoint of its grandiose culmination in Platonic metaphysics. On the contrary, the scene is worth considering inasmuch as it occurs within the context of a controversy about the status of the different kinds of knowledge in the city.

Consider first the paradox behind the Socratic proposition: "Why, on what lines will you look, Socrates, for a thing of whose nature you know nothing at all? Pray, what sort of thing, amongst those that you know not, will you treat us to as the object of your search? Or even supposing, at the best, that you hit upon it, how will you know it is the thing you did not know?"[63] The theory of reminiscence is a response to that paradox, which Plato's master characterizes as "eristic," though historians of philosophy agree it has more value than what is suggested by Socrates's disdain for it.[64] This paradox, in fact, bears the traces of fifth-century Sophistic thought, and some exegetes have even argued that the great Gorgias was the first to have formulated it explicitly.[65] The paradox certainly attests to an empiricist philosophy, according to which experience alone is the source of knowledge. Above all, it belongs to a specific epistemology within the lineage of the Protagorian model, whereby virtue can be taught without a definitive knowledge of what it is.

Socrates challenges the idea that one can know something of virtue without knowing its essence beforehand.[66] For Meno, on the contrary, "the search for definitions reduces us to total ignorance, since we are unable to possess full knowledge."[67] But that powerlessness in the face of knowledge in no way implies a pedagogical powerlessness. The philosophy of Gorgias or Protagoras was altogether capable of reconciling a pessimistic theory of knowledge stipulating it is impossible to know what is[68] and an optimism about education that celebrates the possibility of transmitting knowledge.[69] These great Sophists, distant precursors of the famous "ignorant schoolmaster" Joseph Jacotot, claimed there was no need to possess definitive knowledge in order to dispense it.[70]

To resolve that Sophistic paradox and to demonstrate that a single thing can be both known and unknown, Socrates proceeds in two stages. First, he invokes the myth of metempsychosis, no doubt Pythagorean or Orphic in origin,[71] appealing to the authority of possessors of specialized knowledge, namely, priests and poets: "[The speakers] were certain priests and priestesses who have studied so as to be able to give a reasoned account of their ministry; and Pindar also and many another poet of heavenly gifts."[72] Then Socrates summons one of Meno's young slaves, to whom he submits a geometrical proposition. The slave, who speaks Greek, serves merely as the object of an experiment whose proof is actually addressed to Meno.[73] In discovering on his own the length of the sides of a square with twice the area of a given square, the slave, "recovering the knowledge out of himself"[74] by his own deductive capacities, manages to prove that he already knew what he was supposed to be ignorant of.[75]

The intervention of the slave at that crucial moment in the dialogue has often been interpreted from the angle of the universalism of knowledge. The Socratic cross-examination supposedly demonstrates that personal status or social condition in no way determines access to knowledge, and some historians of philosophy have not hesitated to invoke a hypothetical

Socratic egalitarianism.[76] In reality, the hypothesis is very risky, and on this point one may follow Jacques Rancière, who sees the scene primarily as the founding site of the conflictual relationship that has bound philosophy since its origins to the democratic masses and the world of work. The figure of the slave, who for the duration of an experiment comes to play "the chosen of supreme science" before being brushed aside once more, is destined to bear witness against the false knowledge of the artisan, "man of the multitude," and to liquidate a "popular Socratism." Far from providing a universal horizon for the Socratic dialectic, Meno's slave, because he is not "a social subject or a person of the Republic," is primarily a stand-in for the figure of the democratic masses, the artisan citizen, and his "virtual omniscience" allows Plato to disqualify in advance the hypothesis of a popular or democratic philosophy inextricably linked to the world of artisanship.[77]

In view of the civic epistemology brought to light, the entire scene is open to a different interpretation than that traditionally attributed to it. The episode would not so much attest to the universalism of access to knowledge as attempt to contest radically the democratic epistemology of Protagoras, of which Meno's paradox indirectly bears the marks. In summoning a man lacking an identity of his own, prohibited from speaking out in the city, yet one who can accede to the knowledge from which reminiscence proceeds, Socrates would be contrasting a knowledge that owes nothing to the civic order and its dialogism with Sophistic epistemology—another way of demonstrating that authentic knowledge does not have a place in the democratic city.

Indeed, the form of knowledge to which reminiscence (*anamnēsis*) gives access stands opposed point for point to the deliberative knowledge of the democratic order. Socrates's argument is the following: "Seeing then that the soul is immortal and has been born many times, and has beheld all things both in this world and in the nether realms, she has acquired knowledge of all and everything; so that it is no wonder that she should be able to recollect all that she knew before."[78] This knowledge comes partly from a vision, that of a sun external to consciousness, the "upper sun" toward which rise "glorious kings and men of splendid might and surpassing wisdom," like "holy heroes," in Pindar's words quoted by the philosopher.[79] That "sun," which is nothing other than the world of intelligible realities, is accessible only because of a prior identity between the soul and the realities of which it has knowledge.[80] For the soul, therefore, *anamnēsis* consists of detaching itself from the sensible to reach the intelligible world, its true home. In that respect, the theory of reminiscence inherits and simultaneously reinterprets a set of conceptions and practices proper to the masters of truth of the archaic period.[81] Whereas democratic epistemology conceives of a knowledge whose object has no anteriority other than that constructed by deliberative practice, the theory of reminiscence conceives it as a prior reality that the soul, endowed with an independent life, can revisit.

Hence the famous scene from *Meno* dramatizes two incompatible regimes of knowledge, and the theory of reminiscence, demonstrated—or rather tested—by a slave, is presented primarily as a condemnation of Athenian democratic epistemology. In that sense, the scene is an echo chamber of the regime of knowledge proper to the democratic city, a regime that dissociates a public knowledge resulting from deliberation among equals and a knowledge that owes nothing to the world of the city, so that even someone who lacks a civic identity can be its mouthpiece. The Platonic interpretation suggests that the slave is the figure par excellence through which the distance between these two conceptions of knowledge manifests itself.

A LLOW ME to broaden the focus for a moment and, with the aid of a comparison, attempt to look differently at the issues associated with the figure of the expert *dēmosios*. I take you to the Sokoto Caliphate, founded by Usman dan Fodio in the first decade of the nineteenth century, at the confluence of the Niger River and Lake Chad in the northern part of present-day Nigeria. In the mid-nineteenth century, that vast state, comprising about ten million inhabitants, may have had between 1 and 2.5 million slaves working in every sector of production. Specialists on the region do not hesitate to place the state of Sokoto in the category of "slave societies," to use the expression popularized by Moses I. Finley.[82] Organized around an ancient urban center, the Kano emirate was the most prosperous region of the Sokoto empire throughout the nineteenth century. The emir who ruled it owed his power to the caliph's authority, but he possessed a sufficient margin of autonomy to constitute something like a principality within the caliphal state. In a pioneering book, Sean Stilwell considered the role in the Kano emirate of public slaves, whose power and autonomy grew continually throughout the nineteenth century. They even became a major player in the civil war that would set the caliphate ablaze in 1893. During the first twenty years of British rule, from 1903 to 1926, these royal slaves also managed to hold onto their privileged position within the new colonial order. Stilwell believes that the knowledge possessed by some of these public slaves was central to the autonomization of the slave community in the course of the twentieth century.[83]

In the late twentieth century, a descendant of one of the emir's slaves declared: "[The slaves] taught the [princes] everything, horse-riding, how to live with other people [i.e., politics]. They [were] also fed and clothed by them."[84] The art of politics taught by slaves? Indeed, the tasks entrusted to royal slaves called for the most diverse skills. As the sovereign's chief fiscal agents, the emir's slaves were the only ones who knew the real state of affairs in the different districts under his authority. The emir selected the principal commanders of his army from among them, so that slaves did not fail to develop a knowledge, not only of war strategy, but also of "military technology." The compilation, preservation, and transmission of the royal chronicles of Kano were likewise under their authority.

All these servile skills were defined by the term *san'i*, which designated a specialized knowledge distinguished from the order of the *'ilmi*, to which theoretical knowledge (about religion or the history of Islam) belonged. The transmission of knowledge took place inside the slave community under the supervision of the oldest slaves. It occurred, moreover, under a seal of secrecy (*sirrî*), constitutive as it was of the privileges attached to the status of the emir's slaves.[85] Thus, even though their skills were sometimes denigrated as "servile knowledge" by the free aristocracy, these slaves came to acquire and transmit a "cultural capital," which increased their autonomy from the emir and allowed them to constitute a truly autonomous corps defending its own interests within the state.

The process Stilwell highlights in the Kano emirate clearly has no counterpart in the Athenian city of the classical period. The field of expertise placed in the *dēmosioi*'s hands was doubtless less extensive than that of the emirs of Kano, but that is not the essential thing. The *dēmosioi* enjoyed a "kinship privilege" (though it is difficult to document), but they could never form lasting dynasties or constitute themselves into an autonomous community capable of advancing its own interests in the city. All the documentation suggests that the reproduction of the slave corps through transmission of the status of *dēmosios* was negligible, when compared to the number of public slaves who were purchased at the markets.

That dimension indirectly sheds light on the specificities of the knowledge in the *dēmosioi*'s hands. It is particularly difficult to understand how they could have acquired such specialized skills. There is nothing to suggest there were "state schools" that trained public slaves from an early age, as there were for the slave scribes in the Umayyad administration,[86] much less forms of collective education similar to that dispensed to the Mamluks in the seraglio of the beys of Tunis.[87] In his *Politics*, Aristotle mentions the existence of a slave science (*doulikē epistēmē*) taught in Syracuse in the fourth century.[88] That is the only reference in the ancient sources to an institutional education system for slaves,[89] and nothing in the Stagirite's words allows one to think that this slave science concerned expert knowledge about tasks such as those performed by public slaves.

The hypothesis of a transmission of knowledge among the *dēmosioi* themselves, similar to the system in the Kano emirate, is likewise very fragile. In the case of the two Demetriuses, father and son, working in the sanctuary of Asclepius in the third century, one must no doubt imagine a specific skill passed on to the younger slave, but such cases appear to have been rare. Most public slaves were purchased, and it seems more likely that there were slave markets specialized enough for the cities to find skilled slaves to fit their specific needs. That simple fact meant that the skills in the *dēmosioi*'s hands did not offer them resources for autonomy within the city. Unlike the public slaves of Kano, who could inherit and transmit specialized knowledge constitutive of their status, the *dēmosioi* could not use their expertise to foster a specific identity on which to found their power, which might have gradually increased over time.

But the explanation can also be turned on its head. If the public slaves of classical Athens never formed an autonomous body in the city, it was also because the Athenian democratic ideology, in erecting a barrier between the order of expertise and that of the political, somehow prevented them from using their specific skills to rule. In that sense, Athenian democratic epistemology, in relegating expert knowledge to the margins of the political—a noble activity reserved for citizens—was not simply a defense of public knowledge founded on deliberative practice. Indirectly, its function was also to legitimize the fundamental distinction separating the slave from the freeman and to found the slave structure of Athenian society on reason. In classical Athens, the democratic order of knowledge was also the order of slave society.

CHAPTER FIVE

The Mysteries of the Greek State

> Proud and calm, the State steps before this tribunal and by the hand it leads the flower of blossoming womanhood: the Greek city. For this Helen the State waged those wars—and what grey-bearded judge could here condemn?
>
> —Friedrich Nietzsche, "The Greek State"

To describe an individual whose mere appearance made one's blood run cold, the Greeks of antiquity sometimes used the strange expression "man of Tenedos" (*Tenedios anthrōpos*). The Suda, a famous Byzantine encyclopedia compiled during the ninth century, traces the origin of the expression back to the laws of the legendary king Tennes, who is said to have given his name to the North Aegean island of Tenedos. Obdurate, even inhumane, the king made a law that "the public slave should stand with a raised axe behind those who were making false accusations, where he could immediately execute those convinced."[1] If one is to believe the encyclopedia, it was in memory of the terror caused by that *dēmosios* that the expression "man of Tenedos" came into being.

The ax brandished by a public slave was the emblem of the city of Tenedos during the classical and Hellenistic periods. The image of that double-headed ax was engraved on the reverse of the city's coins, with a two-faced head, combining a male and female profile, represented on the obverse. The Tenedians are even said to have consecrated a double-headed ax as emblem of the city in honor of Apollo at Delphi.[2] The ax of Tenedos, famous among the ancient authors, is at the center of two narratives about the singularity of the power of the founding king, Tennes. Pausanias, retracing the history of the ax consecrated at Delphi in book 10 of his *Description of Greece*, tells of the origins of Tenedos.[3] Tennes, the son of Kychnus and Proclea, was born in the city of Colonae in Troad. Shortly after his mother's death, the attractive young man rejected the advances of his new stepmother, Philonome. Furious, she persuaded Kychnus of his son's guilt, claiming he had tried to rape her. The king, to keep Tennes away from his stepmother permanently, locked him and his sister Hemithea in a wooden chest, which he set adrift off the coast of Troad. But the gods protected the handsome Tennes, and the chest miraculously arrived on the banks of the island of Leucophrys, the future Tenedos. A few years later, Kychnus, realizing his mistake, set off by sea to reunite with his son and beg his forgiveness. But the son, having become the ruler of Tenedos, was little inclined to indulgence and in a mad rage took an ax and severed the rope that moored his father's ship to the shore. "For this reason a by-word has arisen, which is used of those who make a stern refusal: 'So and so has cut whatever it may be with an axe of Tenedos,'" concludes Pausanias.[4] The Suda links the notoriety of the ax of Tenedos to one of Tennes's laws, which condemned to death any man found guilty of adultery. As it happened, the king's son was the first to be convicted of that crime. The obdurate Tennes agreed to apply the law at the expense of his own child, who was beheaded with an ax.[5]

Pausanias's account and the anecdote transmitted by the Suda carve out a coherent field of signification around the figure of the founder Tennes. Pausanias describes the unmitigated violence of sovereign power, ready if necessary to turn against the most sacred bond of kinship, the one uniting a father to his own son, symbolized by the rope attaching Kychnus's ship to the island of Tenedos. The fear inspired by the public slave armed with the ax of Tenedos is the precise emblem for that inflexible power, whose only concern is the higher interest of the state. In the daily life of the ancient cities, of course, most public slaves did not elicit such terror. But this imaginary *dēmosios*, forged by later traditions, reveals in hyperbolic form an essential dimension of public slavery: All *dēmosioi*, in embodying the state and its power of coercion, resembled to a greater or lesser extent the slave of Tenedos. It would therefore be worthwhile to consider the terror elicited by the obscure slave of Tenedos in terms of the problem raised by the very existence of the state in ancient Greece.

Problems of the State in Ancient Greece

Historians of the Greek world long ago adopted the term "city-state" (*Staatstadt* in German) to translate the word *polis* into modern languages. Far from constituting a rigorous analytical category, it is, in its most common usage, an umbrella term for sovereign political communities organized around a city but exerting their domination over the rural territory around them.[6] In that sense, the concept of city-state, because it is comparative, long allowed historians of the Greek world to sidestep the question of the concrete specificities of state organization in the *poleis*. The terms of the debate have been largely rethought in the last twenty years, however, because of the research conducted under the aegis of the Danish historian Mogens Hansen. After a colossal inventory of all the cities of the archaic and classical Greek world and an exhaustive survey of the uses of the term *polis*, that undertaking culminated in several ambitious proposals intended to revisit the traditional conceptual framework for thinking about the Greek city.[7]

The analogy between the Greek *polis* in the classical age and the modern state occupies a central place in this venture, and in that respect at least, Hansen's writings belong to the European historiographical conjuncture of the 1990s, which made the question of the state foremost among its concerns—within a context, paradoxically, of a proclaimed crisis of the welfare state.[8] The analogy rests on a twofold proposition: first, the *polis* was conceived by the Greeks themselves as an abstract, impersonal entity, an "abstract public power above ruler and ruled";[9] on the other, contrary to a long tradition of studies dating back to Fustel de Coulanges, a clear distinction between state and civil society needs to be recognized as central to the *polis*. In the classical city, the equivalents of these two notions are said to be *polis* and *koinōnia*.[10]

Such an analogy has two major stumbling blocks. Just because the *polis* is invoked in the ancient sources as an entity above society does not necessarily imply its existence on the legal scene as a person, endowed with rights and duties and able to contract obligations. The "civil institution of the city" remained a blind spot in Greek law.[11] Furthermore, the analogy between the *polis* and the modern state is dubious when assessed in terms of the existence of a civic administration. Granted, several studies devoted to the civic uses of writing have revealed a city with a denser "bureaucratic" system than was earlier believed.[12] Nonetheless, from the ancien régime officer to the contemporary civil servant, the modern state has primarily been embodied in agents who "form its apparatus because they hold a power in its name."[13] And the bureaucratic structure of the modern state had little equivalent in the ancient cities.[14]

Athenian civic ideology could not conceive of the existence of a body of citizens whose profession would have been the permanent management of public affairs. Direct democracy required that all public posts be in the hands of all citizens, whether elected or, more often, selected by lot. Hence the city's "magistrates" did not "represent" the *dēmos*, they were its delegates or proxies, and throughout their tenure they remained forever under the control of the citizenry as a whole. Every bureaucratic or administrative apparatus was understood at best as a regrettable necessity, incompatible in principle with the democratic ideal, and with the exception of the brief passage in Plato's *Statesman* already considered, Greek political philosophy did not elaborate on it in any way.

It was precisely public slaves who, whether guaranteeing the city's weights and measures, overseeing the city's archives, verifying the coinage in circulation, or reprimanding citizens at the markets, ensured that the civic administration would continue to function despite the regular rotation of magistracies. In a certain way, they embodied the bureaucracy of the Greek city. In that sense, their presence was a reminder of a troublesome intruder—the state—in a civic community that, in claiming to make the order of the *archē* (command) coincide with that of the *koinon* (community), dreamed of being transparent to itself. By their mere existence, these "civil servants" demonstrated the limits of the city's institution of itself. And in entrusting to slaves such tasks—indispensable but kept carefully outside the field of the political—the Athenians sought to conceal the role of bureaucracy or administration inherent in the workings of the democratic system by projecting it onto a figure of absolute alterity. In other words, the use of slaves allowed them to mask the ineluctable distance between the state and society, between the necessary administration of public life and the democratic ideal.

Did the use of slaves render invisible the act of violence and dispossession that the advent of the state always represents? Such a paradigm has useful parallels in social anthropology, which has continually highlighted the role of royal slaves in the construction of a political authority, even a state apparatus, that can be deployed to the detriment of the line of succession.[15] In the early days of Islam, among the Umayyads and the Abbasids, in the African kingdoms that flourished before the colonial conquest, and under the Han dynasty in China, history repeated itself. In each case, the slaves in the sovereign's service became the perfect instruments of his power when he undertook to assert his authority against the members of his own family.[16] The use of slaves can be easily explained: because they were excluded from the order of kinship, slaves found it impossible to exercise in their own name a power that could contest royal power.

The Ideal Servant

In 1871, after two years spent crossing the Sahara, Gustav Nachtigal, famous ambassador of the king of Prussia, finally reached the Bornu Sultanate west of Lake Chad. Assigned the mission of delivering gifts to the sultan, whom William I hoped to make an ally at a time when all the European powers were seeking to divide up Africa among themselves, the young traveler, inspired by the great Herodotus, took advantage of his embassy to describe all the mores and customs of the different peoples he encountered along the way. Nachtigal lived for three years in Kuka, capital of the Bornu Sultanate. Even now, his account of the organization of the sultanate constitutes an invaluable source for historians of the Sahara.

If one is to believe Nachtigal, the sultan's council was organized into two distinct groups, which traditionally occupied symmetrical positions on either side of the royal divan. On one side sat the sultan's brothers and sons, on the other his advisers, which included a number of his slaves. But that admirable balance was a sham, as the ethnographer explains:

> Now only the will of the sovereign and the influence of his favourites count for anything . . . and the free man bowed before the slave if the latter stood higher in the sovereign's favour. . . . It must be borne in mind that most of the court offices, which in view of the autocratic power of the prince originated entirely in personal service to him, just as in civilized states, the offices of Lord High Cupbearer, Lord Camberlain and others have similar origin, were nearly always in the hands of slaves; the ruler had much greater confidence in them than in his own kindred and free fellow-tribesmen, and he could certainly rely more on their loyalty. For these reasons the defence of the country also had since ancient times been entrusted chiefly to slaves, so that we see military posts for the most part in their hands. On the other hand, the rulers of Bornu had very many relatives—brothers, sons, and children of sons and daughters—who had to be looked after. Their brothers were naturally regarded with a certain mistrust, and treated the worst. There

were usually also some of their sons whose power it was prudent to restrain within certain limits, and the same attitude was not infrequently observed towards the *maidogu*, the descendants of the king's sons, who, since the succession follows the male line of descent, might eventually be entitled to rule, and could therefore be suspected of dangerous ambition. We find, accordingly, the most important court offices in Bornu in the hand of slaves, while posts which are remote from the seat of government are in the hands of the princes.[17]

The sultan thus ruled through slaves and at the royal family's expense. The traveler was describing a process copiously documented by ethnography, in which slaves are used to protect the sovereign's personal power from his own family's influence and to establish that power on a foundation other than that of his lineage. All the narratives about Tennes that link the presence of a public slave to the existence of an inflexible power turned against the figures of father and son obscurely trace a similar horizon.

But any reader of Max Weber is well aware that the state apparatus is always at risk of producing a bureaucratic order that can defend its own interests or even constitute an autonomous body at its core. Although royal slaves are necessary for the emergence of a state apparatus, they become a threat once the privileged position offered by service to the sovereign is transmitted as an inheritance. The curialization of royal slaves means that they can become notables, can form an autonomous corps that constructs new family solidarities parallel to traditional lineage structures.[18] This process can lead the sovereign's slaves to seize state power, a situation for which Claude Meillassoux invented the neologism "anceocracy" (the rule of servants).[19] Well beyond the famous Egyptian Mamluks, history abounds in royal slaves who usurped power and founded slave dynasties that gave them control of states, temporarily or over the long term.

That threat in turn sheds light on the privilege given to eunuchs, who embodied the ideal figure of the royal servant.[20] Because they were castrated, they could not exploit their titles as an inheritance for their progeny and thereby convert their power into a dynasty, a state of affairs that increased their dependency on the prince: "The eunuch, unable to reproduce, is of interest to his master inasmuch as he cannot escape the instrumentality that enslaves him."[21] In that sense, the eunuch fulfills remarkably well the potentialities of royal slavery. So long as he does not join forces with any lineage, the royal slave remains fully in the master's hands.

Paradoxically, such dependency on the sovereign was sometimes enhanced by unions between his slaves and princesses of the "royal" line, as in the Ottoman court in the sixteenth century. There, imperial sons-in-law were chosen as a mark of recognition and honor from among the sultan's *kul* slaves and at the expense of princely suitors. But such unions in no way implied an integration into the royal lineage, since they did not grant the slaves "a real place within the ranks of the royal family."[22] The slave, excluded from the sphere of full kinship and with no rights other than those the sovereign conceded to him—and these were always revocable—in no way weakened the charismatic dimension behind the leader's power. He even made it possible to ward off the threat of the bureaucratization and routinization of power. In that sense, his position was the result of a paradox: even as the royal slave participated in the assertion of a sovereign authority emancipated from lineage structures, his purpose was to conceal the scandalous nature of any form of state apparatus.

The *Polis* against the State

This general schema was played out in the Greek city. The development of public slavery at the beginning of the classical period can be analyzed as the mark of a resistance by the *polis* to the emergence of a state apparatus, consistent with the bold paradigm proposed by Pierre Clastres for "primitive society."[23]

Let me briefly recall the two fundamental dimensions of the "Copernican revolution" caused by Clastres's *Society against the State*.[24] First, the author rejects the contractualist tradition of political philosophy regarding the classical period, which conceives the advent of the state as a unification (or universalization) that produces the common good, eliminating the division of the social body. Rather, Clastres views the institution of the state primarily as a force of separation. The essence of the state would lie in the establishment of a power relation that would itself be the source of every form of social division. The state would thus take the form of a "structure separate from society, which divides society from the outside while claiming to unify all its features."[25] Second, Clastres portrays primitive society as a wholly political society, whose profound nature would lie in a continuous process whereby the community as a whole would constantly reassert its control over each of its parts, thus making impossible the formation of a power detached from it: "The essential feature (that is, relating to the essence) of primitive society is its exercise of absolute and complete power over all the elements of which it is composed; the fact that it prevents any one of the subgroups that constitute it from becoming autonomous; that it holds all the internal movements—conscious and unconscious—that maintain social life to within the limits and direction prescribed by the society."[26] In that sense, Amerindian chieftaincies would provide only a simulacrum of separate power, consisting primarily of the embodiment of the community in its unity; the chief, "under the obligation of innocent speech,"[27] would not exercise any form of power.[28]

Pierre Clastres imputes to the Greeks the origin of Western singularity, which always grasped "the essence of the political in the social division between ruler and ruled, between those who know and therefore command and those who do not know and therefore obey." In support of his thesis, he cites Heraclitus, Plato, and Aristotle.[29] The Greek frame of reference would thus be the obstacle that makes the political at work in primitive societies incomprehensible to us.[30] Yet historians of the ancient cities find the Greece depicted by Clastres almost unrecognizable. In invoking the One, he appeals more to Platonic metaphysics than to the reality of the civic communities of the classical and Hellenistic periods. I would even suggest, following Nicole Loraux, that the historian of Greece may feel "in familiar territory among Clastres's Indians."[31]

Could the Athenians of the classical period be the distant relatives of the Tupi-Guarani? It should be noted that, despite what Clastres claims, it was not in terms of "rulers and ruled," "those who command" and "those who obey," "those who know" and "those who do not know" that the city conceived of political authority.[32] Aristotle claimed that political power can be distinguished from domestic power in that "the ruler should learn by being ruled."[33] Therefore, a city in which some would obey and others would command would be "a state consisting of slaves and masters, not of free men."[34] In the ancient city, the principle of reciprocity central to political organization took the form of a regular rotation of posts and selection by lot, two institutional practices at the foundation of the civic body's equality. Finally, as we have seen, the Athenians of the classical period had nothing close to our conception of the government expert. It was inconceivable for them that mastery of a specific knowledge could legitimize the exercise of political authority.

It is clear, then, that nothing is to be gained by considering the nature of the *polis* in terms of a stark alternative between a "stateless" society and one akin to the modern state. Rather, understood from a dynamic perspective, the relation the *polis* maintained with a state form of government entailed a tension, and the very nature of the political in ancient Greece required that that tension remain unresolved. Granted, the *polis* was a community of citizens that exercised its sovereignty over a clearly delimited territory by means of political institutions, and power occupied a very visible place in the city. In that minimalist—if not trivial[35]—sense, the city was a state: there was an authority to which all members of society could appeal, even though that place was not separated out from the community and did not transcend it. But it is no less true that the existence of a state as an administration, a separate agency, was problematic for a civic community that sought to keep every form of power within the immanence of its own existence as a community.

The development of public slavery at the beginning of the classical age can therefore be interpreted as the mark of a resistance on the part of civic society to the emergence of a state apparatus—or, in Clastres's terms, an "encoding."[36] The society sought thereby to preserve its indivision, which was nothing other than "a division glimpsed, its full destructive force assessed and lucidly rejected."[37] Such is the meaning of the astonishing institution of public slavery: even while entrusting posts that granted de facto power and expertise to slaves, the cities tainted these functions with an irrevocable stigma attached to the status of those who performed them. The use of slaves, "living instruments" in the hands of the people, theoretically guaranteed that no administrative apparatus could erect an obstacle to the will of the *dēmos*. The city, in making invisible those in charge of its administration, warded off the danger of a state that could constitute itself as an autonomous agency and, if need be, turn against the city itself. In other words, in the classical city, the state was never embodied except as the pure negativity of the *dēmosios*'s slave body.

That system conferred a peculiar position on the public slave, that of blind spot of the city's very institution. His person was a mirror in which the enigma of sovereignty was reflected. That enigma cannot be approached in the bright light provided by political thought in the classical period or the discourse of the fourth-century orators, which historians habitually recognize as the Athenian "civic ideology." On the contrary, it can be glimpsed in the chiaroscuro of strange scenographies that place figures of the public or royal slave at the center, whether the shepherd slave of Laius in Sophocles's *Oedipus Tyrannus*, the *dēmosios* with whom Socrates converses in prison just before his death in *Phaedo*, or the Ethiopian eunuch converted by Philip in the Acts of the Apostles.[38] Pierre Vidal-Naquet has brilliantly suggested that the artisan was the secret hero of Greek history.[39] What if the public slave were the secret hero of the Greek state?

The Institution of the City as Enigma

And here, with the institution of the city as relation to the enigma, it is as if, in spite of ourselves, we already find ourselves in the middle of Sophocles's *Oedipus Tyrannus*. No other narrative, no other legend dramatizes so precisely the limits of the political order and human knowledge when confronted with what is foreign to it. Indeed, the path that leads Oedipus to a knowledge of his own origins is the same one that gradually reveals the limits of any political community confronted with what irremediably escapes it: the order of gods and heroes and that of beasts and monsters, to which the son of Laius is relegated, having become the *pharmakon* by the end of the tragedy.[40] But Sophocles's narrative is also a meditation on the contradictory nature of power, portrayed as both necessity and plague. Therein lies all the ambiguity of Oedipus's situation from the beginning of the play. The one who had saved the city several times by solving the Sphinx's riddle has defiled it by his crime and provoked the wrath of the gods. In that sense, the riddle Oedipus cannot solve is not merely that of his own identity: it is that of power in its utmost generality. And the task will fall to a royal slave to bring to light the impossibility of power ever being fully conscious of its institution.

To pick up the thread of the Oedipal investigation: it opens with the words of the god, embodied in the "godlike prophet" Tiresias,[41] who characterizes Oedipus as the "unholy polluter" of the city.[42] From the beginning of the tragedy, the confrontation between the king and the seer sets in place the two dimensions of the Oedipal riddle, that regarding Oedipus's origins ("Who among mortals gave me birth?" "This day shall be your parent and your destroyer")[43] and that relating to the discovery of Laius's murderer ("That man is here!" Tiresias announces).[44] But the word of the god is not sufficient in itself to prove the guilt of the son of Laius. The chorus even explicitly refutes the efficacy of the prophet's words: "When it comes to men, one cannot tell for sure that a prophet carries more weight than I; true, the knowledge of one is greater than that of another. But never, till I see the saying made unmistakable, shall I assent to those that find fault with him."[45]

The entire play will take the form of a gradual "veridiction," a truth-telling, within the human order of the divine word incarnated by Tiresias. It will present in succession the accounts of Jocasta and of the Corinthian messenger, who will deliver a portion of the Oedipal riddle, before finding its ultimate resolution in the intervention of a former shepherd of Laius's.

Jocasta first reports to Oedipus the old oracle of Apollo, according to which Laius would be killed by his own son. She reassures the king, informing him that Laius had bound his son's feet together on a remote mountaintop far from the city and had then ordered him put to death: "And so Apollo did not bring it about that he should become the murderer of his father, nor that Laius should suffer the disaster which he feared, death at his son's hands."[46] Jocasta also tells Oedipus of the circumstances of Laius's murder at the place where three roads meet.[47] Oedipus, frightened, remembering he had killed an old man large in stature at that very crossroads, realizes he is no doubt the king's murderer, but he still does not know Laius was his father. A messenger arrives to announce the death of Polybus, king of Corinth, who had adopted Oedipus shortly after his birth. This news temporarily brings relief to Oedipus, who still believes he has escaped the fate of a parricide. Nonetheless, in simultaneously revealing that Oedipus is not Polybus's biological son but a child he had taken from a shepherd on Mount Cithaeron, the messenger relaunches the investigation. At this stage, however, neither Jocasta nor the Corinthian messenger has definitive knowledge about the Oedipal riddle, and their two narratives do not necessarily converge to designate the king of Thebes as the one responsible for the death of his father, Laius.

The two components of the riddle—Who killed Laius? Who is Oedipus's father?—are resolved in tandem by the testimony of a former shepherd of Laius's, who tells that he was both the witness to Laius's murder and the man who entrusted Oedipus to the Corinthian messenger. Only that shepherd is in a position to confirm the word of the god, by reporting that he received the nursling from Laius's hands, that he was supposed to do away with him, and that Polybus then adopted the child. The ruler of Thebes is therefore not the son of Polybus but the child of Jocasta and Laius. As Jean Bollack writes, it is with the shepherd's testimony that the Oedipal investigation "culminates and falls apart."[48]

As it happens, this shepherd is a royal slave. Jocasta uses the term *doulos* (slave) the first time she mentions his existence to Oedipus,[49] telling him that when Oedipus became king of Thebes, this man had asked for her permission to vanish forever from the city.[50] Likewise, it is under threat of torture that the words are dragged out of him by Oedipus, a direct reflection of the *basanos*, an Athenian judiciary practice in the classical period according to which a slave could bear witness only with his own body. But the shepherd, before the Theban king's face, denies he is an ordinary slave, claiming he was not purchased but rather raised in the royal house.[51] As Bollack notes, the shepherd, in invoking his proximity to the king, here expresses his own superiority to the "unavowable son," Oedipus.[52] As a slave, he possesses knowledge about Oedipus's birth that the king himself lacks.

The shepherd, a slave and Laius's property, is never called a *dēmosios*. But that statement needs to be qualified, because the institutions and structures of the classical city never have an exact equivalent in the "broken mirror" of classical tragedy.[53] In particular, the portrayal of the shepherd combines some of the indications I identified regarding the *dēmiourgoi* of the archaic period, but with one fundamental difference: In this case, he really is a slave. The chorus characterizes him as a servant remarkably attached to the person of Laius himself. "More than anyone, he was for Laius like his trusty shepherd."[54] This expression refers as well to the figures of Homeric *dēmiourgoi* who, more than any other servants, were dependent on the royal person. The chorus's turn of phrase, however, has been interpreted by many philologists as a concessive clause: "He was one of Laius's men, more faithful than another, insofar as such praise can befit a mere shepherd."[55] We have already come across this paradox many times. It contrasts the status of slave to the prestige provided by proximity to the one holding political authority.

The God's Double, the King's Shadow

The essential thing is the role played by this slave in the unfolding of the tragedy. Sophocles's *Oedipus Tyrannus* is the account of an investigation, which contrasts two types of knowledge: the incomplete and fragmentary knowledge of Oedipus, Jocasta, and the messenger; and totalizing knowledge, which is embodied in two different characters. The knowledge possessed by the god Apollo and revealed through the mouth of his prophet Tiresias instigates the investigation, while that of the royal slave, whom Laius ordered to kill Oedipus, concludes it. The god and the royal slave, placed in symmetrical positions, mirrors of each other, are the only depositaries of complete knowledge about the Oedipal riddle. The slave's knowledge corresponds to that of the god, and both delimit in negative terms the boundaries of the knowledge in the possession of Oedipus and, more broadly, of the civic community. Furthermore, Tiresias himself is described as a slave belonging not to Oedipus but to Apollo: "I live not as your slave, but that of Loxias,"[56] he boldly exclaims before the king of Thebes.

In 1971 and again in 1980, Michel Foucault studied *Oedipus Tyrannus*, inquiring how the question of power in Sophocles's play was linked to a certain mechanism for elaborating the truth.[57] As "a dramaturgy of multiple truths,"[58] *Oedipus Tyrannus* is said to dramatize a "struggle between kinds of knowledge,"[59] distinguishing in the last instance the divine truth of Tiresias from that proceeding from the slave's first-person testimony, grounded in "seeing." Foucault is led to contrast the "oracular alethurgy" of Tiresias to the "alethurgy of testimony" embodied in the shepherd slave.[60] This distinction must not mask the symmetry set in place between the word of the god and that of the slave, the only figures who possess an absolute knowledge about the Oedipal riddle. As Foucault writes, "The slave's humble memory corresponds word for word to the 'Immortal Voice.'"[61] The shepherd slave, then, is not only the god's adjuvant in that his act of disobedience is necessary for the oracle to be fulfilled; above all, in the human order, the royal shepherd alone possesses a knowledge equal to that of the gods, and it is through his mouth that the oracular word, placed in doubt by the chorus, acquires its veracity in the eyes of the civic community.

In addition, the shepherd slave, the only one in possession of the answer to the riddle, source of Oedipus's power, embodies the limits of power when it claims to establish its foundations on an absolute knowledge. It is his knowledge that enthroned Oedipus as ruler of Thebes, after he solved the Sphinx's riddle: "I shall begin again and light up the obscurity. In taking up at the beginning the investigation, I am going to clarify it once again,"[62] Oedipus proclaims as the investigation of Laius's murder gets under way. As Jean-Pierre Vernant writes, "At first Oedipus is the clear-sighted one, the lucid intelligence that, without anyone's help, without the help of a god or an omen, was able to guess the Sphinx's riddle, solely through the resources of the *gnōmē*."[63] Oedipus, sure in his knowledge, exclaims to Tiresias: "You are sustained by darkness only, so that you could never harm me or any other man that sees the light."[64] The relation between knowledge and power, whose various articulations we have been following—from the Daedalus legend to the figure of the expert *dēmosios* in the classical city—is at the center of the tragedy.[65] Indeed, Oedipus, the one who knows (*oida*), claims to possess a *technē* of *technē*, a knowledge of knowledge, the origin of his own power: "O riches and kingship, skill surpassing skill, how great is the hatred you store up in a life much-envied."[66] So he exclaims to Tiresias, imagining that the prophet is being manipulated by Creon, who wants to seize Oedipus's throne. But the power of the king of Thebes is ignorant of its own origin, and when Oedipus sets out to discover the source of his power, he is blinded by it. The royal slave, the only human being who holds the secret that haunts the fate of "Oedipus the Learned,"[67] indicates the failure of that knowledge of knowledge when it claims to be the foundation of a power.[68] In that respect, the tragedy of *Oedipus Tyrannus*, contemporaneous with the democratic epistemology of Protagoras, recounts the deposition of a power that also thinks of itself as a knowledge—and it is a royal slave who embodies that deposition.

But the royal shepherd is not only the figure through which the divine word proves its truth within the human order. He is also a double for the king of Thebes. Here the tragedy repeats sotto voce the theme of the king as "the people's shepherd" (*poimena laōn*) already present in the Homeric epic.[69] Throughout the play, a secret kinship unites Oedipus and the shepherd.[70] Just as Oedipus saved Thebes while leading the city to its destruction, the shepherd, in saving the newborn entrusted to him, is the source of his ruin: "The shepherd who released me from the cruel fetters of my feet, and saved me from death, and preserved me, did me no kindness!"[71] exclaims Oedipus, blinded at the end of the tragedy. The shepherd's fate, like that of the king of Thebes, takes the form of escape: just as Oedipus fled Corinth to avoid the fulfillment of the prophecy that he would murder his father, the shepherd fled the city of Thebes, understanding that the new sovereign was none other than the child formerly fated to die.[72] And finally, the feeling of pity (*katoikteirō*) that the nursling inspired in the slave is expressed in the same terms when the king attests to his own pity for the residents of Thebes.[73] God's mirror and king's shadow, such is the royal shepherd, in whom Oedipus's omnipotence finds its limit. Revealed here is an imaginary architecture of political sovereignty, secretly linking the royal figure to that of the slave—who, one barely dares whisper, is *like* the king's second body.

The Anonymous Disciple

The shepherd in *Oedipus Tyrannus* is clearly not a *dēmosios*, and it is only in the reflection of a "broken mirror" that his unique place in Sophocles's drama seems to replicate the position of public slaves in classical Athens. By contrast, a very real *dēmosios* makes an appearance in the middle of one of the most famous episodes of the Socratic legend, the last scene of Plato's *Phaedo*.

Evening has fallen on the Athens prison. Socrates, condemned to death by the Athenians, has just expressed his last wishes to his wife and children, who then leave the prison. If one is to believe the narrator, Phaedo, "After that not much was said."[74] Impromptu words, textual excess: the ordinary rules of Socratic dialogue are abolished here, and time seems to stand still. The philosopher receives a visit in his cell from a *dēmosios*, who has come to announce Socrates's imminent execution. This public slave is one of the servants placed under the charge of the Eleven, responsible for overseeing the Athens prison and organizing executions for capital crimes. At this point, a strange dialogue begins. It consists of mutual praise by the slave and Socrates in the presence of the philosopher's assembled disciples. The *dēmosios* tells Socrates: "I have found you in all this time in every way the noblest and gentlest and best man who has ever come here, and now I know your anger is directed against others, not against me, for you know who are to blame. Now, for you know the message I came to bring you, farewell and try to bear what you must as easily as you can." Then, Phaedo recounts, "he burst into tears and turned and went away." He continues: "Socrates looked up at him and said: 'Fare you well, too; I will do as you say.'" It is then that Socrates, turning to his disciples, praises the slave in return: "How charming the man is! Ever since I have been here he has been coming to see me and talking with me from time to time, and has been the best of men, and now how nobly he weeps for me! But come, Crito, let us obey him, and let someone bring the poison, if it is ready; and if not, let the man prepare it."[75] How to understand the sudden appearance of this public slave, just as Socrates is about to face death? What is the meaning of the mutual praise of the *dēmosios* and the philosopher?

This short dialogue, inserted between the Socratic account of the immortality of the soul and the philosopher's enigmatic last words prescribing that Crito sacrifice a rooster to Asclepius—"Crito, we owe a cock to Asclepius"[76]—has elicited little interest in philosophers, who have seen it as one of those literary ornaments devoid of philosophical import of which Plato was so fond.[77] But the lack of interest from Platonic scholars is inversely proportionate to the fascination this public slave character held for eighteenth-century painters who set out to represent the philosopher's last moments.[78] The *dēmosios* occupies a central place in the *Death of Socrates* painted by Jacques-Louis David in 1787 (and exhibited at the Metropolitan Museum of Art in New York since 1931). In fact, the composition is organized around that strange pair, the public slave and the philosopher. As the slave, seen from behind, looks to his left, holding back his tears, the philosopher, viewed frontally, addresses his disciples positioned to the right as the cup of hemlock is passed from one to another. The young slave from the back, the old sage full-face: the genius of Socratic thought is brightly lit, the slave's face plunged in darkness, as if the two characters were the front and back of a single figure. What, then, did David *see* in that scene, which Platonic exegesis persists in ignoring?

It would clearly be absurd to read the praise of the *dēmosios* as an indication of a specific position on slavery in Socratic philosophy. What is at stake lies elsewhere. The *dēmosios* is by no means one of Socrates's disciples, and if, as the philosopher claims, he shared many conversations with Socrates, the *logoi sokratikoi* carefully refrains from reporting their content. The slave's behavior, lauded by Socrates, is in reality constructed to mark a contrast with the attitude of the disciples, paralyzed by the idea of their master's death. Against the dejected disciples, the slave sets the example of the noble behavior to be adopted in the face of that death.

While the disciples bemoan their fate, as Phaedo will acknowledge,[79] the slave grieves for Socrates out of generosity and nobility of soul (*hōs gennaiōs*). The *dēmosios* understands Socrates's behavior better than all the disciples combined. His compassion propels him to the philosopher's side while the disciples stand by powerlessly in the face of their master's death. None of them will be favored with the farewell (*chairē*) Socrates gives the slave,[80] and Phaedo, in concluding his account with a celebration of Socrates as the best (*aristos*), the wisest (*phrōnimotatos*), and the most righteous (*dikaiotatos*) of men, merely echoes the discourse of the slave who, observing the same threefold structure, praised the most noble (*gennaiotatos*), the most gentle (*praotatos*), and the best (*aristos*) of men.

Specters of Socrates

The nameless slave, without a past and barred any future, is twice called by the generic term *anthrōpos*, first by Socrates and then by Phaedo.[81] He is placed in the position of radical exteriority, far from the circle of disciples and also from the civic community that voted to have the philosopher put to death. The very possibility of transmitting Socrates's memory beyond the narrow circle of the disciples is dramatized in his person. Indeed, by his testimony, the *dēmosios* bears witness not only to Socrates's innocence but also and above all to the survival of his teachings beyond the defeat of the year 399. In this scene, which is in some sense the birthplace of what I will call Socratic *hauntology*—borrowing that felicitous neologism from Jacques Derrida[82]—the *dēmosios* plays a determining role. This absolute outsider, for that is what a slave is, is called upon to guarantee Socrates's greatness on a broader scale than the group of disciples alone: "The others curse me; this one blesses me," Diderot will have Socrates say, in his free translation of *Phaedo*. By means of this slave, the Platonic text gestures toward an elsewhere, a future when the true value of Socratic thought will be recognized.

Yet the scene is not only praise for the philosopher. It is also the occasion for a mutual acknowledgment of Socrates and the slave. The philosopher seems to recognize the kindly *dēmosios* as his double, as if a secret bond united the two. The brief dialogue occurs shortly after Socrates has reassured Crito at length about what will happen to his body and soul after death: "After I drink the poison I shall no longer be with you, but shall go away to the joys of the blessed you know of . . ."[83] In this crucial moment, as Socrates prepares for his journey to the underworld, an identical connection to death unites the two characters. It is striking that the metaphor of slavery and emancipation runs through the entire dialogue to convey the passage from life to death. And until the final and mysterious invocation of Asclepius, it borrows a large share of its rhetoric from the acts of manumission in the Greek world.[84] As the soul of Socrates frees itself from his mortal coil to become the slave of the god Apollo,[85] he identifies himself as an *anthrōpos* dispossessed of his own body: The philosopher's death and "social death"—the lot of the slave—are here mirror images of each other. Indeed, this scene *hauntology* can also be read as an encounter between two specters. At a moment when Socratic memory is about to become the specter that will never cease to haunt Athens, it projects itself into a public slave. As a body that does not answer to the name of a person—and in that respect "a body without flesh"[86]—the public slave is himself altogether spectral. His speech seems to come from a place inaccessible to the common mortal, here incarnated in Socrates's poor disciples. His word, therefore, would possess a superior power of veridiction.

The First Christian: "Do You Know What You Are Recognizing?"

Several centuries later, at a great remove from the Athenian agora of 399, a famous scene in the Acts of the Apostles provided an unexpected sequel to that drama. But are we really as far from classical Athens as we tend to think? No doubt—unless one admits that the New Testament actually belongs to what we pedantically call "Greek literature," and that the images and expressions of authors from the classical period enriched its writing.

At the end of the eighth chapter of Acts, Christ's early disciples have suffered the wrath of the Jerusalem church. Peter has appeared before the Sanhedrin; Stephen, the chief representative of the circle of Hellenists, has been stoned to death; and a number of the faithful have dispersed to Judea and Samaria. At that tragic moment, Philip is the first to venture outside Jerusalem to spread the gospel. He goes off to evangelize the Samaritans, who had long been faithful to a Judaism distinct from that of Jerusalem. Then, answering the call of an "angel of the Lord," the evangelist takes the road leading from Jerusalem to Gaza:

> And behold, a man of Ethiopia, a eunuch of great authority under Candace the queen of the Ethiopians, who had charge of all her treasury, and had come to Jerusalem to worship, was returning. And sitting in

his chariot, he was reading Isaiah the prophet. Then the Spirit said to Philip, "Go near and overtake this chariot." So Philip ran to him, and heard him reading the prophet Isaiah, and said, "Do you understand what you are reading?" And he said, "How can I, unless someone guides me?" And he asked Philip to come up and sit with him. The place in the Scripture which he read was this: "He was led as a sheep to the slaughter; And as a lamb before its shearer *is* silent, So He opened not His mouth. In His debasement, His rights were taken away, And who will declare His generation? For His life is taken from the earth." So the eunuch answered Philip and said, "I ask you, of whom does the prophet say this, of himself or of some other man?" Then Philip opened his mouth, and beginning at this Scripture, preached Jesus to him. Now as they went down the road, they came to some water. And the eunuch said, "See, *here is* water. What hinders me from being baptized?" Then Philip said, "If you believe with all your heart, you may." And he answered and said, "I believe that Jesus Christ is the Son of God." So he commanded the chariot to stand still. And both Philip and the eunuch went down into the water, and he baptized him.[87]

This episode, located between Philip's mission to Samaria and Peter's conversion of the Roman centurion Cornelius,[88] is a founding moment in the grand narrative of the spread of the gospel. The Ethiopian eunuch is the first non-Jew to receive baptism. A number of exegetes have believed that Luke was repeating a tradition specific to a circle of "Hellenists," who credited Philip rather than Peter as the first to have evangelized a pagan. The episode thus concerns the expansion of the community beyond the original land of Judea and even prefigures the mission to the far reaches of the world, as the eunuch himself will embark on a mission to Ethiopia.[89] In that sense, the baptism of the Ethiopian eunuch "violates the Law, whose function it is to protect the purity of the chosen people,"[90] and opens the Christian faith to a new horizon, universal in its dimensions. The Acts briefly reports that, after the eunuch's baptism, Philip went from Azotus to Caesarea "and passing through, he preached in all the cities."[91]

Philip teaches the eunuch that the story of Christ's life is the fulfillment of the Old Testament, and this act of recognition transforms the dead letter into the living word. "Do you therefore know [*gignōskeis*] what you are recognizing [*anagignōskeis*] [through reading]?" the evangelist asks the eunuch, who admits he does not and asks for someone to guide him. The episode will provide food for thought for the Church Fathers when they have to legitimize the church's authority through interpretation of the sacred text.[92] The eunuch's innocence may thus provide the model for any person of faith taking up the text. As an orphan, the text requires a word from elsewhere, and only that word can shed light on how the text is to be read. Above all, the Acts demonstrates in eminently Platonic terms the opposition between the dead letter, powerless to say anything on its own, and the living word, which alone can bring about the text's Assumption.[93] The fulfillment of the written text's meaning lies solely in the inspiration of the living word, rooted in the knowledge of revelation. The eunuch slave, whose servile condition is written in his flesh, can receive the revelation of salvation only through the words of Philip, who responds to the call of an "angel of the Lord" (*aggēlos kuriou*) and becomes the mediator of the Holy Spirit.

But the eunuch is no ordinary slave, and this character has not failed to give rise to the most contradictory interpretations. He is nameless, designated by a geographical or "ethnic" identity—"the Ethiopian"—and by a function, officer in charge of Queen Candace of Ethiopia's treasury. Exegetes have not neglected to point out the intertextuality of this episode and Chapter 5 of Second Kings in the Old Testament, concerning the character of Naaman, who may have served as one of Luke's models. Namaan, a powerful commander of the army of the king of Syria, also travels in a chariot. Afflicted with leprosy, he is healed only after the messenger of the prophet Elisha tells him to bathe seven times in the Jordan. Then Naaman must acknowledge that "*there is* no God in all the earth, except in Israel."[94]

The eunuch's religious identity is unclear. He has come to Jerusalem to "worship": Does that mean is he a "god-fearer" (*phoboumenos ton theon*), a pagan whose sympathies lie with Judaism, given that he holds a scroll of Isaiah in his hand?[95] On the long list of peoples present in Jerusalem for Pentecost at the beginning of Acts 2, Luke does not mention the Ethiopians,[96] and whatever the precise religious status of the eunuch, he appears in any case "excluded as a result of his handicap from religious communion with Israel."[97] Above all, this character has sparked a multitude of interpretations based on his ethnicity, gender identity, or social status, often dating back to the patristic literature itself. In that sense, the Ethiopian eunuch is an operator of difference, and his alterity can be interpreted on many different levels.

Some have focused on the fact that he is a man of the outer reaches. For the ancient authors, Ethiopia, even more than the vast territory between

Aswan and Khartoum making up ancient Nubia, was understood to be the ends of the inhabited world. In the *Odyssey*, the Ethiopians are the "farthermost of men."[98] And Augustine, commenting on Psalms, believes they live "at the end of the earth."[99] Through the eunuch's baptism, then, the promise made at the beginning of Acts, that of bringing the good news *eschatou tēs gēs* (to the end of the earth), would be fulfilled.[100]

But the character of the eunuch also lends itself to a reading in terms of gender or queer theory.[101] The sexual neutralization of the eunuch would even be compounded by the uncertain status of his mistress, Queen Candace, whom Strabo claims was an *andrikē gunē*, a woman of the male sex.[102] Some Church Fathers did not fail to see the episode as a justification for the ascetic ideal of monachism.[103]

Finally, the episode has given rise to an interpretation in terms of ethnicity and skin color, providing inspiration for black theology.[104] The Ethiopian eunuch, in this view, is "a *recognizable black African* from ancient Nubia,"[105] and his conversion points toward a different story of Christianity's expansion, toward Africa this time, a story deliberately covered over by Paul's mission to the Western Mediterranean and Rome, capital of the empire, at the beginning of Acts 9. Recently, Patrick Fabien has suggested that the eunuch's "negritude" was the object of Luke's attention.[106] Through that black African's baptism, Luke would have been showing that revelation transcends any distinction of ethnicity or "race." It should be noted that such an interpretive grid was not radically different from that of several Church Fathers, who themselves interpreted the eunuch's baptism in terms of a symbolics of color, as a passage from darkness to brilliance and from black to white.[107]

One thing is certain: The eunuch stands at the crossroads of multiple identities, all of them bearing the mark of alterity. As Patrick Fabien writes, "The Ethiopian eunuch bears the most open identity typology in Acts, which makes him able to take different audiences into account."[108] But whatever the criterion chosen on which to base that "difference," all modern exegetes agree that he is the archetype of the stranger, whose conversion realizes the program of the Gospel: to welcome those excluded from the covenant and held in contempt by society.[109]

The prophecy of Isaiah, which the eunuch reads without understanding its meaning, is significant in that respect: "He was led as a lamb to the slaughter, And as a sheep before its shearers is silent, So He opened not

His mouth. In His debasement, His rights were taken away, And who will declare His generation? For He was cut off from the land of the living."[110] Luke deliberately chooses two verses from the fourth Servant Song of Isaiah, which relate the fate of the Servant of Yahweh, condemned to a death that atones for the "crimes of his people." The distress of the Servant, "overcome in his body and speech,"[111] reflects the eunuch's condition. "And who will declare His generation? For He was cut off from the land of the living." Such is the fate of the eunuch, but also of every slave. In his evocation of the Servant, who Isaiah says bears "the sin of many," Philip invites the eunuch to recognize the suffering of Christ.[112] But Philip also allows the eunuch to recognize his own condition in that of the Servant, one that will find its redemption in the figure of Christ. The "silent sheep," which is to say, the eunuch, has found his voice through Philip. The scene from Acts is thus constructed around a connection between two texts, at whose confluence three identities converge.[113] Juxtaposed in the verses from Isaiah are the destinies of the suffering Servant, of Jesus, and of the Ethiopian eunuch. The life of Jesus sheds light on the prophecy of Isaiah even as the condition of the Ethiopian eunuch is projected onto it.

The eunuch's status, however, cannot be reduced to a position of exclusion. Having stepped down from a chariot he is not driving (we know this because he orders it to stop), then receiving baptism from Philip, the eunuch occupies a position of majesty in Luke's text. He is in charge of Queen Candace's treasury, and John Calvin did not hesitate to portray him as one of the leaders of the kingdom of Ethiopia.[114] Finally, the language the eunuch uses is particularly elegant and refined. Yet the man is unquestionably a slave of the queen of Ethiopia, and that inferior status is compounded by his castration. The character is thus marked through and through by the now-familiar paradox whereby political power is linked to an irremediably low status.

This apparent contradiction disappears when a connection is made to the very status of royal slave. The singularity of the eunuch's status has not been pointed out by exegetes, although it is central to the episode. The eunuch is not only a black man, a man from the ends of the earth, and a sexually mutilated male. He is also not a slave or marginal figure like any other. In reality, all the marks of alterity that define his exclusion combine to form a singular status, that of royal slave, and it is as such that he occupies a preeminent position in the narrative regarding the diffusion of revelation—that of the first convert of the pagan nations. Because he is a public slave, his presence makes him an operator of radical alterity, but it also elevates him to the rank of a third-party guarantor or mediator, "hands of the Holy Spirit" and "herald of the Word"—as Theophylact of Ohrid will write[115]— through whom revelation opens itself to new horizons.

In the figure of the Ethiopian eunuch, the universality of the biblical word is fulfilled. He combines in his person the Old and New Testaments, Jerusalem and the ends of the earth. But in that narrative, because he has the preeminent position of being the first non-Jew to receive the gospel, the eunuch is also placed in the emblematic posture of mediator for all gentiles, called upon to identify with the person of Christ.

IN THREE MONUMENTS of Greek literature—the fall of "Oedipus the Learned," Socrates's last moments in prison, and the baptism of the first gentile—figures of public or royal slaves make their appearance in the middle of the narrative, at moments as decisive as they are unexpected. For Sophocles, the royal slave's word is symmetrical to that of the god, and a mysterious connection unites him to the figure of the sovereign. Oedipus's knowledge— and more broadly, the political order—comes up against its own limit in the person of the royal shepherd, god's mirror and king's shadow. In *Phaedo*, the spectral recognition at work between Socrates and his jailer places the slave in a preeminent position that contrasts with that of the dejected disciples: it is up to him to bear witness to the philosopher's memory beyond Socratic circles. And finally, the Acts of the Apostles places a royal slave at the center of the grand narrative of the universal spread of the Gospel.

Nothing seems to link a priori *Oedipus Tyrannus*, a tragedy about knowledge and sovereignty, to the meditation on death in *Phaedo* or the history of the expansion of the Christian faith. Yet a secret thread joins the Ethiopian eunuch, the royal shepherd, and the guard in the Athenian prison. Each of these three men expresses in his own way a radical alterity that places him in a position to embody a limit. Located on the borderline between two worlds, each man plays the role of go-between: between the order of the gods and that of the political community, between the philosopher's disciples and the city (even between life and death, in the no-man's-land of his servile condition), or between the community of Jerusalem and all those excluded from the covenant.

Above all, the exteriority of their position traces an elsewhere from which the norm can be formulated. Indeed, the "off-field" from which the public slave's word is uttered is irreducible to that of slaves in general or "outcasts." Their public or royal status confers on their person a dimension unlike any other. Whether these slaves are the property of the king, the queen, or the city, their status converts the exclusion characteristic of their servile condition into a third agency, radically exterior, from which the ultimate horizon of the norm, that of the political community or the community of believers, can be formulated. These three figures thus provide a glimpse of a unique mechanism that in the ancient city links the figure of the slave to the enunciation of truth.

From one philosophical testament to another: a few months before his death, Michel Foucault devoted his last classes at the Collège de France to the study of the modalities by which "truth-telling" is constructed and becomes manifest. This was, in his own terms, a rough draft of the history of the different "regimes of truth." Foucault posited four figures of enunciation, all constituting "forms of the subject telling the truth" in the ancient world: the prophet, the sage, the technician (or "man of skill"), and the philosopher.[116] These four figures, according to him, constituted not so much specific social roles as generic forms of veridiction, "fundamental modes of truth-telling," often likely to intersect.[117] It seems to me that the figure of the public or royal slave, embodied in the shepherd in *Oedipus Tyrannus* or the slave in Socrates's prison, ought to be added to that typology.

This figure cannot be reduced to those of prophet, sage, technician, or philosopher. His word does not have the obscurity of prophecy or the apodictic dimension of the sage's word. Unlike the prophet, he does not speak in the name of the gods; unlike the sage, he does not express himself in his own name because he has none. Nor is his word a polemical truth-telling, like that of the parrhesiastic philosopher, ready to risk his life for speaking out. Nor, finally, is it a *technē* that could be proven by a demonstrative argument. The public slave's word is nonetheless a word of truth, rooted in the eminently paradoxical nature of his condition, which combines the radical exteriority from civil society characteristic of the slave and the maximal dependency on the political community characteristic of any public property. That strange condition traces a third space from which truth can arise, irreducible to the sphere of the sacred and, in that respect, entirely immanent. Specter of the philosopher, shadow of the king, phantom body of a community yet to come: from that elsewhere where the public slave resides, a face of truth goes forward.

Conclusion

> Octavian was here again; he stood near the candelabrum, apart from the shadowy swarm, and though he himself was invisible, his dark eyes glanced toward the slave, giving him leave to speak.
> "Speak," directed the slave, "give your permission."
> Thereupon the order, which in reality was nothing of the sort, was given by Caesar.
> —Hermann Broch, *The Death of Virgil*

Somewhere along the edge of the Aegean Sea, several hundred armed men gather at a herald's call. Little by little, their assembly takes the form of an enormous circle, toward the center of which one of them will soon advance. As all eyes converge on him, the man will seize a scepter and begin to talk about an affair that concerns everyone. His speech will be followed by others; then the Assembly, by acclamation, will make a decision to which the entire community will be bound from now on.

If one is to believe historians and anthropologists of the Greek world, the beautiful scenographies of collective deliberation provided by the world of the Homeric epic anticipated the political destiny of Greek civilization in the classical age. Never mind that the orators were usually princes, and that the people (*laos*) expressed their opinion not by voting but by acclamation, unanimous on principle. Already within the folds of these scenes an original trait proper to ancient Greece, the "civilization of political speech,"[1] can supposedly be made out. A continuous line would thus run between the war assembly of the men in the *Iliad*, that of the citizens in the small oligarchic cities of the archaic period, and the Athenian *ecclēsia* of the classical period, three sites of speech where the Greeks are said to have discovered the political.[2]

The birth of the political in ancient Greece would thus consist of the advent of a communitarian order organized around collective deliberation in a central and egalitarian space.[3] And indeed, the public aspect of decision making was certainly a dimension constitutive of a Greek city's organization. Places of assembly were all sites that realized in concrete form the intervisibility of citizens, making the Greek city, in Hannah Arendt's idealist description, "the space of appearance in the widest sense of the word, namely, the space where I appear to others as others appear to me."[4] That public dimension of political life consisted primarily of a set of institutional practices, such as the obligation on the part of magistrates to give a public accounting of their tenure or the civic decrees engraved on stelae and displayed in public spaces accessible to all. In that sense, the Greek city, in making the organizational principles of social life the object of public deliberation, would provide the first example of a fully autonomous society that recognized itself as the "source of its own norms."[5] The memory of the Greek city, the place of a "transparency realized through the identification of the rational with the political," would reassure historians—melancholic by nature—that "in contrast to all the disillusionments of the present time, there was for democracy a time of transparency."[6]

The Political Neutralized

But the bright light that still shines forth from the assemblies and theaters of the Greek cities may have blinded us. The "transparency" of the Greek political was matched by the veil of opacity with which the city covered what, though indispensable to its operation, lay on its margins. As in a shadow play, the dignified gestures and fine words of the citizens gathered at the Assembly had their counterpart in the mute scenography of anonymous beings, voiceless and without an identity. Hidden away in the recesses of the Acropolis, counting and recounting the property of Athena, carefully recording the expenses of the generals on expedition, or rushing about in every direction to orient citizen judges and seat spectators at the tribunals, all these men had to be invisible for the illusory transparency of the civic community to be maintained.

Imagine for a moment that the president of the European Central Bank, the director of the Compagnies Républicaines de Sécurité (French national riot police) and of the French National Archives, the inspectors of the treasury administration, and the court clerks were slaves, the collective property of the French people or, even more improbably, of a European people. Transport yourself, in short, to a republic where the most important "servants" of the state would have been its slaves. What would the Place de la Nation in Paris look like on the evening of major demonstrations, if cohorts of slaves had to move along the stragglers? Suppose that one of these demonstrations was protesting the fiscal austerity imposed by the European treaties: Would the European Union's monetary policy be different if the president of the Central Bank were a slave whom the European Parliament could sell or flog if he performed his job poorly? To continue in that vein, what form would the deliberations between representatives take in that same Parliament, if slaves were the only staff permanently attached to the institution, members of Parliament being replaced every year? The prospect makes you wonder.

This analogy—weak, to be sure—has the virtue of conjuring up, in contrast to our own political condition, a dual dimension constitutive of public slavery in the Greek cities. In the first place, the community as a whole sought to exert direct control over several realms lying fully within its sovereignty (law and order, currency, civic documents), which it was unthinkable to entrust to citizens, even if they were experts. The use of slaves, "living instruments" in the hands of the people, theoretically assured that no constituted body, no administrative apparatus, would be an obstacle to the will of the *dēmos*.

Above all, the analogy sheds light on how rigorously the political field was delimited in the ancient city. No doubt "the political" in Greece was broader than a banal understanding of the term "politics" might suggest, in that it cannot be reduced to competition for power in the context of civic institutions. Citizenship was expressed in multiple realms of civic life (religious practices, economic life, mores) that extend far beyond mere participation in institutions.[7] But it is also true that the delimitation of the political field in the ancient city proceeded from a rigorous division, which relegated to its margins, or "off-field," techniques and bodies of knowledge indispensable to the administration of public affairs.

The ancient authors conferred no name on that sphere of activity in the city, nor did they attempt to inscribe it within a general taxonomy of powers and jurisdictions. This is because the field of activity of the public slaves, while participating fully in the expression of sovereignty, was primarily defined in negative terms, in opposition to political activity. The activities of the *dēmosioi*, which entailed a suspension of the political field's rules of operation, belonged to a *neutralized* political. Invoked as *eleutheria leitourgia*, that mechanism paradoxically placed the public slave in the position of a third party guarantor of collective freedom. But sometimes, in the theater of the city, the curtain separating the stage from the wings was raised, and the public slave advanced toward the spectators to reveal the real story, as if that figure of alterity fleetingly provided a place from which the city could conceive of its own institution.

Life and Death of an Institution

The singularity of Greek public slavery can be seen more clearly through the prism of other slave systems. Because they were public property, public slaves—owners of property who enjoyed a kinship privilege and were sometimes even honored by the cities—enjoyed a privileged status when compared to private slaves. Yet the *dēmosioi* never possessed the autonomy typical of public or royal slaves throughout history. Under the control of the civic community, they did not possess the influence afforded by an advantageous position beside the one who personally held public authority. Above all, their job never became a patrimony, which would have allowed them to constitute an order or a corps that could have advanced its own interests—and that fact can be explained more generally by the way the city conceived the status hierarchies at its core.

The figure of the slave as "public expert," which has many ethnographic parallels, also sheds light on the political uses of the different bodies of knowledge in classical Athens. If the order of the democratic city entailed relegating expert knowledge to the margins of the political field, this was not because the democratic system was the dictatorship of ignoramuses, as Plato claimed. The expert slave was the product of an original civic epistemology, which valorized the horizontal circulation of knowledge among equals, and for which the Sophist Protagoras's "city of auletes" provides the model.

These remarks are a reminder of the obvious: The status of public slaves cannot be understood apart from the general characteristics of the social and political organization of the *polis*. The end of that institution in the cities of the Greek Orient during the imperial age was therefore merely a sign of a much larger change affecting the organization of city life. The decline of public slavery, attested for the early fifth century CE—the date at which the Greek cities definitively stopped using slaves in their administration—is already perceptible in the third century. By the early fourth century, that unique institution was no longer understood by the imperial chancellery: Constantinian laws explicitly conflated slaves of the cities and imperial slaves.[8]

In reality, the end of public slavery in the ancient cities can be explained in terms of the conjuncture of several phenomena. First, it is quite probable that the social prestige associated with the imperial administration redounded on the administration of the cities themselves, gradually leading citizens to covet the *dēmosioi*'s position. Cities therefore came to entrust to freemen public posts formerly reserved for slaves.[9] In Ephesus in the first century CE, some freemen performed on a provisional basis duties usually reserved for the public slaves, although the Roman governor put an end to the practice.[10] Second, a few anecdotes gleaned randomly from inscriptions suggest the difficulties the cities may have encountered in managing their slaves.[11] The imperial rescript of Marcus Aurelius and Lucius Verus of 163/164 CE, for example, indicates that a public slave by the name of Satorneinus, in the service of the Gerusia of Ephesus, whose duties included the collection of debts from public debtors, had misappropriated part of the funds intended for the city.[12] Conversely, a century earlier, an honorary decree from the small Pamphylian city of Cibyra mentions the misappropriation of public property for which a citizen had been convicted: he had taken no fewer than 107 *dēmosioi*.[13] Although a historian hardly has the means to determine how representative these two anecdotes are in the overall evolution of public slavery, I am inclined to think—setting aside all academic prejudices—that these anecdotes would have been inconceivable in the Athens of the fourth or third centuries BCE.

Such difficulties are insignificant, however, when compared to two phenomena whose coincidence announced nothing less than the advent of a new world within which public slavery, as the classical and Hellenistic city had known it, no longer had a place. Beginning in the mid-third century, the decline in the number of circuits supplying slaves to the Mediterranean world clearly had major consequences for public slavery. Because hereditary succession played only a marginal role in the replacement of the contingents of *dēmosioi*, the institution required an extensive and even specialized slave market. A second transformation, slower and more secret, had consequences that lay deeper but were just as decisive: it is likely that the establishment of a state Christianity, and more precisely, the development of a Christological conception of imperial sovereignty, gradually led to a radically new philosophy of the state, far removed from the model of the Greek city in the classical period.

The City's One Body

I indicated that the state never existed in the Greek city, except in the purely negative form of its public slaves; the *dēmosios* therefore constituted the "secret hero" of the Greek state. At first sight, the hypothesis takes the form of a chiasmus: On the one hand, the *dēmosioi* embodied the city's administration and were in that sense its sole civil servants; on the other hand, the use of slaves attested to the resistance of the civic community to the advent of a state conceived as an agency separate from society. The city, in rendering invisible those responsible for its administration, averted the emergence of a state that could constitute itself into an autonomous agency and turn against the city if necessary. The *polis* thus sought to keep every form of power within the immanence of its own existence as a community. In that sense, the public slave was the figure in whom the city encountered the limit of its self-institution and, in the same gesture, repressed it.

One may measure the distance that separated the Greek city at its foundations from the modern state using the conceptual archaeology proposed by Ernst Kantorowicz. In his well-known thesis, the juridico-theological development presiding over the advent of the modern state is said to rest on the fiction of the king's two bodies, composed—in the words of Plowden, a jurist during Elizabeth I's reign—of a "Body natural" and an indivisible "Body politic." The "natural body" of the royal person is born, begets, and dies, but the sovereign's "political body" is both invisible and immortal. That strange fiction of the king's two bodies was necessary for the perpetuation of a political community "from which the individual king might easily be separated, but not the Dynasty, the Crown, and the Royal Dignity."[14] In other words, power had to free itself from its fleshly envelope, and the crown had to cease to be identified completely with the royal person. The immutability in time of the political community thus stemmed from the elaboration of a fiction, that of a monarch's "super-body distinct from his natural mortal body,"[15] which made the royal state a "being of personal physiognomy and impersonal constitution."[16]

At the end of his book, Kantorowicz explores the Greco-Roman roots of this "dichotomous concept of rulership."[17] Did the royal cult in Hellenistic monarchies and the imperial cult in Rome anticipate the fiction of the king's two bodies? The historian's response is no. Never, neither in Pergamon, nor in Alexandria in the second century BCE, nor in the Rome of the Late Empire was the conception clearly formulated of a king or emperor possessing two bodies at once distinct and indivisible. Neither the theorists of royal power within the Hellenistic monarchies nor the jurists of the empire arrived at an explicit concept of the separation between the sovereign's mortal body and the imperishable body incarnating the res publica. The monarch's divinity was a component of his individual being and never took the form of another person who could represent the kingdom or the empire symbolically. In reality, the duality of the king's body, although not entirely reducible to the ontological duality of Christ, is unthinkable without it.

Yet the king's "super-body" was also the site of the *representation* of the kingdom as a whole, and our own experience of democracy actually proceeds from the strange mechanism of the two bodies. If Kantorowicz's book holds "something of the secret of our world's foundations,"[18] it is because it traces an archaeology of the conditions for politics in the modern sense. From that uninhabited place, that void of the king's political body, sovereign power can become a pole of identity and identification for the social body as a whole. In that sense, the fiction of the king's two bodies gives substance to the "idea of an occupation by society of the site of power, instead of simply reflecting back to it, as was earlier the case, the image of an uncontrollable superiority."[19] But if that fiction constructs a place devoid of human beings so that the social body will find a way to identify with power, it does so in accordance with a mode completely unknown to the Greek city, that of representation.

In book 3 of the *Politics*, Aristotle conceives of the perpetuity of the political community, real and symbolic, in very different terms: "For inasmuch as a city is a determinate community, and is in fact a community by constitution among citizens [*koinōnia politōn politeias*], when the form of the constitution has been altered and is different it would appear to follow that the city is no longer the same."[20] It is a bewildering definition: the city as community by constitution shared among citizens. Aristotle establishes a principle of identity between the *koinōnia*, or community, and the political system it has chosen for itself. It would therefore be a misuse of language to persist in calling by the same name ("Athens") the democratic city of 450 and the oligarchic city of 403.

Such a conception, far from being an original feature of Aristotelian philosophy, can be illustrated by certain famous episodes in the history of the ancient cities. At the start of the Peloponnesian War, for example, the Thebans claimed that it was not possible to impute to them the Medism of their ancestors because the *politeia* was no longer the same.[21] The natural substratum of the political community—its territory, the successive generations of its residents—cannot on its own ensure the continuity of a political community. Above all, no immaterial unity, no "super-body," was superimposed on the instituting agreement called *politeia*, under which citizens sought to live together.

I would be tempted to add that this is because the *dēmosios* stands in place of the city's second body, and he neither embodies nor represents the civic community. The city claims to have only one body, in which the sphere of command (*archē*) and that of the community (*koinon*) are identical and perfectly coincide, with nothing left over. That identity, in which the potentiality for political representation is nullified, an identity that in its way constitutes a feature of the city's "primitivism," was the insuperable condition for the democratic experience in ancient Greece.[22]

From the Enlightenment thinkers to contemporary theorists of deliberative democracy, the Athenian regime has persistently constituted a normative ideal—as if the Agora in Pericles's time offered the best seat from which to observe the present moment of any democracy and imagine its future. True, the thesis of the "Greek miracle" is a frayed mantle that no one wants to wear any longer. But there are few discussions about the contemporary crisis of representative democracy to which ancient Athens is not invited. This would seem to prove that Kostas Axelos was right when he wrote that the *polis* is "a prototype, never again equaled, that marks time past, present, and future," adding, in a turn of phrase both sharp edged and obscure, that "the Greeks inaugurated that age, which contains its future in virtuality."[23] Classical Athens, for example, provides an edifying model for those aspiring to reconstruct, in the wake of

Hannah Arendt, a concept of the common good and of the public, supposedly threatened by democratic individualization. And it is also a source of inspiration for conceiving, in the present tense, what an authentic direct democracy founded on the expansion of the deliberative practice and the drawing of lots might look like.[24]

As magnificent as the Greek beginnings may have been, however, we cannot trace an unbroken line from the Athenian political experience to our own: the river running from the direct democracy of the classical period to our democratic systems cannot be navigated in reverse. It's a good bet, in fact, that it was dammed up long ago. The Greek city, inscribed in the contretemps of our own history, and in that respect literally anachronistic, can offer resources of meaning only at a radical distance from our own political condition.

Indeed, if democratic Athens seems to offer "fertile seeds for any conception of the project of an autonomous society"[25] and for any democracy to come, it does so on the basis of a notion of the collective and the state that is radically alien to us, and that notion is inextricably linked to the institution of slavery. The slave, excluded from the civic community, was in fact central to the workings of the political in the ancient city. It is best to move beyond the banal observation that, in the world of the Greek cities, the exercise of political rights was a privilege reserved for a minority of the population. That is obviously indisputable, but it does not in any way compromise the originality, historically speaking, of the model of the *polis*. One would even do well to refrain from noting that, at the center of the civic economy's system of production, the slave was what made the citizen's political activity possible. I would like to speak of something different: the close connection between the absence of political representation and the existence of the slaveholding system. The slave was at the center of the workings of the political precisely because his existence made it possible to ward off every form of representation, which the civic community could conceive of only in terms of separation, even dispossession. And that grandiose exorcism could be achieved only through another dispossession, of which slaves were the victims. In that sense as well, slavery was the price to be paid for direct democracy.

Notes

Introduction

1. E. Merton Coulter, "Slavery and Freedom in Athens, Georgia, 1860–1866," *Georgia Historical Quarterly* 49 (1965): 264–293.
2. Quoted ibid., p. 271.
3. Quoted ibid., pp. 268–269.
4. Aristotle, *The Athenian Constitution*, 50.2.
5. With the notable exception of O. Jacob, *Les esclaves publics à Athènes* (Liège: Champion, 1928).
6. On certain American historians, see P. du Bois, *Slaves and Other Objects* (Chicago: University of Chicago Press, 2008), pp. 13–18. On the historiography of the slavery of antiquity, cf. M. I. Finley, *Ancient Slavery and Modern Ideology* (New York: Viking, 1980).
7. H. Wallon, *Histoire de l'esclavage dans l'Antiquité* (Paris: Robert Laffont, 1988 [1847]), pp. 5–6.
8. See in particular Finley, *Ancient Slavery*, p. 9. The categories were adopted by N. Fisher, *Slavery in Classical Greece* (London: Bristol Classical Press, 1995), pp. 3–4.
9. For a high estimate, see R. Descat and J. Andreau, *Esclaves en Grèce et Rome* (Paris: Hachette, 2009), p. 72; and T. Taylor, "Believing the Ancients: Quantitative and Qualitative Dimensions of Slavery and the Slave Trade in Later Prehistoric Eurasia," *World Archaeology* 33 (2001): 27–43. For a low estimate (between 15 percent and 35 percent of the population), cf. Fisher, *Slavery in Classical Greece*, pp. 35–36.
10. Finley, *Ancient Slavery*, p. 66.
11. A few essential references for Africanism: C. Meillassoux, ed., *L'esclavage en Afrique précoloniale* (Paris: Maspero, 1975); I. Kopytoff and S. Miers, eds., *Slavery in Africa: Historical and Anthropological Perspectives* (Madison: University of Wisconsin Press, 1977); J. R. Willis, ed., *Slaves and Slavery in Muslim Africa* (London: Frank Cass, 1985); S. Beswick and J. Spaulding, eds., *African*

Systems of Slavery (Trenton, NJ: Africa World Press, 2012); P. E. Lovejoy, *Transformations in Slavery: A History of Slavery in Africa* (Cambridge: Cambridge University Press, 2012). Among the specialists in Southeast Asia, see: A. Reid, ed., *Slavery, Bondage and Dependency in Southeast Asia* (St. Lucia: University of Queensland Press, 1983); G. Condominas, ed., *Formes extrêmes de dépendance. Contribution à l'étude de l'esclavage en Asie du Sud-Est* (Paris: École des Hautes Études en Sciences Sociales, 1998); I. Chatterjee and R. M. Eaton, eds., *Slavery and South Asian History* (Bloomington: Indiana University Press, 2007). Within a generalist perspective, see I. Kopytoff, "Slavery," *Annual Review of Anthropology* 11 (1982): 207–230; O. Patterson, *Slavery and Social Death: A Comparative Study* (Cambridge, MA: Harvard University Press, 1982); C. Meillassoux, *Anthropologie de l'esclavage. Le ventre de fer et d'argent* (Paris: Presses Universitaires de France, 1986); A. Testart, *L'esclave, la dette et le pouvoir. Études de sociologie comparative* (Paris: Errance, 2001). Finally and above all, two decisive contributions to the study of public or royal slavery: on the Kano emirate in the nineteenth century, see S. Stilwell, *Paradoxes of Power: The Kano "Mamluks" and Male Royal Slavery in the Sokoto Caliphate (1804–1903)* (Portsmouth: Heinemann, 2004); and on the Mamluks of the beys of Tunis, M. Oualdi, *Esclaves et maîtres. Les Mamelouks des beys de Tunis du XVIIe siècle aux années 1880* (Paris: Publications de la Sorbonne, 2011).

12. See the list proposed by Testart, *L'esclave, la dette et le pouvoir*, pp. 176–182, as well as his general remarks on the problems of definition posed by the notion of slavery, pp. 115–136.

13. Slavery Convention, signed at Geneva, September 25, 1926, article 1.1, http://www.ohchr.org/Documents/ProfessionalInterest/slavery.pdf

14. On this point, see the remarks of P. Lovejoy, "Slavery in Africa," in *The Routledge History of Slavery*, ed. G. Heuman and T. Burnard (New York: Routledge, 2011), p. 43.

15. Lovejoy, *Transformations in Slavery*, pp. 24 and 120–123.

16. See all the cases listed ibid., pp. 111–128, 174–175.

17. See the remarks of O. Patterson in "Slavery, Gender, and Work in the Pre-Modern World and Early Greece: A Cross-Cultural Analysis," in *Slave Systems: Ancient and Modern*, ed. E . Dal Lago and C. Katsari (Cambridge: Cambridge University Press, 2008), pp. 32–69, esp. p. 33.

18. See the 1833 debate in the House of Commons concerning the abolition of slavery in the British Indies. Both the abolitionists and the representatives of the interests of the East India Company spoke euphemistically of the forms of traditional slavery in the Indies, the better to contrast them to the brutality of American slavery: A. Major, *Slavery, Abolitionism and Empire in India (1722–1843)* (Liverpool: Liverpool University Press, 2012), pp. 3–8. For a reinterpretation of the phenomenon of slavery in India and its connections to the caste system, see I. Chatterjee, *Gender, Slavery, and Law in Colonial India* (Oxford: Oxford University Press, 1999), pp. 1–33.

19. Although the magnitude of slavery in precolonial Africa is debatable, the determining role (demographically and economically) it acquired in the interior kingdoms during the eighteenth and nineteenth centuries was in part the

consequence of the Atlantic and trans-Saharan slave trade, which continued to transform the traditional structures of dependency. Cf. Lovejoy, *Transformations in Slavery*, esp. p. 21. See also J. D. Fage, "African Societies and the Atlantic Slave Trade," *Past and Present* 125 (1989): 97–115. In India, likewise, unprecedented forms of slavery came into existence with the first British and Portuguese contacts and reshaped the customary structures of dependency. Yet they were irreducible to New World slavery. Cf. I. Chatterjee, "Renewed and Connected Histories: Slavery and Historiography of South Asia"; and S. Guha, "Slavery-Society and the State in Western India, 1700–1800," in Chatterjee and Eaton, eds., *Slavery and South Asian History*, respectively, pp. 1–43 and pp. 162–186.

20. G. Campbell and A. Stanziani, eds., *Debt and Slavery in the Mediterranean and Atlantic Worlds* (London: Pickering and Chatto, 2013); and idem, *Bonded Labour and Debt in the Indian Ocean* (London: Pickering and Chatto, 2013).

21. Cf. Patterson, *Slavery and Social Death*, p. 13, and his famous definition: "Slavery is the permanent, violent, domination of natally alienated and generally dishonoured persons." At the same time, some anthropologists have drawn new dividing lines between different slave societies. James Watson has proposed a distinction between "closed systems" and "open systems." See J. Watson, "Slavery as an Institution: Open and Closed System," in *Asian and African Systems of Slavery*, ed. J. L. Watson (Oxford: Blackwell, 1980), pp. 1–15. In an "open" system, slaves could much more easily become part of the lineage system, especially through a fictive kinship, and the practice of emancipation would be common. Whereas African slavery is said to belong predominantly to an "open system," American slavery, marked by racial domination, illustrates the extreme case of a "closed" system; several societies in Southeast Asia also provide examples. On this point, see the emendations to Watson's model proposed by A. Reid, "'Closed' and 'Open' Slave Systems in Pre-Colonial Southeast Asia," in Reid., ed., *Slavery, Bondage and Dependency*, pp. 156–181.

22. By way of example in recent historiography: M. Kleijwegt, ed., *The Faces of Freedom: The Manumission and Emancipation of Slaves in Old World and New World Slavery* (Leiden: Brill, 2006); Dal Lago and Katsari, eds., *Slave Systems*; D. Geary and K. Vlassopoulos, eds., *Slavery, Citizenship and the State in Classical Antiquity and the Modern Americas*, special issue of *European Review of History* 16, no. 3 (2009): 295–436; S. Hodkinson and D. Geary, eds., *Slaves and Religions in Graeco-Roman Antiquity and Modern Brazil* (Cambridge: Cambridge Scholars Publishing, 2012); A. Gonzales, ed., *Penser l'esclavage. Modèles antiques, pratiques modernes, problématiques contemporaines* (Besançon: Presses Universitaires de Franche-Comté, 2012). In the field of Roman slavery, however, see the works of Walter Scheidel, particularly "The Comparative Economics of Slavery in the Greco-Roman World," in Dal Lago and Katsari, eds., *Slave Systems*, pp. 105–126; and P. Temin, "The Labor Market of the Early Roman Empire," *Journal of Interdisciplinary History* 34 (2004): 513–538, esp. pp. 522–527. See also the timid attempts of K.-W. Welwei in "Menschenraub und Deportationen in frühen Kulturen," in *Menschenraub, Menschenhandel und Sklaverei in antiker und moderner Perspektive*, ed. H. Heinen (Stuttgart: F. Steiner, 2008), pp. 21–43.

23. For a series of recent studies, see the articles collected in *Faire des sciences sociales*, vol. 2, *Comparer*, ed. O. Renaud, J.-F. Schaub, and I. Thireau (Paris: École des Hautes Études en Sciences Sociales, 2012); and within a much more general perspective, the programmatic ambitions of an experimental comparativism proposed by M. Detienne, *Comparer l'incomparable* (Paris: Seuil, 2009 [2000]).

24. The rich bibliography on the question will be cited in the course of this book.

25. By way of example, see R. S. O'Fahey, "Slavery and Society in Dar-Fur," in Willis, ed., *Slaves and Slavery in Muslim Africa*, pp. 83–100.

26. See, in particular, beginning with the practice of *mort d'accompagnement* (companionship death), A. Testart, *La servitude volontaire* (Paris: Errance, 2004), vol. 1, *Les morts d'accompagnement*; vol. 2, *L'origine de l'État*.

27. Hence, by way of example, see E. Terray, *Une histoire du royaume abron de Gyaman: Des origines à la conquête coloniale* (Paris: Karthala, 1995), pp. 815–816. A distinction is made among the court's captives, between those who are the personal property of the Gyamanhene, acquired by him before he accedes to supreme power, and those who are among the "possessions of the seat," whom the sovereign receives as an inheritance from his predecessor.

28. In Pergamon at the time of the War of Aristonicus: *Orientis Graeci inscriptiones selectae*, ed. Wilhelm Ditterberger (Leipzig: S. Hirzel, 1903–1905), 338 (131 BCE), lines 20–26 and 37–38 [hereafter cited as *OGIS*].

29. See the remarks in G. Boulvert, *Esclaves et affranchis impérieux sous le Haut-Empire romain. Rôle politique et administratif* (Naples: Jovene, 1970), pp. 9–10. The distinction is tenuous, however, because laws at the end of the imperial period conflated the two categories. See N. Lenski, "*Servi Publici* in Late Antiquity," in *Die Stadt in der Spätantike—Niedergang oder Wandel?*, ed. J.-U. Krause and C. Witschel (Stuttgart: F. Steiner, 2006), pp. 335–357, esp. p. 350.

30. Athenaeus, *The Learned Banqueters*, 6.265b–c, p. 221. [Unless otherwise indicated, all quotations from classical sources are taken from the new Loeb Classical Library published by Harvard University Press and available online (by subscription) at http://www.loebclassics.com/. Occasionally, the translation has been modified to better reflect the author's argument.—trans.]

31. Strabo, *Geography*, 8.5.4, p. 135 [translation modified—trans.].

32. Pausanias, *Description of Greece*, 3.20.6, p. 129 [translation modified—trans.].

33. As Jean Ducat reminds us, the Helots can be considered public property only from an external point of view, in that they could not be sold out of the city. J. Ducat, *Les Hilotes* (Athens: École Française d'Athènes, 1990), p. 21; and N. Luraghi, "The Helots: Comparative Approaches, Ancient and Modern," in *Sparta: Comparative Approaches*, ed. S. Hodkinson (Swansea: Classical Press of Wales, 2009), pp. 261–304, esp. p. 275. S. Hodkinson is more skeptical about the possibility of the Helots' alienation within Spartan society itself (*Property and Wealth in Classical Sparta* [Swansea: Classical Press of Wales, 2000], p. 119). But one cannot rule out the possibility that, in the late Hellenistic period, they became "like" *dēmosioi*: see N. M. Kennell, "*Agreste genus*: Helots in Hellenistic

Laconia," in *Helots and Their Masters in Laconia and Messenia: Histories, Ideologies, Structures*, ed. N. Luraghi and S. Alcock (Washington, DC: Center for Hellenic Studies, 2003), pp. 81–105.

34. Jacob, *Les esclaves publics à Athènes*. Jacob's book, however, was preceded by three important studies. Both S. Waszynski, "Über die rechtliche Stellung der Staatsclaven in Athen," *Hermes* 34 (1899): 553–564; and O. Silverio, *Untersuchungen zur Geschichte der attischen Staatsklaven* (Munich: F. Straub, 1900), focus on Athenian public slavery in the classical period. G. Cardinali, "Note di terminologia epigraphica, I. *Dêmosioi*," *Rendiconti della Reale Accademia dei Lincei* 17 (1908): 157–165, is an inventory of all the evidence of public slaves provided by the epigraphic sources. For the imperial period, the standard reference is now A. Weiss's *Sklave der Stadt: Untersuchungen zur öffentlichen Sklaverei in den Städten des Römischen Reiches* (Stuttgart: F. Steiner, 2004).

1. Genesis

1. For example, Harpocration, *dēmosios*.
2. F. Bader, *Les composés grecs du type de* dêmiourgos (Paris: Klincksieck, 1965), p. 108.
3. Homer, *Odyssey* 17.382.
4. Homer, *Iliad*, 7.219.
5. Pliny, *Natural History*, 7.197.
6. Pausanias, *The Description of Greece*, 9.19.1.
7. Hesiod, fragment 282.
8. Homer, *Odyssey*, 3.425–3.427.
9. Homer, *Iliad*, 5.59–5.68.
10. Homer, *Odyssey*, 1.154.
11. Ibid., 19.135.
12. Ibid., 3.269–3.271.
13. Ibid., 19.247.
14. Homer, *Iliad*, 24.674.
15. Homer, *Odyssey*, 18.424.
16. For two radically different approaches, see K. Murakawa, "Demiurgos," *Historia* 6 (1957): 385–415; and B. Quiller, "Prolegomena to a Study of the Homeric Demiurgoi (Murakawa's Theory Re-Examined)," *SO* 55 (1980): 5–21. M. I. Finley, *The World of Odysseus* (New York: Viking, 1954), p. 49, formulated the hypothesis of a "blurred" or "indefinable" status within the social hierarchy of the Homeric world.
17. Homer, *Odyssey*, 18.424.
18. Homer, *Odyssey*, 18.47.
19. Ibid., 22.403.
20. Ibid., 22.321–22.329.
21. Ibid., 22.345 [translation modified—trans.].
22. See P. Pucci, *Odysseus Polutropos: Intertextual Readings in the Odyssey and the Iliad* (Ithaca, NY: Cornell University Press, 1987), pp. 228–235.

23. Homer, *Odyssey*, 22.344–22.353 and 367–370.

24. E. Cantarella, *Ithaque. De la vengeance d'Ulysse à la naissance du droit* (Paris: Albin Michel, 2003 [2002]), p. 250.

25. Homer, *Odyssey*, 21.146–21.147.

26. Ibid., 24.440–24.445.

27. The Doloneia has raised many problems for specialists in Homeric poetry, who usually consider it a more or less late interpolation. See in particular B. Fenik, *Iliad X and the Rhesos: The Myth* (Brussels: Latomus, 1964); and O. M. Davidson, "Dolon and Rhesos in the Iliad," *Quaderni urbinati di cultura classica* (*UCC*) 1 (1979): 61–66. The Homeric authenticity of the episode is incidental here.

28. Homer, *Iliad*, 10.315.

29. Ibid., 10.177.

30. L. Gernet, "Dolon the Wolf," *The Anthropology of Ancient Greece*, trans. J. Hamilton and B. Nagy (Baltimore: John Hopkins University Press, 1981; 1st ed. 1936), pp. 125–139.

31. F. Lissarrague, "Iconographie de Dolon le Loup," *Revue Archéologique* (1980): 3–30.

32. Cf. A. Schnapp-Gourbeillon, *Lions, héros, masques. Les représentations de l'animal chez Homère* (Paris: Maspero, 1981), p. 122.

33. Lissarrague, "Iconographie de Dolon le Loup."

34. See in particular P. Warthelet, "Rhésos ou la quête de l'immortalité," *Kernos* 2 (1989): 213–231.

35. On the formation of the Daedalus legend, cf. F. Frontisi-Ducroux, *Dédale. Mythologie de l'artisan en Grèce antique* (Paris: Maspero, 1975), pp. 89–94.

36. *Die Fragmente der griechischen Historiker*, ed. F. Jacoby (Berlin: Weidmann, 1923–1958), 3, F, 146 [hereafter cited as *FgrHist*].

37. Bacchylides, *Ode*, 26.5–26.7.

38. Diodorus Siculus, *Library of History*, 4.77.1.

39. Bacchylides, *Ode*, 26.

40. The connection between Daedalus and Ariadne already appeared in Homeric poetry, where Daedalus was supposed to have had a dance floor built for the daughter of Minos: cf. Homer, *Iliad*, 18.590–18.592.

41. Diodorus Siculus, *Library of History*, 4.77.5.

42. Pausanias, *Description of Greece*, 9.11.4–9.11.5.

43. *FGrHist*, 323, F, 17.

44. Diodorus Siculus, *Library of History*, 4.29–4.30.

45. Cf. Frontisi-Ducroux, *Dédale*, esp. pp. 180–190.

46. Cf. ibid., pp. 179–190.

47. Hesiod, *Theogony*, line 885.

48. J.-P. Vernant and M. Detienne, *Les ruses de l'intelligence. La* mètis *des Grecs* (Paris: Flammarion, 1974), p. 75.

49. J.-P. Vernant, *Entre mythe et politique* (Paris: Seuil, 1966), p. 315.

50. Ovid, *Metamorphoses*, 8.186–8.187.

51. Xenophon, *Memorabilia*, 4.2.33 [translation modified—trans.].

52. See also Plato, *Laws*, 3.677d, which links the two figures.

53. Cf. H. Van Effenterre, "Le statut comparé des travailleurs étrangers en Chypre, Crète et autres lieux à la fin de l'archaïsme," in *Acts of the International Archaeological Symposium: The Relations between Cyprus and Crete, ca. 2000–500 B.C.* (Nicosia: Department of Antiquities, 1979), pp. 279–293; R. Koerner, "Vier frühe Verträge zwischen Gemeinwesen und Privatleuten auf griechischen Inschriften," *Klio* 63 (1981): 179–206.

54. The status of public doctors lies beyond the scope of this book, in that it never gave rise to the constitution of a lifetime civic appointment. The best-known case is without a doubt Democedes, a renowned doctor who was taken in by the Eginetes, the Samians, and then the Corinthians in the sixth century (Herodotus, 3.131), as well as the doctors mentioned on the bronze Idalion Tablet (E. Samma, *Les médecins dans le monde grec* [Paris: Droz, 2003], p. 456, no. 367).

55. The cosmos was the highest magistracy in most Cretan cities.

56. I reproduce here the main part of the translation by the first editors of the inscription: L. H. Jeffery and A. Morpurgo-Davies, "ΠΟΙΝΙΚΑΣΤΑΣ and ΠΟΙΝΙΚΑΖΕΝ: BM 1969.4–2.1, a New Archaic Inscription from Crete," *Kadmos* 9 (1970): 118–154.

57. On the meaning of the verb *poinikazein*, see the recent clarification in C. Pébarthe, "Spensithios, scribe ou archiviste public? Réflexions sur les usages publics de l'écriture en Crète à l'époque archaïque," *Temporalités* 3 (2006): 37–56.

58. [*Hors-champ*, literally "outside the field," is a cinematographic term meaning "off-screen" or "out of frame."—trans.]. In particular, Spensithius's position was distinct from that of the *gnōmōn*, in charge of the memory of public acts in Gortyna, who was replaced every ten years.

59. F. Ruzé, "Aux débuts de l'écriture politique. Le pouvoir de l'écrit dans la cité," in *Les savoirs de l'écriture en Grèce ancienne*, ed. M. Detienne, repr. in F. Ruzé, *Eunomia. À la recherche de l'équité* (Paris: De Boccard, 2003), pp. 71–79.

60. W. Dittenberger, ed., *Olympia. Die Ergebnisse der von dem Deutschen Reich veranstalteten Ausgrabung (Textband 5): Die Inschriften von Olympia* (Berlin, 1986), 2 [hereafter cited as *IvO*] (Van Effenterre and Ruzé, *Recueil d'inscriptions politiques et juridiques de l'archaïsme grec* [Rome: École Française de Rome, 1994], vol. 1, no. 23).

61. The reading and translation proposed by Henri Van Effenterre and Françoise Ruzé, which I follow for the most part, is not unanimously accepted. It seems to me, however, that it is best able to account for the coherence of a text that would otherwise be altogether incomprehensible. Although nearly all researchers agree that "Patrias" is in fact a personal name and not a dialectal declension of *patris* (country), the entire problem lies in the relation between the central part of the decree, which lists a set of provisions that may extend beyond the case of Patrias, and the beginning and final clauses of the text, both of which concern him. In my view, the philological arguments of S. Minon in *Les inscriptions éléennes dialectales (VIIe–IIe s. av. J.-C.)* (Paris: Droz, 2007), 1:138–1:149, claiming that lines 2–8 do not refer to Patrias, can stand only at the cost of obliterating the general coherence of the decision. How is one to understand that a decree whose object is obviously to guarantee the rights of the scribe, and which ends with the mention of Patrias's activity, should set out to evoke a more general

prescription that concerns him only incidentally? Furthermore, Sophie Minon's interpretation implies that the prescription of the penalty of whipping was standard in the Elean procedure (p. 148), which would be particularly surprising.

62. Minon (*Les inscriptions éléennes dialectales*, p. 503) puts forward the hypothesis that Patrias was not a magistrate and occupied a subordinate position similar to that of the Athenian *hupogrammateus* of the classical period.

63. Van Effenterre, "Le statut comparé des travailleurs étrangers," p. 284, n. 35. By contrast, Minon (*Les inscriptions éléennes dialectales*, p. 144) hypothesizes that this was a slave emancipated by consecration, playing the role of a public servant within the Olympian context, and to whom might have been entrusted, "for example, the bookkeeping for the sanctuary's administration and the inventories of the *iara* [sacred goods]."

64. See T. E. Rihll, "Classical Athens," in *The Cambridge World History of Slavery: The Ancient Mediterranean World*, ed. K. Bradley and P. Cartledge (Cambridge: Cambridge University Press, 2011), p. 60.

65. See, in particular, Testart, *La servitude volontaire*, vol. 2, *L'origine de l'État*.

66. Cf. C. de Oliveira Gomes, *La cité tyrannique. Histoire politique de la Grèce archaïque* (Rennes: Presses Universitaires de Rennes, 2007), p. 144.

67. Herodotus, *The Persian Wars*, 3.39.

68. Ibid., 1.59; and Aristotle, *The Athenian Constitution*, 14.1.

69. Polybius 1.21.3; Nicolas of Damascus: *FGrHist*, 90, F, 58; Plutarch, *Life of Solon*, 30.3.

70. B. M. Lavelle, "Herodotus, Archers and the Doruphoroi of the Peisistratids," *Klio* 74 (1992): 78–97, 80, and 87–92.

71. Aeschines, 2 (*On the Embassy*), 173.

72. Nicolas of Damascus: "He prevented the citizens from acquiring slaves and disposing of leisure time"; and Heraclides Lembus (M. R. Dilts, *Heraclidis Lembi Excerpta Politiarum* [Durham, NC: Duke University, 1971], no. 20): "In addition, he put an end to the acquisition of slaves and to the refined life." On this episode, see the suggestive remarks of O. Picard, "Périandre et l'interdiction d'acquérir des esclaves," in *Aux origines de l'hellénisme, la Crète et la Grèce. Hommage à Henri Van Effenterre* (Paris: Publications de la Sorbonne, 1984), pp. 187–191.

73. Aristotle, *Politics*, 5.11.1313b; and Plato, *Republic*, 563a–d.

74. Herodotus, *The Persian Wars*, 3.123.

75. Cf. Lucian, *Menippus*, 16; and *Charo*, 14.

76. Herodotus, *The Persian Wars*, 3.142.

77. Ibid., 3.123: Polycrates "sent one of his townsmen (*andra tōn astōn*), Maeandrius, son of Maeandrius, to look into the matter; this man was his scribe."

78. That is the position of J. Roisman, "Maiandrios of Samos," *Historia* 34 (1985): 257–277; V. La Bua, by contrast, defends the hypothesis of his slave status: "Sulla Conquista persiana di Samo," *MGR* 4 (1975): 41–102, here pp. 55–58.

79. Herodotus, *The Persian Wars*, 7.170.

80. Diodorus Siculus, *Library of History*, 11.48, 11.59, 11.66, and 11.76.

81. Pausanias, *Description of Greece*, 5.26: "This Micythus, when Anaxilas was despot of Rhegium, became his slave and steward of his property; afterwards, on the death of Anaxilas, he went away to Tegea."

82. On the Great King's domestic staff, which included slaves, see Pierre Briant, *Histoire de l'Empire Perse. De Cyrus à Alexandre* (Paris: Fayard, 1996), pp. 272–306.

83. M. I. Finley, "Was Greek Civilization Based on Slave Labour?" in *Economy and Society in Ancient Greece* (New York: Vintage, 1982), p. 115.

84. The Assembly, open to all Athenian citizens irrespective of fortune, was the only body that could pass laws. The Boulē, whose members were replaced every year, was composed of five hundred citizens (fifty per tribe) drawn by lot, irrespective of fortune; one of its principal functions was to discuss and draft the laws that were subject to the vote of the Assembly. "Heliaia" refers to the tribunals of the city as a whole. Because Athenian justice was fully democratic, the body of judges, who were replaced every year, was composed of six thousand citizens (six hundred per tribe) drawn by lot. Each month, these judges were distributed to all the tribunals constituting what the Athenians called the Heliaia.

2. Servants of the City

1. Plato, *The Statesman*, 289e–290b [translation modified—trans.].
2. Jacob, *Les esclaves publics à Athènes*.
3. *Supplementum epigraphicum graecum* (Amsterdam: J. C. Gieben, 1984), 2, 710, lines 4–6 [hereafter cited as *SEG*].
4. Aristotle, *The Athenian Constitution*, 64.1; 65.1, 65.4; 69.1.
5. Plutarch, *Life of Demosthenes*, 5.3.
6. By way of example, see Harpocration, *dēmosios*: "A public slave is the slave of the city, who is in the service of the courts and public works projects."
7. E. Varinlioglu, "Five Inscriptions from Acmonia," *Revue d'études anciennes* 108 (2006), no. 41, lines 38–39; no. 5, line 13 (64 CE).
8. *Vita Aesopi*, recension G, 81–82.
9. *Inscriptiones graecae. Inscriptiones atticae Euclidis anno posteriores*, ed. Johannes Kirchner (Berlin: W. de Gruyter, 1913–1940), I³ 1390 [hereafter cited as *IG*].
10. They are mentioned for the first time, exceptionally, in a Prytanic decree in 343/342 (*Agora* 15.37, line 4), then on a regular basis beginning in 303/302 (*Agora* 15.62, col. 5, lines 10–18). Beginning in 281/280, they were divided up by tribe at the same time as the prytaneis (*Agora* 15.72, vol. 1, line 5; col. 2, lines 67 and 211; col. 3, lines 83 and 266). Cf. G. J. Oliver, "Honours for a Public Slave at Athens (*IG* II² 502 + Ag. I 1947; 302/1 B.C.)," in *Attika Epigraphika. Meletes pros timōn tou Christian Habicht*, ed. A. Themos and N. Papazarkadas (Athens: Ellīnikī Epigrafikī Etaireíra, 2009), pp. 111–124, esp. p. 123.
11. I follow here the reading of Oliver, "Honours for a Public Slave." On the decree that honors Antiphates, cf. chap. 3.

12. Aristotle, *The Athenian Constitution*, 47.5 and 48.1. On the public slaves assigned to the archives, see the remarks of J. Sickinger, *Public Records and Archives in Classical Athens* (Chapel Hill: University of North Carolina Press, 1999), pp. 140–157.

13. *IG* II² 463, line 28. See also *IG* II² 1492 B line 112; in the late fourth century, Skylax brought the bookkeeping documents necessary to the magistrate.

14. On this point see Sickinger, *Public Records and Archives*, pp. 145 and 158.

15. Demosthenes, 19 (*On the Embassy*), 129, p. 327.

16. *IG* II² 583, lines 4–7. Outside Athens, written evidence is usually from the imperial period, and it is not always certain that the individuals were slaves: cf. A. Weiss, *Sklave der Stadt*, pp. 78–79.

17. *I. Iasos* 93, lines 3–4. See the remarks of L. Robert, *Études anatoliennes. Recherches sur les inscriptions grecques de l'Asie Mineure* (Paris: De Boccard, 1937), p. 453; and for dating, P. Fröhlich, "Les groupes du gymnase d'Iasos et les *presbyteroi* dans les cités à l'époque hellénistique," in *Groupe et associations dans les cité grecques (IIe s. av. J.-C.–IIe s. apr. J.-C.)*, ed. P. Fröhlich and P. Hamon (Paris: Droz, 2013), pp. 59–111.

18. *SEG* 33, 1177, lines 10–15. Cf. M. Wörrle, "Zwei neue griechische Inschriften aus Myra zur Verwaltung Lykiens in der Kaiserzeit," in *Myra: Eine lykische Metropole in antiker und byzantinischer Zeit*, ed. J. Borch-Hardt (Berlin: Gebr. Mann, 1975), pp. 254–300.

19. *SEG* 33, 1177, lines 18–19.

20. *IG* XII 4, 1365, lines 10–11.

21. *IG* II² 120, lines 12–13 (and three years later, *IG* II² 1440, a, lines 6–7).

22. *IG* II², 1492, B, line 111.

23. *IG* II² 839, lines 43–45. Six years later, Demetrius *neoteros* (*IG* II² 1539, lines 9–10), probably the son of that other Demetrius, seems to have played the same role in the sanctuary.

24. *Inscriptions de Délos* (Paris: Honoré Champion, 1926), 1444, Aa, line 54 [hereafter cited as *ID*]; *ID* 1444, Ba, line 20 and line 49. The slave identity of Peritas is certified by *ID* 1442, B, line 75. The inventories of the temple of Apollo during the same period mention the presence of *dēmosioi* in the service of the sanctuary: *ID* 1450, A, line 109.

25. On these slaves of the arsenals (*dēmosioi hoi en tois neoriois*), cf. Demosthenes, 47 (*Against Evergus and Mnesibulus*), 21, 24, 26, with the remarks of B. Jordan, *The Athenian Navy in the Classical Period: A Study of Naval Administration and Military Organization in the Fifth and Fourth Centuries* B.C. (Berkeley: University of California Press, 1975). Opsigonus appears in *IG* II² 1631, B, line 197; C, lines 381–382.

26. K. Clinton, *Eleusis: The Inscriptions on Stone, Documents of the Sanctuary of the Two Goddesses and Public Documents of the Deme*, vol. 1 (Athens: Archaeological Society of Athens, 2005), 177, I, line 12 [hereafter cited as *IE*]. Eucles played the same role a few years later (*IE* 159, lines 60–62, from 336/335 or 333/332).

27. Demosthenes, 8 (*On the Chersonese*), 47; confirmed by the scholiast of Demosthenes, 2 (*Olynthiacs 2*), 9. On the strength of a speech by Demosthenes,

49 (*Against Timotheus*), 6–8, Jacob (*Les esclaves publics*, pp. 123–124) believed he could identify a certain Autonomus, who would have thus worked alongside the *tamias* Antimachus, under the orders of the general Timotheus. The hypothesis is appealing, especially because Autonomus is not subjected to the punishment of Antimachus, which seems to indicate a difference in status. The *dēmosios*, considered neutral, would have been found innocent of the offenses committed by the magistrates.

28. Demosthenes, 22 (*Against Androtion*), 70–71.
29. G. Glotz, *La cité grecque* (Paris: Albin Michel, 1953 [1928]), p. 304.
30. Demosthenes, 22 (*Against Androtion*), 71.
31. Rhodes/Osborne, no. 25. On the precise role of the *dokimastēs* in the law, cf. chap. 4. On the meaning of the verb *dokimazein* (to control) in the inscription, cf. C. Feyel, "À propos de la loi de Nicophon. Remarques sur le sens de *dokimos, dokimazein, dokimasia*," *Revue de philologie* 77 (2003): 37–65.
32. *IG* II² 1388, B, lines 61–62; and *IG* II² 1400, line 57 (390/389). This *dokimastēs* is mentioned again in the late fourth century: *IG* II² 1492, line 137 (305/304).
33. It is very possible that a similar role was played by the *dēmosioi* upon the arrival of wheat in Athens. Several indications suggest that a public slave was in charge of measuring and evaluating the cargos of wheat unloaded at Piraeus (see in particular Dinarchus, fragment 7).
34. *IG* II² 1013, lines 40–41. The *dēmosioi* were placed under the authority of the prytaneis for the Skias, the epimeletes for the emporium at Piraeus, and the hierophante in Eleusis. The position persisted in the imperial period, if the mention of *oiketai tēs Tholou* (*IG* II² 1799, line 25) is to be believed.
35. On the slave's *sphragis*, cf. F. J. Dölger, *Sphragis. Eine altchristliche Taufbezeichung in ihren Beziehungen zur profanen und religiösen Kultur der Alterums* (Paderborn: F. Schöningh, 1911), pp. 23–31.
36. The account of Nymphodorus of Syracuse is transmitted by Athenaeus, *The Learned Banqueters*, 6.265d–266e (*FGrHist*, 572, F4), here 265f. On the episode generally, see the close reading of S. Forsdyke, *Slaves Tell Tales, and Other Episodes in the Politics of Popular Culture in Ancient Greece* (Princeton, NJ: Princeton University Press, 2012), esp. pp. 78–89.
37. By way of example, see the synoecism of the city of Athens under the aegis of King Theseus, in Thucydides, *History of the Peloponnesian War*, 2.15; and Plutarch, *Life of Theseus*, 24.
38. A. Bresson, *Recueil des inscriptions de la Pérée rhodienne* (Paris: Belles Lettres, 1991), no. 102, line 15 (decree of Tymnus regulating the usage of a sanctuary of Zeus and Hera).
39. Cf. L. Robert, *Opera minora selecta VI* (Amsterdam: A. M. Hakkert, 1989), p. 46 and n. 7.
40. Cf. *I. Pergamon* 2.52 (Pergamon, first century BCE, according to Fränkel's hypothesis); *I. Priene*, 112 (Priene, 84 CE), lines 110–112.
41. That is how the positions of *palaistrophulax* (*ID*, 316, line 117; *ID* 338, A. fr. ab, line 67; *ID* 372, A, lines 98–99) and *hupēretēs eis palaistran* (*ID* 290, line 108; *ID* 440, A, line 27; *ID* 444, A, line 27) must be understood. Note that in Thespiae, a *dēmosios* appeared on the list of users of the gymnasium in the

second to first centuries BCE (P. Roesch, *Les inscriptions de Thespies*, 136, line 11, www.hisoma.mom.fr).

42. Lysias, 22 (*Against the Corn Dealers*), 2. See also Aristotle, *The Athenian Constitution*, 52.

43. See esp. Demosthenes, 24 (*Against Timocrates*), 162.

44. Theramenes: Xenophon, *Hellenica*, 2.3.54–2.3.55; and Diodorus Siculus, *Library of History*, 14.5.1–14.5.4; Phocion: Plutarch, *Life of Phocion*, 35.1; 36.1. Also worthy of mention is their intervention in 406 to arrest the Athenian generals who had returned from Arginusae; Diodorus Siculus, *Library of History*, 13.102; Acts of the Apostles 16:23–16:26.

45. Imprisonment, it should be said, was not understood as a penalty but as a waiting period before the judgment was carried out.

46. Pliny the Younger, *Letters*, 19.1: "I pray you, Sir, to advise me on the following point. I am doubtful whether I ought to continue using the public slaves in the various towns as prison warders, as hitherto, or to put soldiers on guard-duty in the prisons." In his response, Trajan confirms the customary use of public slaves.

47. Plato, *Phaedo*, 59c; and Plato, *Crito*, 43a.

48. Plato, *Phaedo*, 116c–117a, here 117a; but also Plutarch, *Life of Phocion*, 36.6.

49. Aeschines, 2 (*On the Embassy*), 126, calls him a *dēmosios*. See all the evidence in Jacob, *Les esclaves publics*, pp. 81–82.

50. In 403 the Thirty may have constituted a variant of that body, recruiting three hundred slaves equipped with whips to control the city (Aristotle, *The Athenian Constitution*, 35.1). On the exact status of these three hundred *mastigophoroi*, see the remarks of P. Tuci, "Arcieri sciti, esercito e Democrazia nell'Atene des V secolo A. C.," *Aevum* 78 (2004): 3–18, esp. 13–14.

51. F. Lissarrague, *L'autre guerrier . . . Archers, peltastes, cavaliers dans l'imagerie attique* (Paris: La Découverte, 1990), p. 130.

52. Ibid., pp. 146–148. In that regard, Sophocles's *Skuthai*, which is known only through fragments, surely played an essential role in the construction of the archetype.

53. In reality, the discussion relies on two distinct sources: first, Andocides, 3 (*On the Peace with Sparta*), 3–7; and second, Aeschines, 2 (*On the Embassy*), 172–174. It is very probable, however, that Andocides based himself on Aeschines: on this point, see J.-C. Couvenhes, "L'introduction des archers scythes, esclaves publics, à Athènes. La date et l'agent d'un transfert culturel," in *Transferts culturels et droit dans le monde grec et hellénistique*, ed. B. Legras (Paris: Publications de la Sorbonne, 2012), pp. 99–119, esp. 109–110. On the role of Speusinius, see Pollux, 8.131–8.132; the Suda and Photius at the entry *Toxotai*; and scholion to Aristophanes, *Acharnians*, 54. See also P. Tuci, "Gli arcieri sciti nell'Atene del V Secolo A. C.," in *Il cittadino, lo stranierio, il barbaro fra integrazione et emarginazione nell'Antichita. Atti del i Incontrao internazionale di Storia Attica (Genova 22–24 maggio 2003)*, ed. M. G. Bertinelli and A. Donati (Rome. Bretschneider, 2005), pp. 375–389.

54. On the number of a thousand archers: the Suda, *Toxotai*; and the scholion to Aristophanes, *Acharnians*, 54. See the dense discussion of Jacob, *Les*

esclaves publics, pp. 64–72; Tuci's count in "Gli arcieri sciti nell'Athene," p. 376; and E. Hall, *The Theatrical Cast of Athens: Interactions between Ancient Greek Drama and Society* (Oxford: Oxford University Press, 2006), p. 233, as well as the summary of Couvenhes, "L'introduction des archers scythes, esclaves publics à Athènes," p. 103.

55. See the hypothesis of P. Gauthier, "Les *xenoi* dans les textes athéniens de la seconde moitié du Ve siècle," *Revue des études grecques* 84 (1971): 44–79, and P. Tuci, "Arcieri sciti, esercito e Democrazia nell'Atene del V secolo A.C.," *Aevum* 78 (2004): 3–18. The hypothesis rests on the likely connection between these Scythian archers and the *toxotai xenoi* (*IG* I³ 138) or *barbaroi* (Thucydides, *History of the Peloponnesian War*, 8.98.1; *Agora*, 17.17, lines 25–29; *IG* I³ 1190, lines 136–138; *Agora*, 17.14, line 35; *Agora*, 17.22, lines 152–159) in the inscriptions from the second half of the fifth century.

56. For all the sources, see Tuci, "Arcieri sciti, esercito e Democrazia," and "Gli arcieri sciti nell'Atene."

57. For a complete list of the comic literature on the Scythian archers, see esp. E. Hall, "The Archer Scene in Aristophanes' *Thesmophoriazusae*," *Philologus* 133 (1989): 38–54, esp. pp. 45–46.

58. See esp. Aristophanes, *Lysistrata*, lines 425–465; and Aristophanes, *Women at the Thesmophoria*, lines 1100–1230.

59. Aristophanes, *Lysistrata*, 463–464.

60. Suda, *Toxotai*. Cf. Tuci, "Gli arcieri sciti nell'Atene," pp. 377–379.

61. Cf. Tuci, "Arcieri sciti, esercito e Democrazia," p. 9. The fragment from Lysias's *Against Theozotides* suggests that the corps of the *hippotoxotai* was about to be increased in size; yet it is quite certain that these were not the Scythian archers (cf. Herodotus, *The Persian Wars*, 6.46.3; and Thucydides, *History of the Peloponnesian War*, 2.96.1).

62. Some, such as Couvenhes in "L'introduction des archers scythes," p. 116, push back the date of their disappearance to the late fifth century. For the most part, however, the date of 378/377 has been accepted because it corresponds to the appearance of the *syllogeis tou dēmou*, who, it appears, henceforth kept order at the Assembly. In *Policing Athens: Social Control in the Attic Lawsuits* (Princeton, NJ: Princeton University Press, 1994), pp. 148–149, V. Hunter is much more circumspect, rightly in my view. In about 325, Demosthenes, 25 (*Against Aristogeiton I*), 23, mentions the cordon protecting meetings of the Council of the Areopagus and the proclamation of the *hupēretēs*, which asked all spectators to leave the public meeting place. This might even be an allusion to the Scythian archers.

63. Aristotle, *The Athenian Constitution*, 50.2 and 54.1. According to Aristotle, these *dēmosioi* were responsible for clearing away the dead bodies lying in the streets of Athens.

64. Scholion to Aristophanes, *Wasps*, line 1007 (Andocides, frag. 3. 2). The location of the mint is unknown; however, see the proposals of C. Flament, *Une économie monétarisée. Athènes à l'époque classique (440–338 av. J.-C.): Contribution à l'étude du phénomène monétaire en Grèce ancienne* (Leuven: Peeters, 2007), p. 249.

65. Rhodes/Osborne, no. 25, lines 53–55: "In the future he shall be eligible for a fee from the same source as the mint workers."

66. *FD* III 3239, line 12 (A. Jacquemin, D. Mulliez, and G. Rougemont, *Choix d'inscriptions de Delphes, traduites et commentées* (Paris: École Française d'Athènes, 2012), no. 166.

67. J. Fournier and C. Prêtre, "Un mécène au service d'une déesse thasienne. Décret pour Stilbôn," *Bulletin de correspondance hellénique* 130 (2006): 487–497, lines 9–12 [hereafter cited as *BCH*].

68. The Delian documentation after the period of independence raises a major problem: no slave is described as a *dēmosios*. The expression *hupēretēs kath hieron* (in *IG* XI 2, 147, A, line 13; *IG* XI 2, 159; A, line 64; *IG* XI 2, 161, A, line 83; *IG* X 12, 162, A, line 46; *ID* 290, line 108) may, however, refer to *dēmosioi*. There is also a certain Dōrus (*IG* XI 2, 161, A, line 84, 279 BCE), called a *hupēretēs*, to whom 156 drachmae were paid. Likewise, the three wage workers Noumenius, Apollonius, and Chresimus, recruited by the city in 200 to work on the sanctuary and remunerated over the entire year, may have been public slaves (*ID* 372, A, lines 97–98). In 179, a certain Apollonius is mentioned with Karpus and Stephanus (*ID* 442, A, line 96). The city paid them an allowance in food and clothing, and several indications suggest they contributed toward the transport of materials to the sanctuary (see the remarks of V. Chankowski, "Le compte des hiéropes de 174 et l'administration du sanctuaire d'Apollon à la fin de l'Indépendance délienne," *BCH* 122 [1998]: 213–238, esp. p. 235).

69. On the *lithagōgountēs dēmosioi*: *IE* 159, lines 49–50, and no doubt as well line 62 (336/335 or 333/332). On the epistates of the *dēmosioi*: *IE* 177, line 62 (329/328) and *IE* 159, line 58 (336/335 or 333/332). On the one who kept the books: *IE* 177, line 12 (329/328). On those who oversaw the weighing of the tools: *IE* 157, lines 26–29 (336).

70. Cf. S. Epstein, "Why Did Attic Building Projects Employ Free Laborers Rather than Slaves?" *Zeitschrift für Papyrologie und Epigraphik* 166 (2008): 108–112 [hereafter cited as *ZPE*].

71. *IE* 159, lines 24–25 (336/335 or 333/332), then, for two *dēmosioi* a few years later: *IE* 177, lines 269–270 (329/328).

72. Cf. Jacob, *Les esclaves publics*, pp. 41–42.

73. *IE* 177, line 266.

74. Cf. J. Crampa, *Labraunda: Swedish Excavations and Researches*, vol. 3, *The Greek Inscriptions*, vol. 2 (Lund: P. Alström Förlag, 1972), p. 60.

75. *IE* 159, line 44.

76. D. Rousset, *Le territoire de Delphes et la terre d'Apollon* (Paris: École Française d'Athènes, 2002), inscriptions no. 31, line 9 and lines 11–12 (102/101 BCE).

77. Cf. Crampa, *Labraunda*, nos. 56 and 59, 60, lines 7–8, and 69. In Patara, see also the case of a *threptos tēs poleōs*, who is also called a *hierodoulos*: H. Engelmann, "Inschriften von Patara," *ZPE* 182 (2012): 179–201, no. 19.

78. See the remarks of Weiss, *Sklave der Stadt*, pp. 151–155.

79. *ID* 2332 (107/106); *ID* 2234 (106/105); *ID* 2249 (107/106); *ID* 2250 (108/107); *ID* 2251 (108/107); *ID* 2252 (108/107); *ID* 2253 (106/105); *ID* 268a (108/107). In the sanctuary of Zeus Kynthios and Athena Kynthia, the name of

the *dēmosios*, who played an identical role, is located in the lacuna (*ID* 1892, 97/96).
80. *ID* 1913.
81. Cf. P. Bruneau, *Recherches sur les cultes de Délos à l'époque hellénistique et à l'époque impériale* (Paris: De Boccard, 1970), p. 363.
82. *ID* 2610, lines 2–3; on the inscription, see L. Bricault, "Les prêtres du Sarapieion C de Délos," *BCH* 120 (1996): 597–616.
83. Weiss, *Sklave der Stadt*, p. 186; Bricault, "Les prêtres de Sarapeion," is more cautious.
84. On the urban sanctuary, Appian, *The Mithridatic Wars*, 26.
85. *IG* XII, 1, 31.
86. Xenophon, *Ways and Means*, 17.
87. Aristotle, *Politics*, 1267b.
88. Ibid. It is also probable that the anecdote about Phaleas shows once again how every political community becomes a slave under a tyrant's leadership.
89. For example, in a Rhodian inscription from the early first century BCE, a certain Sōclēs is described as an *eggēnēs dēmosios (Annuario della Scuola archeologica di Atene e delle Missioni italiane in Oriente* 22 [1939/1940], p. 168, 21, face B, col. 1, line 29) [hereafter cited as *ASAtene*]. For the other *dēmosioi* on this list of subscribers, the native city (generally a dependency of Rhodes) is mentioned, but that is not the case for Sōclēs, which suggests he was born in Rhodes.
90. Demosthenes, 18 (*Against Nicostratus*), 22–24 and 27. If one is to believe the litigant, his adversary's slaves, who are supposed to be confiscated by the city, would become *dēmosioi* and could be subject to torture. The legal argument here mentions only the act of confiscating slaves, without indicating precisely the role these slaves would play in the city's service. The stelae of the Hermocopidai in the late fifth century leave little doubt that these slaves were generally sold off. It was a different matter during the imperial period in the city of Cibyra where, after a trial, 107 slaves became the property of the city (*I. von Kybira*, 41, lines 5–6). In reality, it is very probable that, as J. Nollé has argued ("Epigraphica varia," *ZPE* 48 [1982]: 267–273), in this instance they were public slaves whom a citizen had appropriated. Finally, in Pergamon in the second century BCE, although royal slaves (*basilikoi*) were probably slaves who had been confiscated by the king, there is nothing to indicate that the same was true for the *dēmosioi*: *OGIS* 338, lines 20–26: "The descendants of freedmen shall be transferred to the class of resident foreigners [*paroikoi*], and so too the royal slaves [*basilikoi*], both the adults and the young men, and similarly the women except for those who were bought in the reigns of King Philadelphus and King Philometor and those who were taken from property which became royal [*ek tōn ousiōn tōn gegenēmenōn basilikōn*], and similarly the public slaves [*dēmosioi*]" (trans. M. Austin).
91. Jacob, *Les esclaves publics*, pp. 10–11.
92. On the *servi publici*, cf. W. Eder, *Servitus Publica. Untersuchungen zur Entstehung, Entwicklung und Funktion der öffentlichen Sklaverei in Rom* (Wiesbaden: F. Steiner, 1980), pp. 6–33.
93. Cf. L. Halkin, *Les esclaves publics chez les Romains* (Brussels: Société Belge de Librairie, 1897), pp. 16–18.

94. Rhodes/Osborne, no. 25, lines 36–40 [translation slightly modified—trans.].
95. *ID* 290, line 113.
96. Cf. Aeschines, 2 (*On the Embassy*), 173; and indirectly, Andocides, 3 (*On the Peace with Sparta*), 7.
97. Xenophon, *Ways and Means*, 18.
98. Aristotle, *Politics*, 1299a.
99. *SEG* 33, 1039, lines 68–77 (cf. H. Malay, "Three Decrees from Kyme," *Epigraphica Anatolica* 2 [1983]: 1–20). See also the commentaries of I. Savalli-Lestrade, "Archippè de Kymè la bienfaitrice," in *La Grèce au féminin*, ed. N. Loraux (Paris: Belles Lettres, 2003), pp. 415–432; and on the dating of the decrees, R. van Bremmen, "The Date and Context of the Kymaian Decrees for Archippe," *REA* 110 (2008): 357–382. For a similar case of a bequest of a slave, from an anonymous benefactor in Attaleia, no doubt during the imperial period, see *SEG* 17, 588, lines 3–4.
100. *SEG* 33, 1177, lines 19–23.
101. For Eucles and Telophilus in the fourth century: *IE* 159, lines 60–61; *IE* 177, lines 12 and 205. For Demetrius in the third century: *IG* II² 839, lines 52–35. In the late second century, Sōpatrus was chosen by a show of hands by members of the Boulē to work with the commission in charge of melting down some of the offerings on the Acropolis (*IG* II² 840, line 35).
102. For example, *IE* 177, lines 4–5; and *IE* 159, line 60. See the remarks of W. T. Loomis, *Wages, Welfare Costs and Inflation in Classical Athens* (Ann Arbor: University of Michigan Press, 1998), pp. 11–12. In about 449–447 the *epistatai* of Eleusis were paid four obols a day. In the mid-fifth century, the *misthos dikastikos* was certainly two obols a day: it rose to three obols beginning in 424 and until 322.
103. Aristotle, *The Athenian Constitution*, 56.1.
104. See the general remarks of C. Castoriadis, *La cité et les lois. Ce qui fait la Grèce*, vol. 2, *Séminaires (1983–1984)* (Paris: Seuil, 2008), pp. 55–56.
105. Aristotle, *Politics*, 1299a.
106. The expression is the result of a restitution about which there is little doubt because it is based on a comparison between two versions of the same inscription: in reality, lines 53–54 of *IG* II² 1013 can be reconstituted only in the light of *SEG* 24, 147, line 5; following the proposal of B. Meritt, "Greek Inscriptions," *Hesperia* 7, no. 27 (1938): 77–160.
107. See esp. the translation proposed by M. Austin, *The Hellenistic World from Alexander to the Roman Conquest: A Selection of Ancient Sources in Translation* (Cambridge: Cambridge University Press, 2006 [1981]), p. 240.
108. Cicero, *Pro Sestio*, 91.
109. Y. Thomas, "L'indisponibilité de la liberté en droit romain," *Hypothèses* (2006): 379–389, esp. 387.
110. By way of example, for Umayyad el-Andalus, see S. Kentaro, "Slave Elites and the Saqaliba in al-Andalus in the Umayyad Period," in *Slave Elites in the Middle East and Africa*, ed. T. Miura and J. E. Philips (London: Kegan Paul International, 2000), pp. 25–40, esp. p. 36; in the Sokoto Caliphate of the nineteenth century, Stilwell, *Paradoxes of Power*, pp. 181–182; among the beys of Tunis, Oualdi, *Esclaves et maîtres*, pp. 163–166.

111. For example, on the royal captives of Yatenga, see M. Izard, "Les captifs royaux dans l'ancien Yatenga," in Meillassoux, ed., *L'esclavage en Afrique précoloniale*, pp. 281–296; in the Cambodia of the Middle Period (fifteenth–nineteenth centuries), K. Sok, "L'esclavage au Cambodge à l'époque moyenne à travers les codes, les inscriptions modernes d'Angkor et les chroniques royales," in Condominas, ed., *Formes extrêmes de dépendance*, pp. 315–341, esp. p. 325.

112. By way of example, in the Quiché Maya states, see R. M. Carmack, *The Quiché Mayas of Utatlán: The Evolution of a Highland Guatemala Kingdom* (Norman: University of Oklahoma Press, 1981), p. 516; in the Yoruba kingdoms of the nineteenth century, T. Falola, "Power Relations and Social Interactions among Ibadan Slaves, 1850–1900," *African Economic History* 16 (1987): 95–114; in Savafid Iran, S. Babaie et al., eds., *Slaves of the Shah: New Elites of Savafid Iran* (London: I. B. Tauris, 2004), pp. 49–79; among the Mamluks of the beys of Tunis, Oualdi, *Esclaves et maîtres*, pp. 184–189.

113. See, for Malacca in the fifteenth and sixteenth centuries, P.-Y. Manguin, "Manpower and Labour Categories in Malacca," in Reid, ed., *Slavery, Bondage and Dependency*, pp. 209–215, esp. p. 210.

114. See, for example, C. Perrot, "Les captifs dans le royaume anyi du Ndényé"; and E. Terray, "La captivité dans le royaume abron du Gyaman," in Meillassoux, ed., *L'esclavage en Afrique précoloniale*, pp. 351–188 and 389–453, respectively; or in a completely different context, Oualdi, *Esclaves et maîtres*, pp. 172–175.

115. For an overview, see D. Pipes, *Slave Soldiers and Islam: The Genesis of a Military System* (New Haven, CT: Yale University Press, 1981). On the specifically Islamic character of the military dimension of royal or public slavery, see esp. the remarks of J. E. Philips, "Slave Officials in the Sokoto Caliphate," in Miura and Philips, eds., *Slave Elites in the Middle East and Africa*, pp. 215–234. It is clear that the phenomenon is far from exclusively Islamic: see, for example, the role of the soldier slaves, *tyeddo*, in the Senegambian kingdoms (Lovejoy, *Transformations in Slavery*, p. 73).

3. Strange Slaves

1. Cf. L. F. Thomaz, "L'esclavage à Malacca au XVIe siècle d'après les sources portugaises," in Condiminas, ed., *Formes extrêmes de dépendance*, pp. 357–386, quotations pp. 363, 365–366; and V. Matheson and M. B. Hooker, "Slavery in the Malay Texts: Categories of Dependency and Compensation," in Reid, ed., *Slavery, Bondage and Dependency*, pp. 182–207, pp. 184 and 196.

2. From the verb *bingi*, meaning "to assemble, to gather together, to set aside" (Izard, "Les captifs royaux," p. 282).

3. Ibid., p. 281.

4. Ibid., p. 294.

5. Ibid., p. 289.

6. Testart, *Le servitude volontaire*, vol. 2, *L'origine de l'État*, pp. 48–49 and 75.

7. For the anthropology of precolonial slavery, see many of the articles in Meillassoux, ed., *L'esclavage en Afrique précoloniale*; and Condominas, ed.,

Formes extrêmes de dépendance. More recently, in the very different contexts of the sultanates of northern India and the Sudanese Sokoto Caliphate of the nineteenth century, see S. Kamar, "Service, Status, and Military Slavery in the Delhi Sultanate: Thirteenth and Fourteenth Centuries," in Chatterjee and Eaton, eds., *Slavery and South Asian History*, pp. 83–114, pp. 102–107; and Stilwell, *Paradoxes of Power*. On the subject of the *servi publici* in the Roman Republic, see the remarks of W. Eder, *Servitus Publica. Untersuchungen zur Entstehung, Entwicklung und Funktion der öffentlichen Sklaverei in Rom* (Wiesbaden: F. Steiner, 1980); and J. Zlinsky, "Gemeineigentum am Beispiel des *servi publici*," in *Sklaverei und Freilassung im römischen Recht*, ed. T. Finkauer (Berlin: Springer, 2006), pp. 317–326.

8. L. Darmezin, *Les affranchissements par consécration en Béotie et dans le monde hellénistique* (Nancy: De Boccard, 1999), no. 143.

9. Demosthenes, 22 (*Against Androtion*), 55 [translation modified—trans.].

10. See the recent publication of this regulation in L. Gawlinski, *The Sacred Law of Andania: A New Text with Commentary* (Berlin: De Gruyter, 2012), lines 79–80. See also the regulation for the sanctuary of Apollo Erithaseus in Attica in the late fourth century BCE (*IG* II² 1362, lines 7–13), for Poiessa in Keos in the third century BCE (*IG* XII 5, 569, lines 5–8); and the Astynomic law of Pergamon (*OGIS* 483, col. IV, lines 188–196). See also S. Saba, *The Astynomoi Law from Pergamon: A New Commentary* (Mainz: Verlag Antike, 2012)).

11. Coulter, "Slavery and Freedom in Athens, Georgia," pp. 264–293, here p. 276.

12. Cf. Rhodes/Osborne, no. 25, lines 13–15 [translation slightly modified—trans.]. On the symmetry between the citizen's fine and the slave's flogging, see, by way of example, *CID* IV, line 127. On the use of the whip against slaves, cf. M.-M. Mactoux, "Esclave, fouet, rituel," in *Chemin faisant. Mythes, cultes et société en Grèce ancienne, Mélanges en l'honneur de Pierre Brulé*, ed. L. Bodiou, V. Mehl, J. Oulhen, F. Prost, and J. Wilgaux (Rennes: Presses Universitaires de Rennes, 2009), pp. 59–70; G. Glotz, "Les esclaves et la peine de fouet en Grèce," *Compte-rendu de l'Académie des Inscriptions et Belles-Lettres* (1908): 571–587.

13. *IG* II² 1013, lines 45–49.

14. Demosthenes, 18 (*Against Nicostratus*), 22–24. Cf. Jacob, *Les esclaves publics à Athènes*, pp. 156–157.

15. Cf. Finley, *Ancient Slavery and Modern Ideology*, p. 77.

16. For example, L. Beauchet, *Histoire du droit privé de la république athénienne* (Paris: Chevalier-Marescq, 1897), 2:463.

17. Cf. V. Hunter, "Introduction: Status Distinction in Athenian Laws," in *Laws and Social Status in Classical Athens*, ed. V. Hunter and J. Edmonson (Oxford: Oxford University Press, 2000), pp. 1–29, p. 12; and along the same lines, S. C. Todd, *The Shape of Athenian Law* (Oxford: Clarendon Press, 1993), p. 173.

18. On the debate between order and class and its epistemological impasses, cf. N. Koposov, *De l'imagination historique* (Paris: École des Hautes Études en Sciences Sociales, 2009).

19. F. Bluche and J.-F. Solnon, *La véritable hiérarchie sociale de l'ancienne France: Le tarif de la première capitation (1695)* (Geneva: Droz, 1983).

20. Aristotle, *Nicomachean Ethics*, 8.1159b and 1161a–b: "It is like the relation between a craftsman and his tool, or between the soul and the body [or between master and slave]: all these instruments it is true are benefited by the persons who use them, but there can be no friendship, nor justice, towards inanimate things; indeed not even towards a horse or an ox, nor yet towards a slave as slave. For master and slave have nothing in common: a slave is a living tool, just as a tool is an inanimate slave" [brackets are from the Loeb translation—trans.]

21. Cf. J.-F. Niort, "*Homo servilis:* Essai sur l'anthropologie et le statut juridique de l'esclave dans le Code Noir de 1685," *Droits* 50 (2010): 120–141, esp. 140–141.

22. Aeschines, 1 (*Against Timarchus*), 59.

23. J. Vélissaropoulos-Karakostas, *Droit grec d'Alexandre à Auguste (323 av. J.-C.–14 apr. J.-C.)* (Athens: Centre de Recherches de l'Antiquité Grecque et Romaine, 2011), 1:369–1:378.

24. *IG* II² 1570 (E. Meyer, *Metics and the Athenian Phialai-Inscriptions: A Study in Athenian Epigraphy and Law* [Stuttgart: F. Steiner, 2010], no. 20, lines 78–79). A second case depends on the interpretation of the abbreviation "DHMO" in *IG* II² 1566 (Meyer, *Metics and the Athenian Phialai-Inscriptions*, no. 16), line 33. I concur with the traditional interpretation of the inscription as *dikē apostasiou*, implying freedmen, and not *dikē aprostasiou*, which would refer to metics (contra Meyer, *Metics*; see K. Vlassopoulos's review, convincing in my opinion, in *Bryn Mawr Classical Review* 2011.2.48).

25. Hypereides, 3 (*Against Athenogenes*).

26. On Midas and Athenogenes, see A. Maffi, "Economia e diritto nell'Atene del IV secolo," *Symposion 2007. Akten der Gesellschaft für griechische und hellenistische Rechtsgeschichte* 20 (2008): 203–222; and A. Dimopoulou, "Le rôle des esclaves dans l'économie athénienne. Réponse à Edward Cohen," *Symposion 2011. Akten der Gesellschaft für griechische und hellenistische Rechtsgeschichte* 23 (2012): 225–236.

27. *I. Ephesos* Ia.18c, lines 18–22. The edict uses the term *douloi dēmosioi* to translate the Latin *servi publici*.

28. See B. Dignas's analysis in *Economy of the Sacred in Hellenistic and Roman Asia* (Oxford: Oxford University Press, 2002), p. 153.

29. *IG* XII 1, 383. See the remarks of D. Morelli, "Gli Stranieri in Rodi," *Studi Classici e Orientali* 5 (1956): 126–190, here pp. 137–138.

30. G. Pugliese Carratelli, "Per la storia delle associazioni in Rodi Antica," *ASAtene* 22 (1939–1940): 163, 21, face A, col. III, line 3, line 19, lines 25–26; face B, col. I, line 29, col. III, line 11.

31. *SEG* 49, 1522, line 20.

32. On the category of the "self-established slave" (*esclave casé*), cf. Meillassoux, *Anthropologie de l'esclavage*, pp. 118–119; and Testart, *L'esclave, la dette et le pouvoir*, pp. 124–125.

33. A few dispersed examples: in the Yoruba kingdoms of the nineteenth century, T. Falola, "Power Relations and Social Interactions among Ibadan Slaves, 1850–1900," *African Economic History* 16 (1987): 95–114, pp. 98–99; in the Kano emirate, which was part of the Sokoto Caliphate in the nineteenth century,

Stilwell, *Paradoxes of Power*, p. 192; among the *hamba raja* of the sultan of Malacca, Thomaz, "L'esclavage à Malacca au XVIe siècle d'après les sources portugaises," p. 367; among the slaves of the sultan of Aceh in Java in the late seventeenth century, B. Milceni, "De la notion de dépendance à Java. Quelques remarques," in Condominas, ed., *Formes extrêmes de dépendance*, pp. 388–398, p. 390; within the context of the Ottoman *devshirme* system, D. Ze'evi, "My Slave, My Son, My Lord: Slavery, Family and State in the Islamic Middle East," in Miura and Philips, eds., *Slave Elites in the Middle East and Africa*, pp. 71–79. See also the suggestive remarks about the Mamluks of the beys of Tunis in Oualdi (*Esclaves et maîtres*, p. 185), who claims that "the jurists' slave, reduced to a limited role in the management" of the bey's property, appeared to be a "theoretical illusion."

34. Paulus, *Digest*, 41, 2, 1, 22.

35. Ulpian, *Reg.* 20. 16. See the remarks of Eder, *Servitus publica*, pp. 113–114.

36. Cf. W. Schmitz, "Sklavenfamilien im antiken Griechenland," in *Kindersklaven-Sklavenkinder: Schicksale zwischen Zuneigung und Ausbeutung in der Antike und im interkulturellen Vergleich*, ed. H. Heinen (Stuttgart: F. Steiner, 2012), pp. 63–102; and M. Golden, "Slavery and the Greek Family," in *The Cambridge World History of Slavery: The Ancient Mediterranean World* (Cambridge: Cambridge University Press, 2011), p. 143.

37. I borrow this expression from Finley, *Ancient Slavery and Modern Ideology*, p. 75.

38. *ID* 1913.

39. *IG* II² 1717 and *IG* II² 1720. For that reason, this individual is not to be confused with his polemarch namesake from the deme of Azenia mentioned in *IG* II² 1717.

40. See, by way of example, the slaves listed in *IG* I³ 1032.

41. On this matter, see esp. Cardinali, "Note di terminologia epigraphica. I. Dêmosioi," pp. 161–162; and L. Robert, *Bulletin épigraphique* (France: Les belles lettres, 1981), p. 558.

42. For all the *dēmosioi* with patronymics listed for the imperial age, cf. Weiss, *Sklave der Stadt*, pp. 82–83. In most cases, it is very difficult to decide the matter. The only case in which the *dēmosios*'s citizenship is likely is that of Theophilus son of Philadelphus, who, as an agonothete in Hierapolis, organized the contests in honor of the emperor (cf. H. Pleket, "A Free Demosios," *ZPE* 42 [1981]: 167–170; Robert, *Bulletin épigraphiqe*, p. 558; and Weiss's reservations in *Sklave der Stadt*, p. 169).

43. Thus Beauchet, in *Histoire du droit privé de la république athénienne*, p. 464, claimed, somewhat hastily no doubt, that *dēmosioi* could contract valid marriages, "giving rise" to children able to succeed them.

44. *IG* II² 839, lines 52–35.

45. *IG* II² 1539, lines 10–11. For what is doubtless a similar case in Sparta during the imperial period, see *IG* V 1, 116, lines 16–17.

46. On servile invectives in general, cf. D. Kamen, "Servile Invective in Classical Athens," *Scripta classica Israelica* 27 (2008): 43–56; and K. Vlassopoulos,

"Slavery, Freedom and Citizenship in Classical Athens: Beyond a Legalistic Approach," *European Historical Review* 16, no. 3 (2009): 347–364. These authors, however, see them as proof of the permeability and uncertainty reigning for the different statuses in the ancient city.

47. Lysias, 30 (*Against Nicomachus*), 30 [translation modified—trans.].

48. Ibid., 30, 2: "To tell how Nicomachus's father was a public slave, and what were the man's own occupations in his youth, and at what age he was admitted to his clan, would be a lengthy affair."

49. In that respect, the case of the famous Phormio, Pasion, and Apollodorus, known through Demosthenes, 36 (*For Phormio*), provides a striking contrast. Phormio was a slave, then, after being made a freedman, became a metic, and was finally granted citizenship. By contrast, Apollodorus was the son of a former slave, Pasion, and became a metic.

50. Scholion to Aristophanes, *Wasps*, line 1007 (Andocides, fragment 3. 2).

51. Cf. P. Brun, "Hyperbolos, la création d'une 'légende noire,'" *Dialogues d'histoire ancienne* 13 (1987): 183–198. The comic poet Plato portrayed Hyperbolus as a Lydian (*Poetae comici graeci,* ed. R. Kassel and C. Austin [Berlin: de Gruyter, 1983] VII, frag. 185), hereafter cited as *PCG*); Polyzelus satirized him as a Phrygian (*PCG* VII, fr. 5).

52. Dinarchus, frag. 7, II, Belles Lettres ed.

53. Hypereides, 3 (*In Defense of Euxenippus*), 3.

54. Cf. A. Layish, "Waqfs of Awlād al-Nās in Aleppo in the Late Mamlūk Period as Reflected in a Family Archive," *Journal of the Economic and Social History of the Orient* 51 (2008): 287–326; and R. Amitai, "The Mamluk Institution, or One Thousand Years of Military Service in the Islamic World," in *Arming Slaves: From Classical Times to the Modern Age,* ed. C. L. Brown and P. D. Morgan (New Haven, CT: Yale University Press, 2006), pp. 40–78.

55. Kamar, "Service, Status, and Military Slavery in the Delhi Sultanate," pp. 83–114, esp. pp. 102–107.

56. L. Halkin, *Les esclaves publics chez les Romains* (Brussels: Chevalier-Marescq, 1897), pp. 118–120. On the "kinship privilege" specific to the *servi publici,* see esp. the remarks of Zlinsky, "Gemeineigentum am Beispiel der *servi publici,*" p. 323.

57. Aeschines, 1 (*Against Timarchus*), 54–64.

58. Those who believe Pittalacus was a slave include: E. Cohen, *The Athenian Nation* (Princeton, NJ: Princeton University Press, 2000), pp. 137–139; V. Hunter, "Pittalacus and Eucles: Slaves in the Public Service of Athens," *Mouseion* 6 (2006): 1–13; and before them, Waszynski, "Über die rechtliche Stellung der Staatsclaven in Athen," pp. 554–555. By contrast, Jacob, *Les esclaves publics à Athènes,* p. 162; and N. Fisher, *Aeschines: Against Timarchos* (Oxford: Oxford University Press, 2001), p. 191, portray him as a freedman or a citizen of very lowly station.

59. Cf. Aeschines, 1 (*Against Timarchus*), 54, 59, and the Suda, *Timarchos.*

60. Aeschines, 1 (*Against Timarchus*), 59.

61. Ibid., 62. The expression used by the litigant, however, is not without its obscurity: it is altogether possible that someone else lodged the complaint on

his behalf. On this point, see Beauchet, *Histoire du droit privé de la république athénienne*, pp. 464–465 (contra Waszynski, "Über die rechtliche Stellung der Staatsclaven in Athen," p. 560, who maintains that a *dēmosios* was able to take legal action). By contrast, Fisher's *Aeschines, Against Timarchos*, pp. 199–200, posits the use of the *graphē hubreōs*, supposedly initiated by someone close to Pittalacus.

62. Jacob, *Les esclaves publics à Athènes*, p. 162: "He is a freedman; otherwise, the procedure of *aphairesis eis eleutherian* would have no raison d'être." See also Fisher, *Aeschines, Against Timarchos*, p. 191.

63. If one is to believe Demosthenes, a certain Ctesicles in fourth-century Athens was sentenced to death for "treating freemen like slaves" by whipping a man. Demosthenes, 21 (*Against Meidias*), 180.

64. See Oliver, "Honours for a Public Slave at Athens."

65. *Agora* XV, 62, V, lines 10–18. In 281/280, *Agora* XV, 72; I, line 5; II, line 67, 211; III, line 83, 266.

66. See *IE* 182 (K. Clinton, *Eleusis: The Inscriptions on Stone*, vol. 1 [Athens: Archaeological Society at Athens, 2008], no. 182).

67. See G. J. Oliver, *War, Food, and Politics in Early Hellenistic Athens* (Oxford: Oxford University Press, 2007).

68. *IE* 182, lines 16–18 and lines 18–20. See Oliver's comments, ibid., pp. 258–259.

69. Along the same lines, see Waszynski's comments in "Über die rechtliche Stellung der Staatsclaven," pp. 565–566; and very recently, Clinton, *Eleusis: The Inscriptions on Stone*, 2: 247.

70. Patterson, *Slavery and Social Death*, p. 13.

71. M. Klein, *Slavery and Colonial Rule in French West Africa* (Cambridge: Cambridge University Press, 1998), p. 249. Within the same perspective, see E. Steinhart, "Slavery and Other Forms of Oppression in Ankole," in *Slavery in the Great Lakes Region of East Africa*, ed. H. Médard and S. Doyle (Oxford: James Currey, 2008), pp. 189–209.

72. On this point, see also the counterexample in the Delhi Sultanate: S. Kumar, "When Slaves Were Nobles: The Shamsi *Bandagan* in the Early Delhi Sultanate," *Studies in History* 10 (1994): 23–52.

73. Y. Garlan, "Les esclaves grecs en temps de guerre," *Actes du colloque d'histoire sociale de Besançon, 1970* (Paris: Belles Lettres, 1972), pp. 29–62, quotation p. 45.

74. P. Gauthier, *Un commentaire historique des* Poroi *de Xénophon* (Paris: Droz, 1976), p. 176. On the participation of soldier slaves in combat, cf. P. Hunt, *Slaves, Warfare and Ideology in the Greek Historians* (Cambridge: Cambridge University Press, 1998).

75. *I. Ephesos* 1a, 8, lines 47–48: "The *dēmosioi* who take up arms will become free [*eleutherous*] and *paroikoi*."

76. *I. Ephesos* 1a, 8, lines 43–45.

77. *OGIS* 338, lines 20–26: "The descendants of freedmen shall be transferred to the class of resident foreigners [*paroikoi*], and so too the royal slaves [*basilikoi*], both the adults and the young men, and similarly the women except

for those who were bought in the reigns of King Philadelphus and King Philometor and those who were taken from property which became royal [*ek tōn ousiōn tōn gegenēmenōn basilikōn*], and similarly the public slaves [*dēmosioi*]" and lines 37–38, "concerning the transfer to (the category of) resident foreigners of the [descendants of freedmen and the royal slaves and] the public slaves" (trans. M. Austin)."

78. *IG* XII 1, 383.
79. *OGIS* 338, lines 11–20.
80. P. Ismard, *La cité des réseaux. Athènes et ses associations, VIe-Ier siècles av. J.-C.* (Paris: Publications de la Sorbonne, 2010), pp. 179–185.
81. Y. Garlan, *Les esclaves en Grèce ancienne* (Paris: La Découverte, 1995 [1982]), pp. 46–47.
82. On this matter, see the suggestive remarks about the *servi publici* in Zlinsky, "Gemeineigentum am Beispiel des *servi publici*."
83. Y. Thomas, "L'institution civile de la cité," *Le Débat* 74 (1993), repr. in Y. Thomas, *Les opérations du droit* (Paris: Gallimard-Seuil, 2011), pp. 103–130.
84. Ibid., p. 118.
85. See esp. Marcianus, *Digest*, 1, 8, 6, l; and Ulpian, *Digest*, 48, 18, 1, 7, with the remarks of N. Rouland, "À propos des *servi publici romani*," *Chiron* 7 (1977): 261–278, esp. p. 262. See also Thomas, "L'institution civile de la cité," p. 116.
86. See the remarks of D. Rousset, "Sacred Property and Public Property in the Greek City," *Journal of Hellenic Studies* 133 (2013): 113–133, esp. pp. 122–124.
87. See ibid., esp. pp. 124–129.
88. Xenophon, *Ways and Means*, 4.21. As when it rented out sacred lands, the city required guarantees before renting out the labor of its *dēmosioi*.
89. Rousset, *Le territoire de Delphes*, no. 31, line 9 and lines 11–12 (decree of the Delphians in honor of Nicomedes III and Laodice in 102/101 BCE). See Rousset's remarks on the expression in *Le territoire de Delphes*, pp. 267–268.
90. Rousset, *Le territoire de Delphes*, p. 268, with corrections in Rousset, "Sacred Property and Public Property," pp. 129–130.
91. J. Crampa, *Labraunda*, 2.56, lines 11–12.
92. Ibid., 2.59, C, line 6.
93. Ibid., 2.69, lines 7–8.
94. See the remarks of B. Dignas, *Economy of the Sacred in Hellenistic and Roman Asia*, p. 153, who notes that the Roman governor Persicus, when mentioning how the *dēmosioi* were provided for, makes no distinction between the two funds.
95. Pending a more complete inventory of the sanctuaries of the Greek world, see the remarks of Y. Thomas, "La valeur des choses. Le droit romain hors la religion," *Annales Histoire, Sciences Sociales* 6 (2002): 1431–1462 [hereafter cited as *Annales HSC*].
96. E. Grendi, "Microanalisi e storia sociale," *Quaderni storici* 35 (1977): 506–520, quotation p. 512.
97. Contra E. Cohen, *The Athenian Nation* (Princeton, NJ: Princeton University Press, 2000).

98. M. I. Finley, *The Ancient Economy* (Berkeley: University of California Press, 1973), p. 51.

99. See Finley, *Economy and Society*, p. 148, here and below. On the history of Finley's reading and its reception, see the recent remarks of J. Zurbach, "La formation des cités grecques. Statuts, classes et systèmes fonciers," *Annales HSC* 4 (2013): 957–998; and P. Ismard, "Classes, ordres, statuts. La réception française de la sociologie finleyenne et le cas Pierre Vidal-Naquet," *Anabases* 19 (2014): 39–53.

100. Cf. M. H. Hansen, *Apagoge, Endeixis and Ephegesis against Kakourgoi, Atimoi and Pheugontes* (Odense: Odense University Press, 1976), pp. 55–75.

101. S. C. Todd, *The Shape of the Athenian Law* (Oxford: Clarendon Press, 1993), p. 96.

102. R. Wallace, "Unconvicted or Potential 'Atimoi' in Ancient Athens," *Dikē* 1 (1998): 63–78, p. 65.

103. Andocides, 1 (*On the Mysteries*), 74–76.

104. On this question, see Oualdi, *Esclaves et maîtres*, pp. 37–44.

4. The Democratic Order of Knowledge

1. Scholiast of Demosthenes, 2.134.

2. On the education of young slaves, *oikogeneis*, see the remarks of R. Descat and J. Andreau, *Esclave en Grèce et à Rome* (Paris: Hachette, 2006), pp. 161–163.

3. According to J. Dutisman Cornelius, *When I Can Read My Title Clear: Literacy, Slavery, and Religion in the Antebellum South* (Columbia: University of South Carolina Press, 1991).

4. I borrow the term "epistocracy" from D. Estlund, *Democratic Authority: A Philosophical Framework* (Princeton, NJ: Princeton University Press, 2008).

5. See esp. the reflections of M. Callon, P. Lascoumes, and Y. Barthes, *Agir dans un monde incertain. Essai sur la démocratie technique* (Paris: Seuil, 2001).

6. On social epistemology and its different branches, see the overview of A. Goldmann, "Why Social Epistemology Is Real Epistemology," in *Social Epistemology: Essential Readings*, ed. A. Haddock, A. Millar, and D. Pritchard (Oxford: Oxford University Press, 2010), pp. 1–28.

7. M. Foucault, *Surveiller et punir* (Paris: Gallimard, 1976), p. 36.

8. Demosthenes, 24 (*Against Timocrates*), 213; see also Demosthenes, 20 (*Against Leptines*), 167.

9. Rhodes/Osborne, no. 25. In a vast bibliography, see esp. R. S. Stroud, "An Athenian Law on Silver Coinage," *Hesperia* 43 (1974): 157–188; T. V. Buttrrey, "More on the Athenian Coinage Law of 375/4 B.C.," *Numismatica e antichita classiche* 10 (1981): 71–94; T. R. Martin, "Silver Coins and Public Slaves in the Athenian Law of 376/4 B.C." in *Mnemata: Papers in Memory of Nancy M. Waggoner* (New York: American Numismatic Society, 1991), pp. 21–48; T. Figueira, *The Power of Money: Coinage and Politics in the Athenian Empire* (Philadelphia: University of Pennsylvania Press, 1998); C. Feyel, "À propos de la loi de

Nicophon. Remarques sur les sens de *dokimos, dokimazein, dokimasia*," *Revue de philologie* 77 (2003): 37–65.

10. That was undoubtedly the task already performed by Lacon at the very start of the fourth century (*IG* II² 1388, lines 61–62; but also *IG* II² 1400, line 57); *IG* II² 1401, lines 44–45; *IG* II² 1415, lines 19–20; *IG* II² 1424a, lines 311–312; *IG* II² 1428, line 149; *IG* II² 1443, lines 207–208).

11. Rhodes/Osborne, no. 25, lines 8–12.

12. See the remarks of S. Psoma, "The Law of Nicophon (*SEG* 26, 72) and Athenian Imitations," *Revue belge de numismatique et de sigillographie* 157 (2011): 27–36 [hereafter cited as *RBN*].

13. Cf. Demosthenes, 22 (*Against Androtion*), 71, on the honesty of public slaves.

14. Petronius, *Satyricon*, 56, pp. 115–117.

15. The difficulty was all the greater in that many coins in Athens were privately produced and of very poor quality: cf. C. Flament, "Imitations athéniennes ou monnaies authentiques? Nouvelles considérations sur quelques chouettes athéniennes identifiées habituellement comme imitations," *RBN* 149 (2003): 1–10.

16. Cf. C. Flament, *Le monnayage en argent d'Athènes. De l'époque archaïque à l'époque hellénistique* (Louvain-la-Neuve: Association de Numismatique Professeur Marcel Hoc, 2007), pp. 55–58.

17. See the remarks of Martin, "Silver Coins and Public Slaves," p. 34.

18. Rhodes/Osborne, no. 25, lines 37–40.

19. Ibid., no. 25, lines 14–15.

20. Ibid., no. 25, lines 16–18.

21. On this individual, see, in addition to O. Jacob, *Les esclaves publics à Athènes*, pp. 135–137, V. Hunter's, "Pittalacus and Eucles: Slaves in the Public Service of Athens," *Mouseion* 6 (2006): 1–13.

22. *IG* II² 120.

23. This is the convincing hypothesis of J. Sickinger, *Public Records and Archives in Classical Athens* (Chapel Hill: University of North Carolina Press, 1999), p. 126.

24. *IG* II² 1440, lines 6–7.

25. *IE* 159, lines 60–61. Following Oscar Jacob and Virginia Hunter, I believe this is the same individual.

26. See the remarks of T. Linders, "The Purpose of Inventories: A Close Reading of the Delian Inventories of the Independence," in *Comptes et inventaires dans la cité grecque: Actes du colloque international d'épigraphie tenu à Neufchatel du 23 au 26 septembre 1986 en l'honneur de Jacques Tréheux* (Geneva: Droz, 1988). pp. 37–47. As Tullia Linders has noted, when the Delian inscriptions mention the objects "brought" to the hieropes, one must undoubtedly imagine public slaves performing that task, which required an intimate knowledge of how the sanctuary functioned.

27. *ID* 1444, Aa, line 54.

28. *ID*, 1444, Ba, line 20.

29. *ID* 1442, B, line 76.

30. On the Athenian *paredroi*, see Aristotle, *The Athenian Constitution*, 56.1. On the minor magistracies, an excellent example is provided by V. Chankowski (*Athènes et Délos à l'époque classique. Recherches sur l'administration du sanctuaire d'Apollon délien* [Athens: École Française d'Athènes, 2008]).

31. See the remarks of J.-M. Bertrand, "Réflexions sur l'expertise politique en Grèce ancienne," *Revue historique* 620 (2001): 929–964.

32. It should be noted, however, that a citizen by the name of Hegemon seems to have quickly pushed through a law abolishing the magistracy: Aeschines, 3 (*Against Ctesipon*), 25.

33. *IG* II² 457; *IG* II² 513.

34. On Nichomachus, cf. S. C. Todd, "Lysias against Nicomachos: The Fate of the Expert in Athenian Law," in *Greek Law in Its Political Setting*, ed. L. Foxhall and A. Lewis (Oxford: Clarendon Press, 1996), pp. 101–131, esp. pp. 104–105.

35. Aristophanes, *Frogs*, lines 1505–1506.

36. On the procedure as a whole, cf. E. Volonaki, "The Re-publication of the Athenian Laws in the Last Decade of the Fifth Century B.C.," *Dikē* 4 (2001): 137–167.

37. Lysias, 30 (*Against Nicomachus*), 2 and 4, here 4.

38. Ibid., 3.

39. Ibid., 29, with the comments of Volonaki, "The Re-publication of the Athenian Laws," p. 153.

40. Ibid., 17–22.

41. Ibid., 29.

42. Ibid., 4: "After handling more business than anyone had ever done before he is the only person who has held a magistracy without submitting to an audit" [translation modified—trans.].

43. Lysias, 30 (*Against Nicomachus*), 29 and 5 [translation modified—trans.].

44. Ibid., 27.

45. Plato, *Protagoras*, 309d.

46. Ibid., 318e–319a.

47. Ibid., 319d.

48. On the meanings to be attributed to that fundamental value of archaic and classical society, see the entry *"aidôs"* in *Vocabulaire européen des philosophies*, ed. B. Cassin (Paris: Seuil, 2004).

49. Plato, *Protagoras*, 323c.

50. Ibid., 327c.

51. Ibid., 327a–327b. Protagoras adds: "If we made the same zealous and ungrudging efforts to instruct each other in flute-playing, do you think, Socrates, that the good flute-players would be more likely than the bad to have sons who were good flute-players? I do not think they would."

52. See the remarks of F. Ildefonse in Plato, *Protagoras* (Paris: Flammarion 1997), pp. 30–31.

53. Plato, *Protagoras*, p. 328a.

54. J. Ober, *Democracy and Knowledge: Innovation and Learning in Classical Athens* (Princeton, NJ: Princeton University Press, 2008).

55. On the density of Athenian community life, see P. Ismard, *La cité des réseaux. Athènes et ses associations (VIe–Ier siècle av. J.-C.)* (Paris: Publications de la Sorbonne, 2010).

56. N. de Condorcet, *Essai sur l'application de l'analyse à la probabilité des décisions rendues à la pluralité des voix* (New York: Chelsea, 1972 [1st ed. Paris, 1785]).

57. Aristotle, *Politics*, 1281a–b [translation modified—trans.]. On this passage and its interpretation in terms of social epistemology, see J. Ober, "Democracy's Wisdom: An Aristotelian Middle Way for Collective Judgment," *American Political Science Review* 107 (2013): 104–122.

58. On this point, see the remarks of B. Cassin, *L'effet sophistique* (Paris: Gallimard, 1995), p. 246.

59. Xenophon, *Memorabilia*, 4.2.33: "'Really! Have you not heard how Daedalus was seized by Minos because of his knowledge and forced to be his slave, and was robbed of his country and his liberty, and in trying to escape with his son lost the boy and could not save himself but was carried off to the barbarians and again lived as a slave there?'

'That is the story, of course.'

'And haven't you heard the story of Palamedes? Of course, for all the poets sing of him: how he was envied for his knowledge and done in by Odysseus.'

'Another well-known tale!'

'And how many others, do you suppose, have been kidnapped on account of their knowledge and haled off to the great King's court and live in slavery there?'"

60. Diogenes Laërtius, *Lives and Doctrines of the Illustrious Philosophers*, 2.19.

61. Plato, *Gorgias*, 514a–b: "Then if you and I, Callicles, in setting about some piece of public business for the state, were to invite one another to see to the building part of it, say the most important erections either of walls or arsenals or temples, would it be our duty to consider and examine ourselves, first as to whether we understood the art of building or not, and from whom we had learnt it? Would we have to do this, or not?"

62. Plato, *Meno*, 70a.

63. Ibid., 80d.

64. See esp. R. Weiss, *Virtue in the Cave: Moral Inquiry in Plato's Meno* (Oxford: Oxford University Press, 2001), pp. 52–76; and C. Ionescu, *Plato's Meno* (Plymouth: Lexington Books, 2007), pp. 41–42.

65. See the remarks of M. Canto-Sperber in Plato, *Ménon* (Paris: Flammarion, 1991), pp. 247–248. It should be noted, however, that Thrasyllus of Alexandria placed *Meno* within the sixth tetralogy of the Platonic corpus. And that sixth tetralogy supposedly comprises the dialogues in which Socrates, more explicitly than anywhere else in the Platonic opus, opposed the Sophists of his time, particularly on the question of how to learn excellence (see the remarks of H. Tarrant, *Recollecting Plato's* Meno [London: Duckworth, 2005], pp. 128–193).

66. Plato, *Meno*, 71b.

67. Canto-Sperber, in Plato, *Ménon*, p. 72.

68. The essential document on this point is Gorgias's *Treatise on Nonbeing*, which is known through Sextus Empiricus and the treatise *De Melisso, Xenophane, Gorgia* by Pseudo-Aristotle (cf. G. Kerferd, *The Sophistic Movement* [Cambridge: Cambridge University Press, 1981], pp. 93–99, and Cassin, *L'effet sophistique*, pp. 23–65 and pp. 119–140).

69. See the remarks of P. Woodruff, "Rhetoric and Relativism: Protagoras and Gorgias," in *The Cambridge Companion to Early Greek Philosophy*, ed. A. Long (Cambridge: Cambridge University Press, 1999), pp. 290–310.

70. J. Rancière, *Le maître ignorant. Cinq leçons sur l'émancipation intellectuelle* (Paris: Fayard, 1987).

71. Cf. D. Scott, *Plato's* Meno (Cambridge: Cambridge University Press, 2006), pp. 94–97.

72. Plato, *Meno*, 81a–b.

73. The scene does not in any way give a sample of the Socratic dialectical refutation known as *elenchos*. See the remarks of H. H. Benson, "'Meno,' the Slave Boy and the *Elenchos*," *Phronesis* 35 (1990): 128–158.

74. Plato, *Meno*, 85d.

75. I leave aside the philosophical controversy surrounding the theory of *anamnēsis*: Is it a unified theory running from *Meno* to *Phaedo* to *Phaedrus*, in which the knowledge of Forms is at issue from the start, or does *Meno* propose only a limited version? For a unified approach, cf. L. Brisson, "La réminiscence dans le Ménon (81c5–d5)," in *Gorgias-Menon: Selected Papers from the Seventh Symposium Platonicum*, ed. M. Erler and L. Brisson (Sankt Augustin: Academia Verlag, 2007), pp. 199–203.

76. D. Scott, *Plato's* Meno (Cambridge: Cambridge University Press, 2006), pp. 106–108.

77. J. Rancière, *Le philosophe et ses pauvres* (Paris: Fayard, 1983), pp. 63–65.

78. Plato, *Meno*, 81c.

79. Ibid., 81b–c (Pindar, frag. 133).

80. Ibid., 81c–d.

81. Ibid., 86a. See the remarks of L. Gernet, "Les origines de la philosophie," *Anthropologie de la Grèce antique* (Paris: Maspero, 1964), pp. 415–430, esp. pp. 422–425.

82. Stilwell, *Paradoxes of Power*, p. 6.

83. Ibid., pp. 167–203.

84. The remark is reported in Stilwell, *Paradoxes of Power*, p. 193.

85. See, in a very different context, the rather similar remarks in C. Perrot, "Les captifs dans le royaume anyi du Ndénéyé," in Meillassoux, ed., *L'esclavage en Afrique précoloniale*, pp. 351–388, here p. 380.

86. Y. Ragib, "Les esclaves publics aux premiers siècles de l'Islam," in *Figures de l'esclave au Moyen Âge et dans le monde moderne*, ed. H. Bresc (Paris: L'Harmattan, 1996), pp. 7–30.

87. Cf. Oualdi, *Esclaves et maîtres*, pp. 102–107.

88. Aristotle, *Politics*, 1255b: "The term 'master ' therefore denotes the possession not of a certain branch of knowledge but of a certain character, and similarly also the terms 'slave ' and 'freeman.' Yet there might be a science of

mastership and a slave's science—the latter being the sort of knowledge that used to be imparted by the professor at Syracuse."

89. But it can also be understood as education relating to the management of slaves.

5. The Mysteries of the Greek State

1. Suda, *Tenedios anthrōpos*. The Suda uses the term *dēmios* to refer to the executioner: he is of course a public slave. On the same anecdote, see also Photius, *Tenedios*.

2. Plutarch, *Moralia*, 399f. According to Plutarch, in Tenedos even crabs bore the imprint of an ax on their shell.

3. Pausanias, *Description of Greece*, 10.14.

4. Ibid., 10.14. See also Cicero's joke (*Letter to Quintus*, 14 [2.10].2: "The liberties of the good folk of Tenedos have been chopped by their own axe." Cicero is referring to the liberties the Tenedians demanded from the new Roman authorities, which were unceremoniously rejected.

5. Suda, *Tenedios xunēgoros*.

6. On the notion of the city-state and its heuristic limits, see J.-J. Glassner's remarks in "Du bon usage du concept de cité-État," *Journal des Africanistes* 74 (2004): 35–48.

7. For an overview of this collective work, see, in addition to M. H. Hansen and T. Heine Nielsen, eds., *An Inventory of Archaic and Classical Poleis* (Oxford: Oxford University Press, 2004); M. H. Hansen, "95 Theses about the Greek Polis in the Archaic and Classical Period," *Historia* 52, no. 3 (2003): 257–282; and M. H. Hansen, *Polis and City-State: An Ancient Concept and Its Modern Equivalent* (Copenhagen: Munksgaard, 1998). For a critical introduction, see P. Fröhlich, "L'inventaire du monde des cités grecques. Une somme, une méthode et une conception de l'histoire," *Revue historique* 655 (2010): 637–677.

8. A. Guéry, "L'historien, la crise et l'État," *Annales HSC* 52, no. 2 (1997): 233–256.

9. M. H. Hansen, *Polis: An Introduction to the Greek City-State* (Oxford: Oxford University Press, 2006), p. 64.

10. Ibid., pp. 132–133.

11. I borrow this expression from Y. Thomas, "L'institution civile de la cité," *Le Débat* 74 (1993): 23–44. In that respect, G. Anderson's "The Personality of the Greek State," *Journal of Hellenic Studies* 192 (2009): 1–22, although it claims a "categorical kinship" between the modern state and the Greek city, does not examine the status of the city in the law. The fact that the *dēmos* is one of the metaphors for the *polis* in its unity says nothing about its existence as a legal subject. As Yan Thomas has shown, it is essential that the city's different institutions not be conceived as different "organs" with the capacity to appeal in the last instance to a state conceived as a unity that subsumes them.

12. M. Faraguna, "A proposito degli archivi nel mondo greco. Terra e registrazione fondiarie," *Chiron* 30 (2000): 65–115: "Scrittura e amministrazione

nelle città greche. Gli archivi pubblici," *Quaderni urbinati di cultura classica* 80 (2005): 61–86; C. Pébarthe, *Cité, démocratie et écriture. Histoire de l'alphabétisation d'Athènes à l'époque classique* (Paris: De Boccard, 2006).

13. Guéry, "L'historien, la crise et l'État," 250.

14. Cf. Fröhlich, "L'inventaire du monde des cités grecques," p. 670. This led Finley to describe the city as a state with "no mediating bureaucracy" (M. I. Finley, *Politics in the Ancient World* [Cambridge: Cambridge University Press, 1983], p. 8).

15. A few examples taken from very different contexts: in the Bambara kingdom of Ségou in the nineteenth century, J. Bazin, "Guerre et servitude à Ségou" in Meillassoux, ed., *L'esclavage en Afrique précoloniale*, pp. 135–181; in the Delhi Sultanate during the thirteenth and fourteenth centuries, S. Kamar, "Service, Status, and Military Slavery in the Delhi Sultanate: Thirteenth and Fourteenth Centuries," in Chatterjee and Eaton, eds., *Slavery and South Asian History*, pp. 83–114; in precolonial Yatenga, Izard, "Les captifs royaux dans l'ancien Yatenga," pp. 283 and 296; in the small Zinder Sultanate of Nigeria, P. Mounier, "La dynamique des interrelations politiques. Le cas du sultanat de Zinder," *Cahiers d'Études Africaines* 39 (1999): 367–386; in Savafid Iran in the sixteenth and seventeenth centuries, S. Babaie et al., eds., *Slaves of the Shah: New Elites of Savafid Iran* (London: I. B. Tauris, 2004), pp. 2–19; in the Yoruba states during the modern period and the nineteenth century, T. Falola and M. M. Heaton, *A History of Nigeria* (Cambridge: Cambridge University Press, 2008), pp. 50–52, and E. C. Enogu, "State Building in the Niger Basin in the Common Era and Beyond: 1000–mid 1800, the Case of Yorubaland," *Journal of Asian and African Studies* 46 (2011): 593–614; in the Bamum kingdom (Cameroon) during the nineteenth century, C. Tardits, "Le royaume amoum," in *Princes et serviteurs du royaume. Cinq études de monarchies africaines*, ed. C. Tardits (Paris: Société d'Ethnographie, 1987), pp. 107–135, esp. pp. 131–134; in the Songhay empire, J.-P. Olivier de Sardan, "Captifs ruraux et esclaves impériaux de Songhay," in Meillassoux, ed., *L'esclavage en Afrique précoloniale*, pp. 99–134; in Umayyad Andalusia, S. Kentaro, "Slave Elites and the Saqaliba in al-Andalus in the Umayyad Period," in Miura and Philips, eds., *Slave Elites in the Middle East and Africa*, pp. 25–40; within the context of the Ottoman *devshirme* during the sixteenth century, B. Tezcan, *The Second Ottoman Empire: Political and Social Transformation in the Early Modern World* (Cambridge: Cambridge University Press, 2010), pp. 91–93. See also the general remarks of Meillassoux, *Anthropologie de l'esclavage*, pp. 185–188, and Testart, *La servitude volontaire*, vol. 2, *L'origine de l'État*, p. 48.

16. For a different approach, which understands the recourse to the royal slaveholding institution not in terms of a break with the order of lineage but rather as a means to reinforce the chief's lineage at the expense of the free aristocracy, see, in two distinct contexts, E. Terray, *Une histoire du royaume Abron du Gyaman. Des origines à la conquête coloniale* (Paris: Karthala, 1995); and for the Ottoman *devshirme* in the sixteenth century, the remarks of Tezcan, *The Second Ottoman Empire*, pp. 91–96.

17. G. Nachtigal, *Sahara and Sudan*, trans. A. G. B. Fisher and H. J. Fisher (London: Hurst, 1974–1980), vol. 2, *Kawar, Bornu, Kanem, Borku, Ennedi*, pp. 245 and 247–248.

18. See, for example, the process described concerning, precisely, the history of the Sokoto Caliphate (northern Nigeria) in the nineteenth century, in Stilwell, *Paradoxes of Power*, esp. pp. 117–166; and the general remarks of Meillassoux, *Anthropologie de l'esclavage*, pp. 196–197.

19. Meillassoux, *Anthropologie de l'esclavage*, p. 187. But the case of the Mamluks of the beys of Tunis, studied in Oualdi, *Esclaves et maîtres*, shows that the extension of the sovereign's authority and its privatization to the benefit of his servants can go hand in hand.

20. I borrow this expression from K. Ringrose, *The Perfect Servant: Eunuchs and the Social Construction of Gender in Byzantium* (Chicago: University of Chicago Press, 2004). On the use of eunuchs in very different contexts, see the general reflections of Patterson, *Slavery and Social Death*, pp. 299–333; and S. Tougher, *The Eunuch in Byzantine History* (London: Routledge, 2008), pp. 36–53.

21. Mounier, "La dynamique des interrelations politiques," p. 381. Meillassoux, *Anthropologie de l'esclavage*, p. 190, claims that the eunuch "pushes the anti-family character of slavery to its limit."

22. J. Dumas, "Les perles de nacre du sultanat: Les princesses ottomanes (mi-XVe–mi-XVIIIe)" (PhD diss., École des Hautes Études en Sciences Sociales, 2013), p. 121.

23. C. de Oliveira Gomes (*La cité tyrannique. Histoire politique de la Grèce archaïque* (Rennes: Presses Universitaires de Rennes, 2008) has suggested reading the opposition to the tyrannical model in the classical city in terms of resistance, based on Clastres's writings. I am doubtful, however, that it is possible to speak of a growth of the state apparatus in the tyrannical cities (cf. my review in *Annales HSC*, Sept.–Oct. 2009). But the perspective of Oliveira Gomes, who does not address the question of public slavery, points to something altogether true about the classical city, particularly when she evokes the existence of a "state-inflected ideology of the stateless society" (p. 148).

24. P. Clastres, *Society against the State: Essays in Political Anthropology* (New York: Zone Books, 1989 [1st ed. Paris: Minuit, 1974]). The term "Copernican revolution" is a reference to the first chapter of his book, "Copernicus and the Savages" pp. 7–26.

25. P. Clastres, *Recherches d'anthropologie politique* (Paris: Seuil, 1980), pp. 204–206.

26. Clastres, *Society against the State*, p. 212. Clastres adds: "Primitive society, then, is a society from which nothing escapes, which lets nothing get outside itself, for all the exits are blocked" (p. 212).

27. Ibid., p. 217.

28. Clastres, *Recherches d'anthropologie politique*, pp. 105 and 175–177.

29. Ibid., p. 104; and Clastres, *Society against the State*, p. 217.

30. Clastres, *Recherches d'anthropologie politique*, p. 148.

31. N. Loraux, "Notes sur l'un, le deux et le multiple," in *L'esprit des Lois sauvages. Pierre Clastres ou une nouvelle anthropologie politique*, ed. M. Abensour (Paris: Seuil, 1987), pp. 155–171, quotation p. 157. *Society against the State* played a determining role in the psychoanalytic turn in the historian Nicole Loraux's

writings. She saw the "aversion to the state," as understood by Clastres, as a process that could be formulated in terms of the unconscious and repression. Hence the "division" of the city (N. Loraux, *The Divided City: On Memory and Forgetting in Ancient Athens* [New York: Zone Books, 2002 (1st ed. Paris: Payot, 1997)]) is worth reading in light of the Clastrian notion of indivision, which Loraux interprets as "division glimpsed, assessed in terms of its full destructiveness, and lucidly rejected" (Loraux, "Notes sur l'un, le deux, et le multiple," p. 164).

32. Loraux, "Notes sur l'un, le deux et le multiple," p. 162.

33. Aristotle, *Politics*, 3.1277b.

34. Ibid., 4.1295b19–4.1295b22.

35. See the remarks of C. Castoriadis, *Les carrefours du labyrinthe. La montée de l'insignifiance* (Paris: Seuil, 1996), p. 22: "There may be, there was, and we hope there will again be stateless societies, that is, those without a hierarchically organized bureaucratic apparatus separated from society and dominating it. . . . But a society without explicit institutions of power is an absurdity, into which both Marx and anarchism sank."

36. Clastres, *Society against the State*, p. 212; and Clastres, *Recherches d'anthropologie politique*, p. 109.

37. Loraux, "Notes sur l'un, le deux et le multiple," p. 164.

38. See the suggestive remarks of P. Legendre, *De la société comme texte. Linéaments d'une anthropologie dogmatique* (Paris: Fayard, 2001), esp. p. 24: "Every society, in order to exist, transposes and transcends a logical void by making it the place of darkness and shadow, which we call a scene, where the equivalent of a scenario will be written, the discourse of images that bear within them the workings of institutions; in other words, it elaborates by means of montage a constitutive scenography."

39. P. Vidal Naquet, "Une civilisation de la parole politique," in his *Le chasseur noir. Formes de pensée et formes de société dans le monde grec* (Paris: Maspero, 1981), p. 31.

40. See esp. J.-P. Vernant, "Ambiguïté et renversement. Sur la structure énigmatique d'*Oedipe roi*," in J.-P. Vernant and P. Vidal-Naquet, *Mythe et tragédie en Grèce ancienne*, vol. 1 (Paris: Maspero, 1972), pp. 99–132.

41. Sophocles, *Oedipus Tyrannus*, line 298.

42. Ibid., line 353.

43. Ibid., lines 437–438.

44. Ibid., line 451.

45. Ibid., lines 500–505 [translation modified—trans.].

46. Ibid., lines 720–722.

47. Ibid., line 716.

48. J. Bollack, *L'Oedipe roi de Sophocle. Le texte et ses interprétations* (Lille: Presses Universitaires de Lille, 1990), vol. 4: *Commentaire, troisième partie*, p. 748.

49. Sophocles, *Oedipus Tyrannus*, line 764.

50. Ibid., lines 760–762: "He clasped my hand in supplication, begging me to send him to the fields and to the pastures, so that he could be as far as possible from the city."

51. Sophocles, *Oedipus Tyrannus*, line 1123.
52. Bollack, *L'Oedipe roi de Sophocle*, 4: 733.
53. P. Vidal-Naquet, *Le miroir brisé. Tragédie athénienne et politique* (Paris: Belles Lettres, 2002).
54. Sophocles, *Oedipus Tyrannus*, lines 1117–1118 [translation modified. The Loeb translation reads, "He was as trusty a servant of Laius as any, although but a shepherd"—trans.].
55. See the discussion in Bollack, *L'Oedipe roi de Sophocle*, 4: 729–730.
56. Sophocles, *Oedipus Tyrannus*, line 410.
57. M. Foucault, "Le savoir d'Oedipe," *Leçons sur la volonté de savoir. Cours au Collège de France (1970–1971)* (Paris: Gallimard-Seuil, 2011 [1971]), pp. 223–253; and *Du gouvernement des vivants. Cours au Collège de France (1979–1980)* (Paris: Gallimard-Seuil, 2012 [1980]). Foucault formulates the object of inquiry as follows: "One cannot lead men without performing operations in the order of the true, operations that are always in excess of what is useful and necessary to govern effectively. The manifestation of truth is required by, or entailed by, or linked to the activity of governing and exercising power in a way that always extends beyond the aim of government and the effective means to achieve it" (*Du gouvernement des vivants*, p. 18).
58. Foucault, *Du gouvernement des vivants*, p. 26.
59. Foucault, "Le savoir d'Oedipe," p. 225. Foucault adds: "It is therefore not so much the 'ignorance' or 'unconsciousness' of Oedipus that appears in the foreground of Sophocles' tragedy as the multiplicity of kinds of knowledge, the diversity of the procedures that produce them, and the struggle on the part of the authorities that is played out through their confrontation" (p. 245).
60. Foucault, *Du gouvernement des vivants*, p. 40.
61. Foucault, "Le savoir d'Oedipe," p. 229.
62. Sophocles, *Oedipus Tyrannus*, line 132.
63. Vernant, "Ambiguïté et renversement," p. 108.
64. Sophocles, *Oedipus Tyrannus*, lines 374–375.
65. Cf. C. Segal, Oedipus Tyrannus: *Tragic Heroism and the Limits of Knowledge* (Oxford: Oxford University Press, 2001).
66. Sophocles, *Oedipus Tyrannus*, line 380 [translation modified—trans.].
67. Vernant, "Ambiguïté et renversement," p. 114.
68. Foucault ("Le savoir d'Oedipe," p. 250) asserts: "What disappears with the defeat of Oedipus is that old Oriental form of the scholar king, the king who, by virtue of his knowledge, holds, governs, guides, and puts right the city and keeps disasters and plagues away from it."
69. See all the evidence in J. Haubold, *Homer's People: Epic Poetry and Social Formation* (Cambridge: Cambridge University Press, 2000), p. 197.
70. Cf. Segal, Oedipus Tryannus, p. 103; and esp. C. Segal, *Sophocles' Tragic World: Divinity, Nature, Society* (Cambridge, MA: Harvard University Press, 1995), p. 153.
71. Sophocles, *Oedipus Tyrannus*, lines 1350–1353 [translation modified—trans.].
72. Ibid., lines 118 and 756–762.

73. Ibid., lines 13 and 1178.
74. Plato, *Phaedo*, 116b.
75. Ibid., 116c–d.
76. Ibid., 118 [translation slightly modified—trans.]
77. Commentaries on *Phaedo* devote only a few lines at most to this dialogue. Cf. R. Loriaux, *Le* Phédon *de Platon. Traduction et commentaire*, vol. 2 (84b–118a) (Namur: Presses Universitaires de Namur, 1975); K. Dorter, *Plato's* Phaedo: *An Interpretation* (Toronto: University of Toronto Press, 1982); D. Bostock, *Plato's* Phaedo (Oxford: Clarendon Press, 1986); R. Gotschalk, *Loving and Dying: A Reading of Plato's* Phaedo, Symposium *and* Phaedrus (Lanham, MD: University Press of America, 2001).
78. In addition to J.-L. David's famous painting *The Death of Socrates* (1787), see esp. Benjamin West's 1756 painting of the same name.
79. Plato, *Phaedo*, 117c: "Up to that time most of us had been able to restrain our tears fairly well, but when we watched him drinking and saw that he had drunk the poison, we could do so no longer, but in spite of myself my tears rolled down in floods, so that I wrapped my face in my cloak and wept for myself; for it was not for him that I wept, but for my own misfortune in being deprived of such a friend."
80. On this point, see the remarks of R. Burger, *The* Phaedo: *A Platonic Labyrinth* (New Haven, CT: Yale University Press, 1984), pp. 211–212.
81. Plato, *Phaedo*, 116d and 117e.
82. J. Derrida, *Spectres de Marx. L'État de la dette, le travail du deuil et la nouvelle Internationale* (Paris: Galilée, 1993), pp. 31–32. By "hauntology," Derrida means the specter's mode of presence—beyond the distinction between presence and absence, life and death, visible and invisible—which corresponds to the logic of haunting.
83. Plato, *Phaedo*, 115d.
84. D. Kamen, "The Manumission of Socrates: A Rereading of Plato's *Phaedo*," *Classical Antiquity* 32 (2013): 78–100.
85. Cf. Plato, *Phaedo*, 85b. Socrates claims to be the *homodoulos* and *hieros* of Apollo.
86. Derrida, *Spectres de Marx*, p. 27. See the "visor effect" produced by the spectral apparition invoked by Derrida, pp. 26–27: "That thing is looking at us, however, and sees us not seeing it even when it is there."
87. Acts 8:27–8:38, New King James Version [translation modified—trans.].
88. Acts of the Apostles 10:1–10:48.
89. Acts of the Apostles 10:39, with the commentary of P. Fabien, *Philippe "l'evangéliste" au tournant de la mission dans les Actes des apôtres. Philippe, Simon le Magicien et l'eunuque éthiopien* (Paris: Cerf, 2010), p. 261. "The event anticipates prophetically the universal destiny of the Gospel," writes Daniel Marguerat in *Les Actes des Apôtres 1–12. Commentaires du Nouveau Testament* (Geneva: Labor et Fides, 2007), p. 312.
90. Marguerat, *Les Actes des Apôtres 1–12*, p. 312.
91. Acts of the Apostles 8:40.
92. According to Fabien, *Philippe "l'évangéliste" au tournant de la mission*, the scene also provides an interpretive key to the Acts itself, as Luke believed it

would be read: Philip plays the role of the author (Luke) and the Ethiopian eunuch that of the implied reader.

93. See, for example, Plato, *Protagoras*, 329a, and the condemnation of orators who, "just like books, [are] incapable of either answering you or putting a question of their own"; and Plato, *Phaedrus*, 275d, on the subject of written discourses: "You might think they spoke as if they had intelligence, but if you question them, wishing to know about their sayings, they always say only one and the same thing." Through that "deathly repetition," "writing moves far from the truth of the thing itself, the truth of speech and the truth that opens onto speech" (J. Derrida, "La pharmacie de Platon," *La Dissémination* [Paris: Seuil, 1972], pp. 169 and 171).

94. II Kings 5. On the connections, cf. Fabien, *Philippe "l'évangéliste" au tournant de la mission dans Les Actes des apôtres*, pp. 180–181.

95. On the different readings proposed, see ibid., pp. 192–195.

96. Acts of the Apostles 2:1–2:13.

97. Marguerat, *Les Actes des Apôtres 1–12*, p. 302.

98. Homer, *Odyssey*, 1.22–1.23.

99. Saint Augustine, *Exposition of the Psalms: The Works of Saint Augustine, a Translation for the 21st Century*, ed. John E. Rotelle, trans. Maria Boulding, 20 vols. (Hyde Park, NY: New City Press, 1990–), 17: 463.

100. Acts of the Apostles 1:8. Cf. F. Jabini, "Witness to the End of the World: A Missional Reading of Acts 8:26–40," *Conspectus* 13 (2012): 51–72.

101. See M. B. Kartzow and H. Moxnes's recent article "Complex Identities, Ethnicity, Gender and Religion in the Story of the Ethiopian Eunuch (Acts 8:26–40)," *Religion & Theology* 17 (2010): 184–204; and S. D. Burke, "Reading the Ethiopian Eunuch as Eunuch: Queering the Book of Acts" (PhD diss., University of California Berkeley, 2009).

102. Strabo, *Geography*, 17.1. 54.

103. On the Church Fathers' reading, cf. Kartzow and Moxnes, "Complex Identities," pp. 194–195, and the remarks of Burke, "Reading the Ethiopian Eunuch as Eunuch," pp. 12–15.

104. See esp. G. L. Byron, *Symbolic Blackness and Ethnic Difference in Early Christian Literature* (London: Routledge, 2002), pp. 109–115; and C. Davis, "Black Catholic Theology: A Historical Perspective," *Theological Studies* 61, no. 4 (2000): 656–671.

105. D. K. Williams, "Acts," in *True to Our Native Land: An African-American Commentary on the New Testament*, ed. B. K. Blount (Minneapolis: Fortress Press, 2007), pp. 225–228, quotation p. 227, emphasis in the original.

106. Fabien, *Philippe "l'évangéliste" au tournant de la mission*, p. 205.

107. Cf. Byron, *Symbolic Blackness and Ethnic Difference*, pp. 44–45 and 50.

108. Fabien, *Philippe "l'évangéliste" au tournant de la mission*, p. 303; in *Symbolic Blackness and Ethnic Difference*, Byron evokes a "social and cultural and ethnic outsider" (p. 112).

109. Marguerat, *Les Actes des Apôtres 1–12*, p. 313.

110. Isaiah 53:7–53:8 [translation modified—trans.].

111. Marguerat, *Les Actes des Apôtres 1–12*, p. 309.

112. Isaiah 53:12.
113. Cf. Marguerat, *Les Actes des Apôtres 1–12*, pp. 309–310.
114. J. Calvin, *Commentaires bibliques. Les Actes des Apôtres* (Aix-en-Provence: Kérygma, 2006).
115. Theophylact of Ochrid, *In Defense of Eunuchs*.
116. M. Foucault, *Le courage de la vérité. Le gouvernement de soi et des autres II (cours au Collège de France, 1984)* (Paris: Gallimard-Seuil, 2009), pp. 3–31.
117. Ibid., pp. 26–27.

Conclusion

1. Vidal-Naquet, *Le chasseur noir*, pp. 21–35.
2. J.-P. Vernant, *Les origines de la pensée grecque* (Paris: Presses Universitaires de France, 1962), p. 44.
3. Cf. M. Detienne, "Des pratiques d'assemblée aux formes du politique. Pour un comparatisme expérimental et constructif entre historiens et anthropologues," in *Qui veut prendre la parole*, ed. M. Detienne (Paris: Seuil, 2003), pp. 13–30.
4. Arendt, *The Human Condition*, p. 198.
5. C. Castoriadis, "La *polis* grecque et la création de la démocratie," in *Les carrefours du labyrinthe*, vol. 2, *Domaines de l'homme* (Paris: Seuil, 1986), pp. 325–382.
6. N. Loraux, "Aux origines de la démocratie. Sur la 'transparence démocratique,'" *Raison Présente* 49 (1978): 3–13, quotation p. 4.
7. V. Azoulay and P. Ismard, "Les lieux du politique dans l'Athènes classique. Entre structures institutionelles, idéologie civique et pratiques sociales," in *Athènes et le politique. Dans le sillage de Claude Mossé*, ed. F. de Polignac and P. Schmitt (Paris: Albin Michel, 2007), pp. 271–309.
8. Weiss, *Sklave der Stadt*, pp. 180–183; and Lenski, "*Servi Publici* in Late Antiquity," pp. 348–350.
9. Lenski, "*Servi Publici* in Late Antiquity," p. 351.
10. *I. Ephesos*, Ia, 18c, lines 13–18. The mention of *dēmosioi douloi*, however, does not in this case indicate the existence of a particular category of *dēmosioi*; it is merely the Greek translation of the Latin term *servi publici*.
11. Ibid., pp. 352–353.
12. *I. Ephesos*, Ia, 25, lines 28–40.
13. *I. Kybira* 41, lines 5–6, following the reading proposed in J. Nollé, "Epigraphica varia," ZPE 48 (1982): 267–273.
14. E. Kantorowicz, *The King's Two Bodies: A Study in Mediaeval Political Theology* (Princeton, NJ: Princeton University Press, 1957), pp. 7 and 272.
15. Ibid., p. 272.
16. A. Boureau, *Histoires d'un historien, Kantorowicz* (Paris: Gallimard, 1990), p. 149.
17. Kantorowicz, *The King's Two Bodies*, p. 497.

18. M. Gauchet, "Des deux corps du roi au pouvoir sans corps. Christianisme et politique," *Le Débat* 14 (1981): 133–157, quotation p. 134.

19. Ibid., p. 146.

20. Aristotle, *Politics*, 1276b [translation modified—trans.].

21. Thucydides, *The History of the Peloponnesian War*, 3.62.3–3.62.4.

22. Democratic cities, in the sense that most historians understand that notion, certainly had no monopoly on public slavery. I do not believe, however, that the classical city, and especially that of the Hellenistic period, can be understood in terms of the distinction between oligarchic regimes and democratic systems forged by Athenian political thought in the fifth century BCE. In fact, historians often consider cities that, in the Hellenistic period, thought of themselves as entirely democratic to have been oligarchic regimes. I believe rather that there is a single way of conceiving the link between the community and the sphere of power, one that transcends the canonical distinction between democratic system and oligarchic regime, and which, for example, unites fourth-century Athens and second-century Miletus beyond the differences in their institutions. At its core lies the principle of coincidence between the sphere of the *koinon* and that of the *archē*, which rules out any principle of representation.

23. K. Axelos, *Lettres à un jeune penseur* (Paris: Minuit, 1996), pp. 57–58.

24. See esp. J. Fishkin's writings, esp. *Democracy and Deliberation: New Directions for Democratic Reform* (New Haven, CT: Yale University Press, 1991).

25. Castoriadis, *La montée de l'insignifiance*, p. 192.

Bibliography

This bibliography does not include all the works (sources and historical studies) required in the writing of this book; for these, readers may refer to the notes. It is simply an obviously nonexhaustive overview of the recent studies that open the way for a new history of slavery in ancient Greece, one that is not confined to a comparison with the colonial societies of the New World. For an exhaustive bibliography, one may now refer to the Web site "Bibliography of Slavery and World Slaving," run by the Virginia Center for Digital History at the University of Virginia, which reproduces with annual updates Joseph Calder Miller's *Slavery and Slaving in World History: A Bibliography*, 2 vols. (New York: M. E. Sharpe, 1999), begun in the 1970s.

Listed as well are the principal works on public slavery in the Greek cities and those on public or royal slavery that can accommodate a comparative analysis.

For a Decompartmentalized History of Slavery

Allain, J., ed. *The Legal Understanding of Slavery: From the Historical to the Contemporary.* Oxford: Oxford University Press, 2012.
Beswick, S., and J. Spaulding, eds. *African Systems of Slavery.* Trenton, NJ: Africa World Press, 2010.
Botte, R., and A. Stella, eds. *Couleurs de l'esclavage sur les deux rives de la Méditerranée. Moyen Âge–XXe siècle.* Paris: Karthala, 2012.
Campbell, G., ed. *The Structure of Slavery in Indian Ocean Africa and Asia.* London: Frank Cass, 2004.
Campbell, G., and A. Stanziani, eds. *Debt and Slavery in the Mediterranean and Atlantic Worlds.* London: Pickering and Chatto, 2013.

———. *Bonded Labour and Debt in the Indian Ocean.* London: Pickering and Chatto, 2013.
Chatterjee, I. *Gender, Slavery and Law in Colonial India.* Oxford: Oxford University Press, 1999.
Chatterjee, I., and R. M. Eaton, eds. *Slavery and South Asian History.* Bloomington: Indiana University Press, 2007.
Condominas, G., ed. *Formes extrêmes de dépendance. Contributions à l'étude de l'esclavage en Asie du Sud-Est.* Paris: École des Hautes Études en Sciences Sociales, 1998.
Cottias, M., A. Stella, and B. Vincent, eds. *Esclavage et dépendances serviles. Histoire comparée.* Paris: L'Harmattan, 2007.
Dal Lago, E., and C. Katsari, eds. *Slave Systems, Ancient and Modern.* Cambridge: Cambridge University Press, 2008.
Dias, M. S. F., ed. *Legacies of Slavery: Comparative Perspectives.* Cambridge: Cambridge Scholars Publishing, 2007.
Droits, l'esclavage, la question de l'homme. L'Histoire, religion, philosophie, droit. 4 vols. Paris: Presses Universitaires de France, 2009–2011.
Finley, M. I. *Ancient Slavery and Modern Ideology.* New York: Vintage, 1980.
Fisher, A. G., and H. G. Fisher. *Slavery and Muslim Society in Africa: The Institution in Saharan and Sudanic Africa and the Trans-Saharan Trade.* London: C. Hurst, 1970.
Flaig, E. *Weltgeschichte der Sklaverei.* Munich: Beck, 2009.
Geary, D., and K. Vlassopoulos, eds. *Slavery, Citizenship and the State in Classical Antiquity and the Modern Americas.* Special issue of the *European Review of History* 16, no. 3 (2009).
Grenouilleau, O. *Qu'est-ce que l'esclavage? Une histoire globale.* Paris: Gallimard, 2014.
———, ed. *Esclaves. Une humanité en sursis.* Rennes: Presses Universitaires de Rennes, 2012.
Hanss, S., and J. Schiel, eds. *Mediterranean Slavery Revisited (500–1800). Neue Perspektiven auf mediterrane Sklaverei (500–1800),* Zurich: Chronos, 2014.
Heinen, H., ed. *Menschenraub, Menschenhandel und Sklaverei in antiker und moderner Perspektive.* Stuttgart: F. Steiner, 2008.
Hernaes, P., and T. Iversen, eds. *Slavery across Time and Space: Studies in Slavery in Medieval Europe and Africa.* Trondheim: Dept. of History, 2002.
Hodkinson, S., and D. Geary, eds. *Slaves and Religions in Graeco-Roman Antiquity and Modern Brazil.* Cambridge: Cambridge Scholars Publishing, 2012.
Kleijwegt, M., ed. *The Faces of Freedom: The Manumission and Emancipation of Slaves in Old World and New World Slavery.* Leiden: Brill, 2006.
Klein, M. *Slavery and Colonial Rule in French West Africa.* Cambridge: Cambridge University Press, 1998.
Klein, M. A., ed. *Breaking the Chains: Slavery, Bondage, and Emancipation in Modern Africa and Asia.* Madison: University of Wisconsin Press, 1993.
Kolchin, P. *Unfree Labor: American Slavery and Russian Serfdom.* Cambridge, MA: Harvard University Press, 1988.
Kopytoff, I. "Slavery." *Annual Review of Anthropology* 11 (1982): 207–230.

Kopytoff, I., and S. Miers, eds. *Slavery in Africa: Historical and Anthropological Perspectives*. Madison: University of Wisconsin Press, 1977.
Lovejoy, P. E. *Transformations in Slavery: A History of Slavery in Africa*. 3rd ed. Cambridge: Cambridge University Press, 2012.
Major, A. *Slavery, Abolitionism and Empire in India, 1722–1843*. Liverpool: Liverpool University Press, 2012.
Médard, H., and S. Doyle, eds. *Slavery in the Great Lakes Region of East Africa*. Oxford: James Currey, 2008.
Meillassoux, C., ed. *L'esclavage en Afrique précoloniale*. Paris: Maspero, 1975.
———. *Anthropologie de l'esclavage. Le ventre de fer et d'argent*. Paris: Presses Universitaires de France, 1986.
Miller, J. *The Problem of Slavery as History: A Global Approach*. New Haven, CT: Yale University Press, 2012.
Patterson, O. *Slavery and Social Death: A Comparative Study*. Cambridge: MA: Harvard University Press, 1982.
Reid, A., ed. *Slavery, Bondage and Dependency in Southeast Asia*. St. Lucia: University of Queensland Press, 1983.
Rotman, Y. *Les esclaves et l'esclavage. De la Méditerranée antique à la Méditerranée médiévale (VIe–XIe siècle)*. Paris: Belles Lettres, 2004.
Slavery and Abolition: A Journal of Slave and Post-Slave Studies. 1980–.
Stanziani, A. *Sailors, Slaves and Immigrants: Bondage in the Indian Ocean World, 1750–1914*. New York: Palgrave Macmillan, 2014.
Stilwell, S. *Slavery and Slaving in African History*. Cambridge: Cambridge University Press, 2014.
Testart, A. *L'esclave, la dette et le pouvoir. Études de sociologie comparative*. Paris: Errance, 2001.
Watson, J. L., ed. *Asian and African Systems of Slavery*. Oxford: Blackwell, 1980.
Willis, J. R., ed. *Slaves and Slavery in Muslim Africa*. London: Frank Cass, 1985.
Witzenrath, C., ed. *Eurasian Slavery, Ransom, and Abolition in World History, 1200–1860*. Farnham, Surrey, U.K.: Ashgate, 2015.
Yates, R. D. "Slavery in Early China: A Socio-Cultural Approach." *Journal of East Asian Archaeology* 3 (2002): 283–331.
Zeuske, M. *Handbuch Geschichte der Sklaverei. Ein Globalgeschichte von den Anfängen bis zu dem Gegenwart*. Berlin: de Gruyter, 2013.

Public and Royal Slavery: Bases for Comparison

Amitai, R. "The Mamluk Institutions, or One Thousand Years of Military Service in the Islamic World." In *Arming Slaves, from Classical Times to the Modern Age*, edited by C. L. Brown and P. D. Morgan, pp. 40–78. New Haven, CT: Yale University Press, 2006.
Ayalon, D. *Studies on the Mamluks of Egypt (1250–1517)*. London: Variorum Reprints, 1977.
———. *Le phénomène mamelouk dans l'Orient islamique*. Paris: Presses Universitaires de France, 1996.

Babaie, S. et al., eds. *Slaves of the Shah: New Elites of Savafid Iran*. New York: I. B. Tauris, 2004.
Bazin, J. "Guerre et servitude à Ségou." In *L'esclavage en Afrique précoloniale*, edited by C. Meillassoux, pp. 135–181. Paris: Maspero, 1975.
Boulvert, G. *Esclaves et affranchis impériaux sous le Haut-Empire romain. Rôle politique et administratif*. Naples: Jovene, 1970.
Eder, W. Servitus Publica. *Untersuchungen zur Entsetehung, Entwicklung und Funktion der öffentlichen Sklaverei in Rom*. Wiesbaden: F. Steiner, 1980.
Falola, T. "System Power Relations and Social Interactions among Ibadan Slaves, 1850–1900." *African Economic History* 16 (1987): 95–114.
Izard, M. "Les captifs royaux dans l'ancien Yatenga." In *L'esclavage en Afrique précoloniale*, edited by C. Meillassoux, pp. 281–296. Paris: Maspero, 1975.
Kamar, S. "Service, Status, and Military Slavery in the Delhi Sultanate: Thirteenth and Fourteenth Centuries." In *Slavery and South Asian History*, edited by I. Chatterjee and R. M. Eaton, pp. 83–114. Bloomington: Indiana University Press, 2007.
Kentaro, S. "Slave Elites and the Saqaliba in al-Andalus in the Umayyad Period." In *Slave Elites in the Middle East and Africa*, edited by T. Miura and J. E. Philips, pp. 25–40. London: Kegan Paul International, 2000.
Loiseau, J. *Les Mamelouks (XIIIe–XVIe siècle). Une expérience du pouvoir dans l'Islam médiéval*. Paris: Seuil, 2014.
Miura, T., and J. E. Philips, eds. *Slave Elites in the Middle East and Africa*. London: Kegan Paul International, 2000.
Mounier, P. "La dynamique des interrelations politiques. Le cas du sultanat de Zinder." *Cahiers d'Études Africaines* 39 (1999): 367–386.
Olivier de Sardan, J.-P. "Captifs ruraux et esclaves impériaux du Songhay." In *L'esclavage en Afrique précoloniale*, edited by C. Meillassoux, pp. 99–134. Paris: Maspero, 1975.
Oualdi, M. *Esclaves et maîtres. Les Mamelouks des beys de Tunis du XVIIe siècle aux années 1880*. Paris: Publications de la Sorbonne, 2011.
Perrot, C. "Les captifs dans le royaume anyi du Ndénýé." In *L'esclavage et Afrique précoloniale*, edited by C. Meillassoux, pp. 351–388. Paris: Maspero, 1975.
Philipps, J. E. "Slave Officials in the Sokoto Caliphate." In *Slave Elites in the Middle East and Africa*, edited by T. Miura and J. E. Philips, pp. 215–234. London: Kegan Paul International, 2000.
Pipes, D. *Slave Soldiers and Islam: The Genesis of a Military System*. New Haven, CT: Yale University Press, 1981.
Ragib, Y. "Les esclaves publics aux premiers siècles de l'Islam." In *Figures de l'esclave au Moyen Âge et dans le monde moderne*, edited by H. Bresc, pp. 7–30. Paris: L'Harmattan, 1996.
Ringrose, K. *The Perfect Servant: Eunuchs and the Social Construction of Gender in Byzantium*. Chicago: University of Chicago Press, 2004.
Sok, K. "L'esclavage au Cambodge à l'époque moyenne à travers les codes, les inscriptions modernes d'Angkor et les chroniques royales." In *Formes extrêmes de dépendance: Contributions à l'étude de l'esclavage en Asie du Sud*, edited

by G. Condominas, pp. 315–341. Paris: École des Hautes Études en Sciences Sociales, 1998.
Stilwell, S. *Paradoxes of Power: The Kano "Mamluks" and Male Royal Slavery in the Sokoto Caliphate (1804–1903)*. Portsmouth, NH: Heinemann, 2004.
Tardits, C., ed. *Princes et serviteurs du royaume. Cinq études de monarchies africaines*. Paris: Société d'Ethnographie, 1987.
Terray, E. "La captivité dans le royaume abron du Gyaman." In *L'esclavage en Afrique précoloniale*, edited by C. Meillassoux, pp. 389–453. Paris: Maspero, 1975.
———. *Une histoire du royaume abron du Gyaman. Des origines à la conquête coloniale*. Paris: Karthala, 1995.
Testart, A. *La servitude volontaire*. Vol. 1, *Les morts d'accompagnement*. Vol. 2, *L'origine de l'État*. Paris: Errance, 2004.
Thomaz, L. F. "L'esclavage à Malacca au XVIe siècle d'après les sources portugaises." In *Formes extrêmes de dépendance. Contributions à l'étude de l'esclavage en Asie du Sud-Est*, edited by G. Condominas, pp. 357–386. Paris: École des Hautes Études en Sciences Sociales, 1998.
Tougher, S. *The Eunuch in Byzantine History and Society*. London: Routledge, 2008.
Ze'evi, D. "My Slave, My Son, My Lord: Slavery, Family and State in the Islamic Middle East." In *Slave Elites in the Middle East and Africa*, edited by T. Miura and J. E. Philips, pp. 71–79. London: Kegan Paul International, 2000.
Zlinsky, J. "Gemeineigentum am Beispiel der *servi publici*." In *Sklaverei und Freilassung im römischen Recht*, edited by T. Finkauer, pp. 317–326. Berlin: Springer, 2006.

Public Slavery in Ancient Greece

Bradley, K., and P. Cartledge, eds. *The Cambridge World History of Slavery: The Ancient Mediterranean World*. Cambridge: Cambridge University Press, 2011.
Cardinali, G. "Note di terminologia epigraphica. I. Dêmosioi." *Rendiconti della Reale Accademia dei Lincei* 17 (1908): 157–165.
Descat, R., and J. Andreau. *Esclaves en Grèce et à Rome*. Paris: Hachette, 2009.
Fragiadakis, C. *Die Attischen Sklavennamen von der spätarchaischen Epoche bis in die römische Kaiserzeit*. Athens: n.p., 1998.
Finley, M. I. *Economy and Society in Ancient Greece*. New York: Viking, 1982.
Fisher, N. *Slavery in Classical Greece*. London: Bristol Classical Press, 1995.
Garlan, Y. *Les esclaves en Grèce ancienne*. Rev. ed. Paris: La Découverte, 1995.
———. *Guerre et économie en Grèce ancienne*. Paris: La Découverte, 1989.
Heinen, H., ed. *Handwörterbuch der antiken Sklaverei* (HAS). CD-Rom. Stuttgart: F. Steiner, 2006.
Hunter, V. "Pittalacus and Eucles: Slaves in the Public Service of Athens." *Mouseion* 6 (2006): 1–13.
———. *Policing Athens: Social Control in the Attic Lawsuits, 420–320 B.C.* Princeton, NJ: Princeton University Press, 1994.
Jacob, O. *Les esclaves publics à Athènes*. Liège: Champion, 1928.

Klees, H. *Sklavenleben im klassischen Griechenland.* Stuttgart: F. Steiner, 1998.

Martin, T. R. "Silver Coins and Public Slaves in the Athenian Law of 375/4 B.C." In *Mnemata: Papers in Memory of Nancy M. Waggoner,* pp. 21–48. New York: American Numismatic Society, 1991.

Oliver, G. J. "Honours for a Public Slave at Athens (*IG* II² 502 + *Ag.* 1 1947; 302/301 B.C.)." In *Attika epigraphika. Meletes pros timèn tou Christian Habicht,* edited by A. Mathaiou. Athens: Ellīnikī Epigrafikī Etaireíra, 2009.

Plassart, A. "Les archers d'Athènes." *REG* 26 (1913): 151–213.

Schumacher, L. *Sklaverei in der Antike. Alltag und Schicksal der Unfreien.* Munich: C. H. Beck, 2001.

Silverio, O. *Untersuchungen zur Geschichte der attischen Staatsklaven.* Munich: Druck der Akademischen Buckdruckerei von F. Straub, 1900.

Stroud, R. S. "An Athenian Law on Silver Coinage." *Hesperia* 43 (1974): 157–188.

Tuci, P. "Arcieri sciti, esercito e Democrazia nell'Atene del V secolo A. C." *Aevum* 78 (2004): 3–18.

———. "Gli arcieri sciti nell'Atene del V Secolo A. C." In *Il cittadino, lo straniero, il barbaro fra integrazione et emarginzaione nell'Antichita,* edited by M. Gabriella, A. Bertinelli, and A. Donati, pp. 375–389. Rome: Bretschneider, 2005.

Waszynski, S. "Über die rechtliche Stellung der Staatsclaven in Athen." *Hermes* 34 (1899): 553–567.

Weiss, A. *Sklave der Stadt. Untersuchungen zur öffentlichen Sklaverei in den Städten des Römischen Reiches.* Stuttgart: F. Steiner, 2004.

Welwei, K.-W. "Öffentliche Sklaven *(dêmosioi, servi publici) I. Grieschisch.*" In *Handwörterbuch der antiken Sklarverei* (HAS), edited by H. Heinen. CD-Rom. Stuttgart: F. Steiner, 2006.

Acknowledgments

I benefited from privileged conditions while writing this book, something rarely achieved in academic life. This was particularly thanks to six months studying in a magical place—a Thebaid, as Pierre Vidal-Naquet said: Harvard University's Center for Hellenic Studies in Washington, DC. I would like to thank all the members of the Center and in particular its president, Gregory Nagy; the head of the library, Temple Wright; and his associate, Lanah Koelle.

I wish to thank the two editors of the French version of this book, Séverine Nikel and Patrick Boucheron, who supported the project from the beginning, and whose advice and expansive intuitions contributed toward fashioning a book from a vague research interest. I am also profoundly honored to see this book enjoy a second life in English. I would particularly like to thank Sharmila Sen, executive editor-at-large at Harvard University Press, and Jane Marie Todd, who in my view has produced a wonderful translation.

All my gratitude extends as well to Sara Forsdyke and Josiah Ober, who invited me to present the first results of this research at their respective universities, the University of Michigan in Ann Arbor and Stanford University, and who encouraged me to pursue this study.

This book is not the revised version of a thesis or dissertation already produced within an academic context. If, as is customary, I were to express my thanks to the members of a committee for their valuable advice, that committee would be only imaginary. For better or for worse, it would include more accomplices and friends than austere and rigorous teachers. Among the friends and colleagues who helped me with their expertise and encouragement, I would like especially to thank for their attentive reading, critiques, and suggestions—in a word, for their great intellectual generosity—two friends who played the role of first readers: Vincent Azoulay, once again and always, as I write almost nothing that is not the result of a long dialogue with him; and Marie Goupy, a philosopher and specialist in Carl Schmitt, who takes no small interest in anything having to do with the question of the state.

Finally, this imaginary committee would invite to its table two men who, sadly, are no longer with us. The initial inspiration for this book came from a diligent reading of the works of these extraordinary figures, both jurists and anthropologists, to whose memory I express my gratitude: Alain Testart and Yan Thomas.

Index

abolitionists, 4, 81–82
accounting processes, 39–40, 86–88, 128
Acts of the Apostles, 112, 120–125
Aeschines, 31, 38, 51, 62, 68–70
Aeschylus, 91
Afonso de Albuquerque, 57
Against Timarchus, 68–69
Agamemnon, 17
Agasicles, 67
Alcinous, 17
Alexander, 17
anagrapheus, 87, 89–90
anamnēsis, 99–100
Anaxilas, 31–32
anceocracy, 108
Ancient Economy, The, 76
Andocides, 46, 67, 78
antiliteracy laws, 80–81
Antiphates, 38, 70
antiquity references, 4–7
Apollo, 39, 59, 75, 103, 113, 115, 120
Apollonius, 52, 65
archē, 12, 52–53, 83–85, 90, 106, 134
archē basilikē, 27, 35–36
Archippe, 51
Arendt, Hannah, 128, 135

Aristonicus War, 73
Aristophanes, 14, 37, 45, 67, 89
Aristotle: civic institutions and, 37; philosophy of, 1–2, 133–134; on public slavery, 50–53, 61, 102; on rulers, 110; writings by, 51, 53, 95, 102, 133–134
Artemis, 39, 46, 63, 75, 87
artisans, 11, 16, 23–25, 46–47
Asclepius, 39, 48, 66, 102, 118, 120
atimia, 68, 77–78
Augustine, 123
Axelos, Kostas, 134

Bacchylides, 20
Barros, João de, 57
Berry, Henry, 80
Black Code of 1865, 62
"body politic," 132–133
Bollack, Jean, 114
bookkeeping operations, 40–42, 46–47, 86–88, 128

Calvin, John, 124
Candace, Queen, 120, 122–124
Chremonidean War, 71
Christianity, 4, 112, 120–125, 132
Christy, John, 1

Cicero, 54–55
citizenship: defining, 27, 55–56; full, 73, 77–79; granting of, 65–68, 73–79
city-state, 104–105, 109–112
civic ideology, 71, 88, 106, 111–112. *See also* democratic ideology
civic institutions, 28, 37–38, 89, 94, 129
civic life: functions for, 53–54; operation of, 5, 33, 40; realms of, 129; workings of, 76–77, 88, 93, 133–134
civic order, 3–5, 13, 36–42, 55, 99
civic organization, 36–37
civic seals, 40–42
civic stamps, 40–42
civil servants, 2–4, 8, 105–106, 132
Civil War, 1, 2, 5
Clastres, Pierre, 109–111
Cleidemus, 23
Clytemnestra, 17
Cobb, Thomas, 2
Cocalus, King, 23–24
colonial slavery, 4–7, 57–58, 81, 100–101. *See also* slavery
commercial activities, 40–42, 83–88
Cornelius, 121
counterfeit money, 40–41, 83–86
Cratinus, 45
Creon, 116
Crito, 118–119
currency verifier, 3, 40–41, 49, 55, 60, 83–87

Daedalus, 11, 20, 22–25, 65–66, 96
Dataleis, 26–27
David, Jacques-Louis, 118
Death of Socrates, 118
Demetrius, 39, 65–66, 102
dēmiourgikai technai, 92–93, 96
dēmiourgos, 11, 15–26, 29–34
democratic ideology, 54, 81–83, 88–92, 102
democratic system: foundation for, 92, 135; order of knowledge and, 3, 11, 80–102; philosophy and, 96, 106, 134–135; public slavery and, 3–4, 11–12, 25, 33–34, 130–131
Demodocus, 17, 18
dēmosioi, 2–4, 8–12, 15, 21–22. *See also* public slavery
Demosthenes, 38, 40, 50, 60, 68, 81
Derrida, Jacques, 119
Description of Greece, 103
Diderot, Denis, 119
Diodorus Siculus, 22–23, 32
Diomedes, 17, 20–21
Dion, 71
Dionysus, 37, 45
Diophantus, 38, 50
discipline, 42–43
Dolon, 17, 20–21
Douglass, Frederick, 81
Drimacus, 41–42

eleutheria leitourgia, 12, 54, 130
Eleven, the, 43, 117
Elisha, 122
Elizabeth I, Queen, 132
Epicrates, 70
Epigonus, 64, 73
Epimetheus, 91
Erechtheus, 22
Eucles, 39, 86–88
Eumaeus, 15–16, 18, 26
Eumedes, 20
Eumenus II, 46, 51
Eupalamus, 22
Eupolis, 45
Eurybates, 17
Eutuchides, 48, 52

Fabien, Patrick, 123
Finley, Moses I., 4–5, 33, 76–78, 100
Fisher, Nick, 69
Foucault, Michel, 82, 115, 126
freedmen, 63, 67–73, 76–79

INDEX

Frogs, 89
Frontisi-Ducroux, Françoise, 24

Garlan, Yvon, 72
Gauthier, Philippe, 72
Geneva Convention, 6
Gernet, Louis, 21
Glaucon, 69
Glotz, Gustave, 40
Gorgias, 97–98
Greco-Roman slavery, 4–13, 74, 133. *See also* slavery
Greek literature, 120, 125
"Greek miracle," 5, 55, 76, 134
Greek political philosophy, 3, 31, 54, 106, 109, 127–130

Halkin, Léon, 68
Hansen, Mogens, 105
hauntology, 119–120
Hector, 20–21
Hegesander, 69–70
Hemithea, 104
Heraclides Lembus, 31
Heraclitus, 110
Hermogenes, 53
Herodotus, 30–32, 107
Hesiod, 24, 91
Hippocrates, 91
Histoire de l'esclavage dans l'Antiquité (History of slavery in antiquity), 4
Homer, 15–17
hupēresia, 53, 90
Hyperbolus, 46, 67

Iliad, The, 17, 20, 127
Isaiah, 121–124
Izard, Michel, 58

Jacob, Oscar, 10–11, 36, 46, 50, 69
Jacotot, Joseph, 98
Jesus Christ, 120–121, 124–125, 133
Jocasta, 113–115

Kallicratēs, 59
Kallinous, 59
Kantorowicz, Ernst, 132–133
"kinship privilege," 65–68, 72, 78, 101–102, 130
Klēomēnēs, 59
knowledge: education and, 81, 96–102, 115; order of, 3, 11, 80–102; power and, 24, 34, 81–92, 98–101, 116; servile, 100–102; slavery and, 80–102, 115; specialized , 100–102
koinōnia, 61, 105–106, 133–134
Kronos, 24
Kychnus, 103–104

Laerces, 17
Laius, 112–114
Lamian War, 70
Laodice, Queen, 47
Lavell, Brian, 30–31
leitourgia, 12, 54, 130
Leodes, 19–20
Leōn, 39
Life of Aesop, The, 37
Lissarrague, François, 44
Loraux, Nicole, 110
Luke, Saint, 121–124
Lysias, 66, 89–90
Lysistrata, 45

Maeandrius, 31–32
magistracy: functions of, 35–42, 48, 52–53, 106; priests and, 47–49; responsibilities of, 27–28, 83–90
"man of Tenedos," 103–104
Marcus Aurelius, 131
Median Wars, 31, 44
Medon, 18–20
Meillassoux, Claude, 108
Melantheus, 18
Memorabilia, 96
Meno, 97–100
Merion, 17

Metis, 24
Micythus, 31–32
military operations, 39–40
military service, 30–31, 56, 107
military technology, 101
Milledge, John, 1
Minos, 22–25, 96
Mithridatic War, 72

Naaman, 122
Nachtigal, Gustav, 107
"natural body," 132–133
Nicolas of Damascus, 31
Nicomachean Ethics, 61
Nicomachus, 66–67, 88–90
Nicomedes III, 47, 51, 75
Nicophon, 46, 51

Ober, Josiah, 93–94
Odysseus, 15–21, 25
Odyssey, The, 16–17, 20, 123
Oedipus, 112–117, 125–126
Oedipus Tyrannus, 112–117, 125–126
Opsigonus, 39, 52
Ovid, 24

Palamedes, 25
Pasiphaë, 22
Patrias, 15, 28–29, 34
Patterson, Orlando, 71
Paul, Saint, 43, 123
Pausanias, 9, 23, 32, 103–104
Peisistratus, 30–31
Peloponnesian War, 134
Penelope, 17
Periander, 31
Pericles, 2, 7, 36, 65, 76, 134
Peritas, 87
Persicus, Paullus Fabius, 63
Peter, Saint, 120–121
Petronius, 85
Phaedo, 43, 97, 112, 117–119, 125
Phaleas, 50

Phemius, 15, 17, 19–20
Phereclus, 17
Pherecydus, 20, 22
Philip, 112, 120–124
Philippus, 64
Philoitius, 18
Philonome, 104
Phocion, 43
Pittalacus, 62, 69–70, 74
plantation slavery, 1–6, 81–82. *See also* slavery
Plato: philosophy of, 36, 96–99, 110–112, 118–119, 122; on public slavery, 53, 62, 130; writings by, 36, 43–45, 97–100, 106, 112, 117–119, 125
Pliny the Younger, 43
Plowden, 132
police officers, 12, 42, 44–45
polis, 42, 56, 104–105, 109–112, 130–135
politeia, 77, 133–134
political activities, 50, 92–93, 129–130, 135
"political body," 132–133
political competence, 35–36, 91–93
political order, 8, 27, 92–95, 110–112, 125, 130
political philosophy, 3, 31, 54, 106, 109, 127–130
political representation, 134–135
Politics, 51, 53, 95, 102, 133
Polybus, 113–114
Polycrates, 30–32
Poseidon, 22
Praxō, 59
priests, 47–49
Proclea, 103
Prometheus, 91
property ownership, 62–65, 73–74
Protagoras, 91–99, 116, 130
public seals, 40–42
public service, 12–13, 52–56
public slavery: among ancient people, 4–8; democratic system and, 3–4,

11–12, 25, 33–34, 130–131; end of, 130–132; explanation of, 8–10; institution of, 3–8; and modern slavery, 4–5; origins of, 14–25, 29–33; privileged slaves and, 11–12, 57, 60–63, 68–77, 101–102, 106–116; public service and, 12–13, 52–56; slave roles and, 35–56; slave systems and, 4–8, 55–56, 130–135; tyranny and, 29–30. *See also* slavery

public writings, 38–40

Quintus Veranius, 39

Rancière, Jacques, 99
Rousseau, Jean-Jacques, 54
Rousset, Denis, 75
royal shepherd, 112–117, 125–126
"royal slavery": children and, 68, 73; description of, 8–9; history of, 78–79; privileged positions, 101–102, 106–116; slave systems and, 55–58; status of, 101–102, 111–114, 124–126. *See also* slavery
"rule of servants," 108
rulers, 11, 36, 104–111, 114–115

san'i, 101
Satorneinus, 131
Satyricon, 85
"servile knowledge," 100–102. *See also* knowledge
shepherd slave, 112–117, 125–126
slave body, 59–60
slaveholding system, 1–8, 55–58, 83, 130–135
slave king, 41–42
slave ownership, 62–65, 73–74
slave roles, 35–56
slavery: acquiring slaves under, 49–52; among ancient people, 4–8; colonial, 4–7, 57–58, 81, 100–101; cruel treatment of slaves under, 4, 81, 116;

explanation of, 8–10; Greco-Roman, 4–13, 74, 133–135; humane treatment of slaves under, 4, 14, 81; institution of, 3–8; knowledge and, 80–102; modern, 4–5; origins of, 14–25, 29–33; plantation, 1–6, 81–82; privileged slaves under, 11–12, 57, 60–63, 68–77, 101–102, 106–116; "royal," 8–9, 25, 55–58, 68, 73, 78–79, 101–102, 106–116, 124–126; slave ownership under, 62–65, 73–74; slave status under, 3–4, 11–12, 25, 29, 44, 50, 58–62, 67–79, 90, 97–102, 111–114, 124–126; slave systems under, 1–8, 55–58, 83, 130–135. *See also* public slavery
slaves, acquiring, 49–52
"slave's knowledge," 81, 96–102, 115. *See also* knowledge
"slave society," 4–8, 55–56, 62–63, 81, 100–103
slave structures, 2–3, 6, 102
slave systems, 1–8, 55–58, 83, 130–135
Social Contract, 54
Socrates: death of, 117–120; *hauntology* scene and, 119–120; on humane treatment, 14; last days of, 14, 43, 117–120, 125; philosophy of, 25, 35–36, 39, 91–99, 112, 118–120, 125–126; public service and, 52–54
Solon, 31, 59, 84
Sophocles, 112, 114–117, 125
Southern Watchman, 1
Spensithius, 26–29, 38
Speusinius, 44
Statesman, The, 36, 106
status: defining, 76; personal, 12, 33, 36, 61, 76–78, 98–99; of resident aliens, 33, 61, 72–73; of royal slaves, 101–102, 111–114, 124–126; of slaves, 3–4, 11–12, 25, 29, 44, 50, 58–62, 67–79, 90, 97–102, 111–114, 124–126
Stephen, Saint, 120

Stilbōn, 46
Stilwell, Sean, 100–101
Strabo, 9, 123
Stratocles, 88

technai, 92–93, 96
technē, 28, 88, 92–93, 116, 126
Telemachus, 17, 19
Tenedios anthrōpos, 103–104
Tennes, King, 103–104, 108
Testart, Alain, 58
Theodorus, 35
Theogony, 24
Theophylact of Ohrid, 125
Theopompus, 9, 41
Theramenes, 43
Thomas, Yan, 54–55, 74
Timarchus, 68–70
timia, 77–78
Tiresias, 112–116
Todd, Stephen, 90
Trajan, Emperor, 43
truth-telling, 113, 126

Tryphōn, 39
Tychius, 16
tyranny, 29–30

Usman dan Fodio, 100

Van Effenterre, Henri, 26, 29
Vernant, Jean-Pierre, 24, 116
Verus, Lucius, 131
Vidal-Naquet, Pierre, 112

Wallace, Robert, 78
Wallon, Henri, 4
war strategy, 39–40, 101
Ways and Means, 72, 75
Weber, Max, 108
William I, 107–108

Xanthippus, 65
Xenophon, 24–25, 49, 51, 72, 75, 96

Zeus, 19–20, 24, 28, 48–49, 92
Zōpyrion, 39